KIBBUTZ

VENTURE IN UTOPIA

STUDIES IN THE LIBERTARIAN

AND UTOPIAN TRADITION

KIBBUTZ

Venture in Utopia

Melford E. Spiro

NEW, AUGMENTED EDITION

SCHOCKEN BOOKS · NEW YORK

Permission to quote from copyrighted material is gratefully acknowledged to: Grove Press for Howard Becker, *German Youth: Bond or Free* (1946); Harcourt, Brace for T. S. Eliot, "The Hollow Men," in *Collected Poems* (1936) and for Karl Mannheim, *Ideology and Utopia* (1936); Henrik F. Infield for *Cooperative Living in Palestine* (1944); International Universities Press for Mark Zborowski and Elizabeth Herzog, *Life is With People* (1952); Macmillan for George Peter Murdock, *Social Structure* (1949); National Committee for Labor Israel for Samuel Kurland, *Cooperative Palestine* (1947).

First SCHOCKEN *edition 1963*

New, augmented edition 1970

This edition is published by arrangement with Harvard University Press

Library of Congress Catalog Card No. 70-132260

Printed in the United States of America

To Kiryat Yedidim

CONTENTS

PREFACE

THIS IS an anthropological study of Kiryat Yedidim, the fictitious name of a collective settlement (*kibbutz*) in Israel. Although in itself but a modest investigation of the culture of one *kibbutz*, this book is intended as a case study in the possibilities of social cooperation. The author's interest in this subject was first aroused while conducting field work among the cooperative people of Ifaluk, an atoll in the Central Carolines in Micronesia. It was then that he became eager to explore, in a modern society, the nascent and barely formulated notions concerning cooperation and aggression that he had derived from his research in this "primitive" society. The kibbutz suggested itself almost immediately as the locus for such a project. It could not only satisfy his curiosity concerning social cooperation and aggression, but it would offer a unique opportunity to investigate the ontogenetic development of aggressive and cooperative behavior within a novel socialization context—collective education. As a case study it is the author's hope that this volume be not only an honest portrayal of Kiryat Yedidim but that, like any useful case study, it achieve its aim of illuminating the universal through an examination of the particular.

All statements in this book which have reference to Israeli politics or to the Israel Government refer to conditions prior to the 1955 national elections. Since then there have been new political alignments, and a new Government has been formed.

The field work on which this study is based was conducted in Kiryat Yedidim from February 1951 to December 1951. The author wishes to take this opportunity to acknowledge his gratitude to the Social Science Research Council for making his study possible by granting him a post-doctoral Research Training Fellowship. He also wishes to express his indebtedness to Professor James H. Barnett, Professor and Mrs. A. Irving Hallowell, Professor Jules Henry, Professor Elihu Katz, Professor Raphael Patai and Professor Evon Z. Vogt, Jr. for their important suggestions concerning, and criticisms of, the manuscript. Professor Patai, moreover, contributed generously of his detailed knowledge of Zionist history and Israeli culture. The author's greatest debts are to Mr. William Zev Brinner and to Audrey Goldman Spiro. The former, a storehouse of information concerning the history and structure of the kibbutz movement in general and of Kiryat Yedidim in particular, was of invaluable assistance both in the course of the field work and as a critic of the manuscript. The latter collected much of the data and provided many important insights concerning interpersonal relations in the kibbutz. Finally, the author is grateful to the members of Kiryat Yedidim, whom he cherishes as personal *chaverim* for reasons too numerous to mention.

November 1955   Melford E. Spiro

PREFACE TO THE NEW EDITION

A BOOK—or, more pedantically, the ideas and descriptions which comprise it—constitutes one of the very few exceptions to the general law of change. This can be more than a little disconcerting to an author who is aware of the changes that have occurred in the phenomenon which his book purports to describe. Even a brief visit in the summer of 1962 to Kiryat Yedidim, the *kibbutz* described in this volume, was sufficient to indicate that although the basic structure of kibbutz society had remained stable since my departure in 1952, many changes had ensued in this ten year period. And since it is the kibbutz 1951, not of 1963, that is portrayed in this book, the reader of this edition should be made aware that this book describes the kibbutz at one period—and a critical period, at that—in its historical development. It would be well, therefore, to note briefly some of the changes that I witnessed during my three day visit. That other, perhaps more important, changes had occurred during this interval is not unlikely. But since I returned to Kiryat Yedidim to visit with old comrades, not to gather new materials, this information was gleaned, in passing, while reminiscing over "old times," and it is most certainly not complete.

The physical changes were the most dramatic. The new dining room attracts attention almost as soon as one enters the kibbutz. This spacious and tasteful structure, which contrasts so forcefully with its dingy and unattractive predecessor, is symbolic of the changes that have occurred in kibbutz living. It alone would be sufficient to signal the end of the ascetic orientation which characterized Kiryat Yedidim at an earlier period in its history (pp. 23, 67ff., 176). The dining room, however, is but one of the changes that has served to raise the kibbutz standard of living and to render the lives of its members more comfortable and pleasant. The new housing, which is restricted for the moment to veteran settlers, but which will gradually become the norm, consists of attractively furnished room-and-a-half units, each with its own plumbing, and with an ingeniously contrived mechanical "air-conditioning" system. These conveniences, combined with such universal innovations as electric fans and radios, provide a startling contrast with the conditions I knew in 1951. The importance of these changes for the social scientist lies not only in the productivity which has made these improved consumption standards possible—there can be little question about the viability of this socialist economy—but in the changing ideology which has rendered them acceptable, if not desirable, to even the traditional ideologists. Asceticism is no longer an ideal.

Although concerned with changes in ideology, I must point out that the new consumption patterns of Kiryat Yedidim are taking place in a country that is enjoying wide prosperity, relative to the economic conditions of 1951. The relationship between the more general socio-economic conditions in Israel and shifts in kibbutz attitudes is, in this instance, overdetermined. On the one hand, increasing Israeli prosperity has made many consumer goods available that had not been on the market in 1951. At the same time their availability has served to increase the economic wants of many kibbutz members, thereby widening the gap between their economic achievements and aspirations, and between *their* achievements and those of other sectors of Israeli society. This is surely one—though only one—of the conditions that must be considered in attempting to explain the kibbutz' change from its earlier ascetic tradition.

Other ideological changes must be noted. Although the socialism of Kiryat Yedidim continues to be manifested in its economic system and expressed in its ideology—indeed, a non-socialist kibbutz would be a contradiction in terms—some of its earlier commitments, which formerly had been conceived to be central to its socialist ideology, have been discarded. Thus, with the exception of a few die-hards who are viewed with a mixture of pity and contempt, the Soviet Union is no longer perceived as the leader of the socialist camp nor as the ideal to which a socialist society must aspire (pp. 179 ff.). The Khrushchev revelations of Stalinist tyranny at the Twentieth Communist Congress began the process, not only of de-Stalinization, but of de-Sovietization. Pictures of Stalin and Lenin no longer grace the kibbutz dining room during May Day celebrations. I was obviously wrong when I wrote (p. 186) that the Soviet Union was so important for the kibbutz faith in socialism, that its own socialist experiment would be "seriously shaken" if faith in the Soviet Union were to be destroyed. I was also wrong, incidentally, when I predicted (p. 199) that the political party with which the kibbutz is affiliated could not—because of its unwillingness to become a politically responsible party —long remain in the Government. It remained for almost ten years.

It must be noted, however, that other changes in the quality of kibbutz socialism have occurred which I would interpret as consequent upon the change in its Soviet orientation. Kiryat Yedidim seems to have lost some of its sectarian quality (pp. 128-129), and to the extent that it can still be accurately described as a sect, it is more of a "withdrawing" than a "militant" sect (pp. 171-172). That is, although still concerned with the transformation of the world, its orientation seems to have shifted from a major concern with external, to an important concern with internal, affairs. It seems to be more concerned with making kibbutz socialism an attractive way of life for its own members and less concerned with attempting to remake the rest of the world in its image—although this remains an ideal to which it aspires. In short, Kiryat Yedidim has shifted much of its emphasis from its role as a cell in an international revolutionary movement to that of a community seeking internal stability and achievement. It seems to be more concerned with solving its own domestic problems than with solving the problems of the world.

This reorientation is reflected primarily, of course, in the kibbutz' greater concern with the standard of living of its members. It is reflected, too, in its de-emphasis on the "group dynamics" aspects of its collectivism, in its changing attitude to the professions and "careerism," and to industrialization—to choose only three of the changes revealed by my brief visit last year.

Early kibbutz collectivism comprised three distinct but, from the early-kibbutz' point of view, related values (pp. 30-32, 246-247). These were: group ownership of all economic goods, the primacy of group over individual interests, and group experience as intrinsically valuable (the latter is what I have referred to as its "group dynamics" emphasis). In 1951, an important source of tension in Kiryat Yedidim was to be found in the conflict between this mystique of group experience, derived from the romantic currents which had fed into and been expressed in its Youth Movement traditions, and the strong desire for privacy created by the reality of kibbutz living. Today Kiryat Yedidim appears to be much more inclined to view collective living within the context of its present social reality, rather than from nostalgic distortions of its youth movement past; and the demand for privacy seems to have been recognized as legitimate.

Another important change has occurred in the attitude of Kiryat Yedidim to non-agricultural occupations. At the time of our study, and despite the intellectualism of the kibbutz, the mystique of agricultural labor resulted in a diminution of the importance of those who, like teachers, did not work on the land; and, partly because of its emphasis on the primacy of the group, those who expressed an interest in professional activities which would take them away from the kibbutz were labeled "careerists," a nasty word in the kibbutz lexicon (pp. 31, 156-159). But the teachers with whom I spoke last year claimed that they no longer felt the ambivalence which had characterized people's perceptions of them in the past, and certainly the younger people who have become teachers do not feel the need—as their elder colleagues had in the past—to demonstrate their ability to work as hard and as skillfully as the next fellow in some physical activity.

What is more dramatic, however, is the kibbutz' retention, as members, of two of its *sabras* who work outside Kiryat Yedidim, in highly specialized, technical professions. One, with whom I spoke, said that the decision to permit him to remain in the kibbutz was taken only after a number of town meetings devoted to his case. At these meetings he had argued—and was able to convince a large majority—that Kiryat Yedidim was his home and that a home should welcome all of its children; that the kibbutz did not have a secure future if it limited the interests of its members to agriculture; and that all should be welcome, regardless of occupation, as long as they remained loyal to the basic Socialist-Zionist ideals on which the kibbutz was based.

The realization in Kiryat Yedidim that agriculture cannot remain the sole occupational interest, nor—it should be added—the only source of kibbutz income, is shown in its new factory. This, for Kiryat Yedidim, is a radical departure from its traditional stance concerning industrialization (p. 71). Although some kibbutzim had already introduced various types of industry even prior to my 1951 study, Kiryat Yedidim had resisted this trend as inimical to some of its important values. Today its factory is not only an economic success but, in providing comfortable work for its older members, it also constitutes a partial contribution to the solution of one of the problems of aging (pp. 217-221).

The psychological problems of aging comprised one of the indices of "crisis" noted in this study (ch. 7). I cannot say to what extent the other critical problems have been solved. There is some reason to believe that pressure for the acquisition of consumer goods through private channels has diminished because of the higher standard of living which the kibbutz itself has provided. Some of the features comprising the "problem of the woman" may have achieved solution in the smaller proportion of women in the agricultural labor force, in the obviously greater and guilt-less attention which is now devoted to women's dress and grooming, in the improved working conditions, particularly in the kitchen, and—again—in the general increase in creature comforts. But these are questions to which research alone can provide the answers.

If, however, Kiryat Yedidim is still experiencing a crisis, it is likely that much of the perceived crisis resides in the status of the entire kibbutz movement within the larger Israeli society. Aside from the demotion of the *kibbutznick* from the role of culture hero, the relative strength of the kibbutz movement has been progressively declining with the flow of new immigrants—primarily Asian and African— into the country, immigrants who are either indifferent or hostile to the aims and character of kibbutz life. The new immigration is urban-oriented, and to the extent that it has been induced to settle on the land, it has preferred the *moshav* (p. 4) to the kibbutz. The inescapable fact is that the growth of the kibbutz movement has virtually ceased. In the five year period from 1954-59, the total kibbutz population increased by only 2,000 persons; and, since only two new kibbutzim were settled, this increase is almost exclusively internal. Barring unforeseen circumstances, the fiftieth anniversary of the kibbutz movement—Dagania, the first kibbutz, was founded in 1909—also marks the end of kibbutz expansion. This is bound to have repercussions for the kibbutz' self image, and possible consequences for its future. It is, to say the least, sobering to realize that one's own conception of the good life is rejected by others, despite great efforts to induce them to share in it.

But the future of the kibbutz movement depends not only on external, but on internal recruitment, as well. Although its ability to keep pace with the rapidly increasing Israeli population is, of course, dependent on external recruitment, its survival depends on its ability to hold its young people,

and to motivate them—in our jargon—to occupy the statuses
and perform the roles of their predecessors (pp. 251-252).
In short, the real recruitment problem is not one of biological replacement or of increase, but of social recruitment
and, implicitly, of cultural transmission. In this respect,
Kiryat Yedidim seems to have been more successful than
many other kibbutzim.

In *Children of the Kibbutz* (Harvard University Press,
1958), I pointed out that however else the success or failure
of the kibbutz system of "collective education" was to be
measured, the extent to which it achieved its intended aims
was surely foremost among the criteria by which any as-
sessment was to be made. Since the oldest child of Kiryat
Yedidim was only twenty-eight years old in 1951, it was
premature to say with confidence whether the "children
of the kibbutz" would prefer to remain in Kiryat Yedidim,
rather than move to an urban environment; whether they
would prefer to live in a community whose economy was
based on collective ownership or in one in which private
property characterized economic life; and whether—granted
that the first two questions could be answered affirmatively
—they could responsibly assume the leadership positions
that would eventually be relinquished by the "generation of
the desert." It is still premature, of course, to answer these
questions with confidence, but present information would
certainly lead one to expect that Kiryat Yedidim, as a
physical entity as well as a sociocultural system, will be
perpetuated.

Kibbutz research is in its infancy, and comparative data
from other kibbutzim are meager. In Israel, in the summer
of 1962, I was told of the "increasing percentage" of kibbutz children who were being attracted to towns and cities;

pessimists were sceptical about the future of the kibbutz movement. In my brief stay I had no opportunity to check the accuracy of these reports. If they are reliable, Kiryat Yedidim most certainly constitutes an exception to the reports, as well as to the conclusions drawn concerning the future. Although children of Kiryat Yedidim, too, have left the kibbutz since I completed my study, the number has been so small that these defections have aroused little concern in a community that is, what might be termed, "concern-prone." What is, perhaps, of greater importance, is that some of those who left Kiryat Yedidim later returned to the kibbutz, finding the non-kibbutz style of life wanting.

Impressive to me during my brief visit was the degree to which kibbutz *sabras* have taken primary responsibility for most facets of kibbutz life. In local administration, in education, in central economic posts, in cultural activities, the new generation has taken the place of its elders; and, at least in the case of those with whom I had an opporunity to talk, they perform efficiently and with pride. I was especially impressed with the *élan* expressed in my conversations with some of the sabras. One, a young woman now teaching art in the kibbutz high school, had clearly inspired her students—working in a number of media—to do original and creative work; at the same time she was consciously aware of the social and therapeutic functions of her efforts. What began as a brief visit to her studio extended into the greater part of the afternoon. I have in mind, too, a sabra in his late thirties, to whom I have alluded, revealing firmness and resolution in his determination to continue in his chosen work and, yet, telling me quietly and with humor, of his rootedness in the kibbutz and of his determination to live nowhere else. He then excused himself to attend a meeting of the nominations committee, of which he was a member. Finally, there is a female sabra, also in her late thirties. As I knew her twelve years ago, she seemed discontented and unsettled. The outside world was a lure difficult to resist and her ambitions for her young child burst beyond the confines of a small agricultural village in an Israeli valley. A few months ago, however, she spoke movingly of her work and of her general contentment with life in Kiryat Yedidim. When I reminded her of the discontent she had expressed at the time of my study, she seemed surprised. Where else, she asked, could she find the fellowship and stimulation she enjoys in the kibbutz? If she wants to understand the current economic crisis, she goes to *chaver X;* if she wants to discuss a current book, she talks with *Y;* and so on. She spoke with conviction and with maturity; and I believed her. It would be rash to draw any definite conclusions from these three conversations. They were brief, and even if they accurately reflected the sentiments of these three sabras, I do not know to what extent these three are typical of the group. Here again, only research can provide the answer.

All social movements, as Max Weber has pointed out, pass from a "charismatic" into a "routine" phase in the course of their development. The "routinization of charisma" has a number of possible consequences, among which are the dissolution of the movement, on the one hand, and stabilization at a new equilibrium, on the other. If it is still premature to predict the consequences of kibbutz routinization, it will be possible within the next five or ten years—when the generation that "knew not Pharaoh" becomes the kibbutz movement—to arrive at a considered judgment concerning the future of Kiryat Yedidim in particular and of the kibbutz movement in general. I would hope that both the substantive and theoretical issues which are raised by what is surely a unique movement in voluntary communal living will not be ignored by social science research during this important interval.

January, 1963   Melford E. Spiro

GLOSSARY

Hebrew Terms and Names Frequently Used

aliya (aa-lee-ya'): literally, ascent; immigration. Each successive wave of Jewish immigration to Palestine is known as an aliya. Thus, Zionist immigration history is divided into the First Aliya, Second Aliya, and Third Aliya.

chalutz (chaa-lootz'),* feminine, *chalutza;* plural, *chalutzim:* pioneer. Those Zionists who migrated to Palestine to establish a Jewish Homeland and, specifically, those who settled on the land.

chaver (chaa-vare'),* f., *chavera;* pl., *chaverim:* comrade, companion. A member of a kibbutz.

chevra (chev-raa')*: society. Used in the kibbutz as synonymous with a *gemeinschaft*-type of social group.

The Federation: that federation of collective settlements with which Kiryat Yedidim is affiliated.

hakkara (haa-kaa-raa'): literally, consciousness. Used in the kibbutz to refer to one's sense of moral responsibility for the realization of both the socialist and Zionist goals of the kibbutz.

kevutza (k-voo-tzaa'): literally, group. Used in the kibbutz to refer to the age-graded peer groups into which the children are organized.

* "ch" as in the German gutteral

kibbutz (kee-bootz') pl., *kibbutzim:* literally, a gathering or
a company. Term used in Israel to refer to a collective settlement.

Kiryat Yedidim (Keer-yaat' Ye-dee-deem'): the fictitious
name used to refer to the kibbutz discussed.

kollectiviut ra-ayonit (ko-lek-tee'-vee-yoot raa-aa-yo-
neet'): literally, ideological collectivism. Term used
by The Federation to refer to the acquiescence in a
majority decision on matters of politics and ideology.

The Movement: the youth movement with which the
members of Kiryat Yedidim were affiliated while
still in Europe, and of which their children are members today.

The Party: the national political party to which the members of Kiryat Yedidim belong.

sabra (saa'-bra): term used in Israel to refer to any native-
born Jewish Israeli. In this monograph it is used to
refer to any person born in Kiryat Yedidim.

shabbat (shaa-baat'): Saturday, or the Sabbath.

shtetl (shte'-tl): term used to refer to the small villages in
which the Jews lived in Eastern Europe.

vattik (vaa-teek') f., *vattika;* pl., *vattikim:* veteran. Term
used in Israel to refer to the early pioneers, and in
the kibbutz to refer to its founders.

KIBBUTZ

VENTURE IN UTOPIA

CHAPTER 1

INTRODUCTION

MAN'S QUEST for a more perfect society is probably as old as man himself. This quest has, typically, taken two forms. On the one hand, there have been social theorists and philosophers who projected in literary form their visions of the ideal society, but who did not themselves attempt to establish one. On the other hand, there have been men and women, fired with conviction and purpose, who banded together in order to found utopian societies. Despite the many differences among and between the dreamers and the founders, a common premise underlies most of their dreams and their activities: raw human nature, if nourished in the "proper" social environment, can give rise to that kind of human being who approximates, at least, man's noblest image of himself. This premise, whether viewed as naïve or as realistic, serves to remind us that man is not always concerned with the real and the given, but may, at times, be motivated by the ideal and the novel. Man's purposes, in other words, are not limited by fixed structures, whether biological or social, but may be directed towards the creation of emergent structures. This study is an attempt to describe a society which was founded by people whose level of aspiration involved the creation of such a structure. Where others were content to perpetuate the cultural heritage of the past, they were motivated to found a new culture—a *kibbutz*.

A kibbutz represents one of the three types of cooperative agricultural villages in Israel. These types differ in the extent of their communal living and in the degree of their collective ownership. The *moshav ovdim*, or worker's settlement, is an agricultural village in which all land is owned by the Jewish National Fund,[1] but in which each family works its own alloted plot and retains its income for itself. No family, however, is allowed to hire labor. The agricultural products of the moshav are marketed collectively, and consumer's goods—personal and agricultural alike—are bought collectively.[2] The moshav ovdim in short, represents an example of "segmental cooperation," as Infield has termed it. "Segmental cooperation" is practiced "for the better attainment of specific economic ends . . . (only) when it promises economic benefits."[3]

The kibbutz, (plural, *kibbutzim*) or collective, as the name itself indicates, represents a much more drastic departure from traditional individualistic farming. It is an agricultural village in which all property, with minor exceptions, is collectively owned, in which work is collectively organized, and in which living arrangements—including the rearing of children—are, to a great degree, collective. The kibbutz, therefore, represents "comprehensive cooperation" because "all the essential interests of life are satisfied in a cooperative way . . . (Here) cooperation becomes a new way of life."[4]

[1] The Jewish National Fund is an arm of the Jewish Agency. It buys land, which it holds in the name of the Jewish People, for settlement and rents it to settlers on long-term leases for a nominal fee.

[2] For a description of the moshav, see Dayan, *Moshav Ovdim*.

[3] Infield, p. 20.

[4] *Ibid.*

The third type of settlement, known as *moshav shittufi*, is relatively new and represents a compromise between the kibbutz and the moshav. It combines the collective work and ownership of the kibbutz with the private living of the moshav. Since it is a new development, there are few settlements of this kind, but it is not unlikely that this is the form which many kibbutzim will eventually assume.

There are, of course, important differences among the kibbutzim, so that the 227 kibbutzim which existed in 1954, with a total population of 76,000[5] members, were divided into three major federations and four minor groupings. Although the general principles, as well as the broad outlines of their social structures, are similar in all kibbutzim, there are important differences among them. It is well to stress these differences, since the kibbutz which is described in this study and which we have called Kiryat Yedidim represents a minority of the kibbutzim with respect to certain important cultural variables.

Kiryat Yedidim and its Federation,[6] whose members make up one-third of the total kibbutz population, differ from the majority of kibbutzim in the following salient features of culture. (1) Unlike the majority of kibbutzim, which are

[5] These figures were kindly supplied by the Israel Office of Information in New York. It should be noted, too, that the moshav movement is much larger than the kibbutz movement; its membership totals 112,000.

[6] In order to preserve the anonymity of this kibbutz, its name, as well as the names of the various groups with which it is affiliated, the names of its members, the names of books and authors, and any other information that might serve to identify it, have either been changed or rendered anonymous. Hence, the name of the kibbutz has been changed to Kiryat Yedidim; the kibbutz federation with which it is affiliated is termed, The Federation; the political party in which it is active is termed, The Party; and the youth movement from which it sprang is termed, The Movement. Scholars who are interested in the true names of these groups or who wish to check the bibliographic references may obtain such information from the author.

anti-Marxist and anti-Soviet, Kiryat Yedidim is affiliated with a Federation which is Marxist in ideology and pro-Soviet in the current East-West conflict. This is probably the most important difference among the three major federations and is the most important impediment to inter-federation cooperation. (2) Although some type of collective rearing of children is to be found in all kibbutzim, the system of "collective education" which is found in Kiryat Yedidim is atypical in its duration from infancy through high school. (3) Although all three of the large kibbutz federations are anti-clerical, Kiryat Yedidim and its Federation are atypical in their hostility to any type of religious expression. (4) Unlike the other federations, The Federation is unique in its rule of "collective ideology," with its insistence on ideological and political conformity. (5) Although all three federations have been under severe pressure to introduce changes in their social structures, The Federation is atypical in its extreme resistance to any innovations which might compromise its original values. Hence, the absence in Kiryat Yedidim of "luxuries," hired labor, and industry.

This monograph was originally conceived as an introduction to a detailed study of socialization and personality development in Kiryat Yedidim. It was intended as a brief ethnographic chapter against which the development of the children could be projected. Since the founders of Kiryat Yedidim, as well as its later settlers, were almost all European immigrants who had migrated to Palestine as mature persons, it was assumed that the culture of the kibbutz has had little influence on their personality structure; their formative years had been spent in European culture. It was further assumed that they, and the kibbutz culture which they had created, were the primary determinants of the personality development of their children who were born and raised in Kiryat Yedidim. Hence it was felt that the personality development of their children—the oldest of whom was twenty-eight at the time of the study—could be understood only in terms of the social and cultural history of their parents, of the new culture which the latter had created, and of the motives which had prompted them to create it. This monograph, therefore, is a study of the parental generation and of *their* kibbutz. The impact on Kiryat Yedidim of their adult children, and of the young adults of the latter's age who have become kibbutz members, has been considerable. But this impact, which has resulted in change, conflict, and tension, is not discussed here. It is restricted, rather, to a description of the cultural and psychological base-line from which cultural and psychological changes in the second generation may be measured.

Although intended as a brief historical and ethnographic introduction to the larger personality study, the author began to feel as it unfolded that the introduction had become an independent study—independent, that is, of its function as an introduction to the personality study. Since the latter study will not be completed for several years, it was decided to publish this introduction as a separate monograph. Because of its original conception, however, it is difficult to classify this study within any of the scientific rubrics—community study, ethnography, ethno-history—if, indeed, it deserves the appellation of "science," at all. Few of the materials presented here were collected by means of those techniques which have become *de rigueur* in the scientific investigation of society. The author employed neither schedules nor questionnaires; he used neither formal interviews nor statistics; and he administered no tests, whether sociometric, psychometric, or projective. The absence of these traditional tools may be explained by the fact that these materials were collected only incidentally to the investigation of personality development in children.

I should not like to convey the impression, however, that this monograph represents the free associations of the author. If his associations have intruded themselves into the text, they are, for the most part, controlled associations—controlled, that is, by the data. Whether the data constitute "evidence," or are merely suggestive anecdotes, the author does not presume to judge. All the information, with the exception of that obtained from printed sources, was collected by the author and his wife in the course of their eleven-month residence in Kiryat Yedidim. During that eleven-month period, in which we were mainly preoccupied with our study of the kibbutz children, we became *de facto* members of Kiryat Yedidim. Like other kibbutz members we were called by our first names (Hebraized), and like them we were referred to as *chaverim*—comrades. We each had our daily work assignment which, like that of *de jure* members, was posted every evening on the bulletin board in the dining room. Unlike regular members, however, we worked only half days (four-and-one-half hours) and conducted our formal research on the children the other half. Our work assignments were varied, although the nature of the work was always the same—unskilled labor. We worked in the vegetable gardens, the grapefruit and olive orchards, the vineyards, the kitchen, and (in the case of the author's wife) the infants' house. Our participation in the economic life of the kibbutz was not only a prerequisite for permission to live in Kiryat Yedidim; it was the source of our most important information, and the primary basis for the gaining of rapport. It was only when we were perceived as fellow-workers that the people began to talk with us about those aspects of their lives that were relevant to our research interests.

We not only worked with the people, but also ate with them in the communal dining room; we bathed with them in the communal shower rooms; we attended their meetings and their celebrations; and we spent most of our evenings visiting in their rooms, or entertaining them in ours. Almost always, however, we were participant-observers, and our data, therefore, consist of conversations heard in the fields, speeches recorded at meetings, behavior observed in most situations, and direct information given us by many members who were willing to discuss with us their lives and thoughts.

This, then, is a kind of "clinical" study, in that it used the case-method rather than a statistically-controlled sample to obtain its data. If such a study possesses any merit, it consists in the merits of its defects. That is, since the data are not limited to information obtained by statistically-controlled techniques, they consist of much information that is usually not obtained through formal schedules—information that usually arises only in the context of living. Moreover, since most of our information on attitudes and values is based on inferences drawn from behavior or from statements made in the course of conversations, they were not screened through the defenses which subjects usually set up in a formal interviewing situation.

CHAPTER 2

The strength of the kibbutz lies in its essential social nature which strives for the complete harmony of the individual and the group in every sphere of life, for the maximum development of each individual ... and for the constant deepening of human ethical relations.

From a kibbutz statement of principle[1]

THE MORAL POSTULATES
OF KIBBUTZ CULTURE

TO HAVE BEGUN this monograph in the usual fashion, with a description of the natural environment or of the subsistence economy of Kiryat Yedidim, would do violence to the inner meaning of its culture, as the above quotation indicates. Kiryat Yedidim, to be sure, is an agricultural village consisting of men and women who inhabit a common geographic area and who make their living by tilling the soil in a cooperative fashion. But Kiryat Yedidim is also— and primarily—a fellowship of those who share a common faith and who have banded together to implement that faith. To live *in* Kiryat Yedidim means to become a member *of* a kibbutz, and membership in a kibbutz entails more than voting at town meetings, or driving a tractor in the wheat

[1] All quotations from official kibbutz and Federation publications and speeches have been translated from their original Hebrew by the author.

fields, or living in a lovely village. It means, primarily, becoming a *chaver kibbutz* (a comrade of the kibbutz), that is,
a person who is dedicated to the social, economic, and national ideals for which the kibbutz stands.[2] These ideals
were formulated before Kiryat Yedidim came into being
and, indeed, it was founded with the purpose of bringing
these ideals into being.[3] Hence, these ideals must be understood, if Kiryat Yedidim is to be understood.

Probably the single most important ideal upon which the
entire kibbutz culture is based is what might be termed the
moral value of labor. It is no accident, for example, that
today, when the entire kibbutz movement is experiencing a
profound crisis, it is this principle of *avodah atzmit*, or self-
labor, which has become the measure of the devotion of a
kibbutz to its original ideals. The founders of Kiryat Yedidim, in many instances, were intellectuals for whom labor
was a "calling" rather than a habit. For them, labor was not
merely a means for the satisfaction of human needs; rather,
labor itself was viewed as a need—probably man's most
important need—the satisfaction of which became an end
in itself. *Ki ha-avodah hi chayenu* is the way the kibbutz

---

[2] A chaver (pl., chaverim) is a kibbutz member. The term, literally,
means "companion" or "comrade."

[3] In *Cooperative Living in Palestine*, Infield writes that, the kibbutz
"unlike the utopian communities, did not originate in a deliberate attempt
to mold a new form of social organization on the foundation of a pre-
conceived theory. It came into being, rather, in much the same way as
any other normal community. Basically, what shaped its character was
the necessity for adaptation to the unusual conditions obtaining in Palestine. Hence, the peculiar social structure was necessary to ensure survival."
(p. 25.) Although this statement may characterize the earliest kibbutzim,
it does not apply to Kiryat Yedidim or to most of the other kibbutzim
that were founded by members of the various European Zionist youth
movements. In the case of Kiryat Yedidim, as we shall see, its ideals, and
the social structure which was evolved to implement these ideals, took
shape much before it was founded.

expresses it. "For labor is (the essence of) our life"; and this phrase may be said to be the *leitmotif* of kibbutz living.

This attitude toward labor did not, of course, originate with the vattikim,[4] the founders, of Kiryat Yedidim. Emphasis on labor had long been integral to the *chalutz*, or pioneering, tradition in Zionism. As early as 1882, when one of the first contingents of Russian Jews migrated to Palestine, the ideal of labor on the land was already in process of formulation.[5] As one pioneer put it:

> Farmer! Be a free man among men, but a slave to the soil . . . Kneel and bow down to it every day. Nurse its furrows—and then even its stony clods will yield a blessing! And in this "slavery" remember that you are a tiller of the soil! A tiller of the soil in Palestine! This must become a badge of honor among our people.[6]

But the most important influence came from the pioneers of the Second Aliya (1904–1914) and, specifically, from the seer of the Palestinian labor movement, A. D. Gordon (1856–1922). It was Gordon who invented the term, *dat ha-avodah*, "the religion of labor." For him labor was a

---

[4] A *vattik* (pl., vattikim) is, literally, a "veteran." This term is used in Israel to refer to the early pioneers and settlers. In the kibbutz it refers to the founders of the kibbutz in contrast to those who joined it at a later date.

[5] Palestinian immigration history, since the beginnings of the Zionist movement, is conventionally divided into a series of successive waves of immigration. The first wave, known as the "First Aliya" (1882–1904), consisted for the most part of gentlemen-farmers who settled in villages and managed their plantations which were worked by hired Arab labor. Only a small number professed the ideal of labor, but the germ of this ideal is to be found as early as this Aliya, as the quotation indicates. The ideal of labor and the various labor institutions were forged, however, by the "Second Aliya" (1904–1914) and by the "Third Aliya" (1919–1924). The founders of Kiryat Yedidim were early participants in the latter wave of immigration. See Lotta Levensohn, *Outline of Zionist History*.

[6] Kurland, p. 7.

uniquely creative act, as well as an ultimate value. Through labor, he taught, man became one with himself, society, and nature. But, he warned, it would not be easy:

A people that has become accustomed to every mode of life save the natural one—the life of self-conscious and self-supporting labor—such a people will never become a living, natural laboring people unless it strain every fibre of its will to attain that goal. Labor is not merely the factor which establishes man's contact with the land and his claim to the land; it is also the principle force in the building of a national civilization. Labor is a great human ideal for the future, and a great ideal is like the healing sun. We need fanatics of labor in the most exalted sense of the word.[7]

Gordon's "religion of labor" not only influenced his own generation of Zionist pioneers, but it served to shape the subsequent history of Jewish labor enterprise in Palestine. Hence, the stress in Kiryat Yedidim on labor as a "calling" is an ideal which it shares, not only with other collective and cooperative settlements, but with the entire labor movement in Israel.

This attitude to labor is particularly significant and, in a profoundly psychological sense, explicable only in view of the *petit bourgeois* backgrounds of the vattikim. Before their immigration to Israel, they had not engaged in physical labor; moreover, they were reared in a culture that demeaned labor, as well as the laborer. The persons who were looked down upon in the *shtetl*, the Eastern European villages in which the vattikim were born, were the *proste*. *Prost* is the Yiddish equivalent of "crude" or "vulgar," and the attitude towards unskilled workers on the part of the shtetl is revealed most clearly in its appellation of these workers as the proste. In the shtetl:

[7] *Ibid.*, p. 9.

It is better . . . to be a salesman than to be an artisan. A salesman works with his brain, an artisan merely with his brawn.

For a man who "comes from yikhus" (a respected family)
to engage in manual labor, even under stress of economic necessity, is a calamity for manual labor has come to symbolize the
antithesis of the social ideal—a life devoted entirely to study.[8]

Hence, the ideal of work as an ultimate value—the dat
ha-avodah—represents, in the case of the vattikim, a cultural
revolution; to achieve it they had to overcome the resistance
of both their trained values and their untrained muscles. It
is little wonder that one of their first goals was *kibbush ha-
avodah*, "the conquest of labor."[9]

Kiryat Yedidim, then, is not a worker's community in
the same sense that many of the utopian societies of nineteenth-century America were. This is a community which
was founded, for the most part, by middle-class intellectuals
who deliberately chose to be workers; by so choosing, they
reversed both the traditional prestige hierarchy and the historical aspiration of upward mobility. Instead of aspiring to
"rise" in the social ladder, they aspired to "descend." For
the chaverim, then, it is not business (as in European bourgeois culture) or scholarship (as in the shtetl culture), but
labor which is the highest vocational goal. This goal, it must
be stressed, is primarily a spiritual goal—it is a means to
self-realization. As the chalutz folk-song has it: "To Palestine we have come, to build and to be built in it (the land)."
This Tolstoyan attitude toward work could be evolved, it

[8] Zborowski and Herzog, p. 247.

[9] Kibbush ha-avodah had another meaning, in addition to the one attributed to it here. In the early days of Second Aliya, when Jewish land-
owners preferred to employ cheap Arab labor, a major aim of the Jewish
labor movement was to gain a foothold in those sectors of the economy
which were closed to them. And this was another sense in which the
"conquest of labor" was used.

is not hazardous to say, only by romantic, urban intellectuals.

The "moral value of labor" stresses not only the latter aspect of the principle of avodah atzmit, self-*labor;* the former aspect, which emphasizes *self*-labor, is equally important. This general principle of the labor movement, when applied to the kibbutz, means that no one may be employed from the outside to work in the kibbutz, and that all work must be performed by the members of the kibbutz. Exceptions might be made in certain kinds of labor for which chaverim may have had no training, such as house construction or language instruction in the high school, but no exception may be made in the case of other kinds of labor, no matter how difficult or repulsive they might be. The opposition to hired labor is based on three ethical considerations. First, there is the *mystique* of labor—already hinted at— which stresses the dignity and creativeness of labor and the need to strike roots in the soil. Then, there is the fear, which first arose when the Arabs were the majority group in Palestine, that the introduction of hired labor would open the way to the employment of cheap Arab *fellah* labor. If this happened, it was thought, the kibbutz would eventually become a plantation, worked by Arab labor for the benefit of (what would then become) the leisure class kibbutz owners. The socialist ideology of Kiryat Yedidim, with its abhorrence of "surplus value" and its notion that all wage labor entails exploitation, is the third ethical opposition to hired labor and the insistence on self-labor.[10]

[10] The opposition to hired labor has created many tensions for Kiryat Yedidim, in both its intra- and extra-kibbutz relations. With the great movement of mass immigration into the country, the government of Israel has been hard pressed to find employment for the immigrants (the majority of whom do not wish to become members of kibbutzim), and

The chaverim, in short, constitute a class conscious proletariat, *par excellence;* and it is not surprising that one's
prestige in Kiryat Yedidim is determined primarily by
excellence in and devotion to one's work.

Not all work, however, is equally valued. Physical labor
enjoys the greatest prestige. The further removed it is from
physical labor, the less prestige a job confers. This means,
of course, that pure intellectual work does not confer great
prestige, despite the fact that Kiryat Yedidim is a highly
cultured community, one which is devoted to intellectual
and artistic experience. Of the various categories of physical
labor, agricultural labor is valued the most. Even among the

---

has appealed to the kibbutzim to hire them. The refusal of many of the
kibbutzim to comply with this request has created considerable resentment against them, and has led to charges of "anti-Zionism" and "irresponsibility." Nevertheless, The Federation has remained firm in its opposition to the use of hired labor, insisting that the entire structure of the
kibbutz would change as a result of this innovation; for the members of
the kibbutz would then become a "leisure class" of experts and managers,
who would supervise the work of others. This prediction has been confirmed in the case of those kibbutzim—members of the other two federations—who have adopted the policy of hiring workers.

But the use of hired labor would solve not only a governmental problem; it would solve an equally pressing kibbutz problem. The most acute
economic problem of Kiryat Yedidim, for example, is a shortage of manpower. As its services have expanded, women have been removed from
the agricultural branches of the economy, resulting in a critical labor
shortage. The obvious solution to this problem is the hiring of workers,
and there are some chaverim who openly advocate this solution. Thus
far, the economy has not suffered too much, because of temporary solutions to the problem: (1) the drafting of high school students for special
assignments, such as a special grapefruit or potato harvest; (2) the suspen-
sion of a sabbath for some special task that must be done immediately,
and the drafting of the entire kibbutz for the job; (3) the work performed by the youth groups living in the kibbutz, as well as that performed by various training groups which are sent to the kibbutzim to
work. If this third source of labor were to dry up, the kibbutz would
have little alternative but to hire labor or to devise some compromise
solution.

agricultural branches, however, differential stereotypes have arisen. Those who work in the orchards and vineyards are thought to be intellectual, easygoing people, who are not particularly energetic. Shepherds are supposedly romantic, and inclined to be a bit lazy. On the other hand, the *falachim*, those who work in the grain fields, are presumably hard, energetic workers. They enjoy a national reputation, moreover, for the stereotype has it that the falachim of the past have become the country's leaders, and have built the important labor institutions. It is difficult to assess the relative physical difficulty of these various occupations. It is probably true that, in many respects, the falach has the hardest job, and there are certain periods—such as the harvest, when the combines work almost twenty-four hours a day—which demand almost superhuman effort. But there is another, and probably more cogent, reason for his prestige which has little to do with the difficulty of his work. The kibbutz, as will be noted in the discussion of economic organization, distinguishes between "productive" work and "services." The former enjoys the greater prestige, and (or, perhaps, because) it yields a cash income. Hence, *falcha*—cereal crops—is the most important agricultural branch in the kibbutz economy, for it normally yields the highest economic return. The economic importance of the branch has been generalized to the social importance of the person who works in that branch.

The importance attached to work is in constant evidence in Kiryat Yedidim and almost everyone responds to it. Work has become almost a compulsive habit, so that absence from work, even for good cause, elicits feelings of guilt. For three months, for example, the author had been working in the fields with a chavera whose work was characterized by drive and great energy, and who seldom took a break. He was amazed to discover somewhat later that this labor was tortuous to her; she could not tolerate the heat, and she suffered constant pains in her arms and hands. Again, a chavera of the kibbutz donated one day a week to work in an immigrants' camp. She became quite ill, and was ordered to bed by the doctor. She complained, however, that she must return to her work, and when she heard that there was no one to take her place in the camp, she insisted on rising from her sickbed and returning to the camp. It is interesting to note in this connection that, according to the kibbutz nurse, there are no cases of malingering or of "goldbricking." How compelling this drive for work can become, even for an outsider, is illustrated by an experience of the author. It was mutually decided that he would pay for his expenses by working half a day and by paying the kibbutz for the other half-day. Toward the end of the study, it became apparent that it would be impossible to complete his projected research aims, unless he had more free time for his research. He obtained permission from the Secretariat to work only one-quarter time for two months and to make up the difference in cash payment. As soon as he started his quarter-time schedule, however, the author realized that he would accomplish little work. His own guilt feelings were too great. No one mentioned the fact that he was not working regular hours, and probably few knew of it; nevertheless, he felt that he was shirking his responsibility. He stayed away from public places during the day, trying to avoid the chaverim. The influence of this dominant attitude is so great, that a complete stranger becomes acculturated to it within a few months.[11]

[11] The author's personality must, of course, be taken into account here. But these reactions are particularly significant by contrast with his ex-

Since labor is of such great importance, it follows that the individual who shirks his work responsibilities, or who is inefficient in his work, does not enjoy the respect of his fellows. Regardless of his other talents, the *batlan*, or the lazy person, occupies the position of lowest prestige in the prestige hierarchy of Kiryat Yedidim.

A second moral principle of kibbutz culture is that the property used and produced by the entire community rightfully belongs to the entire community. Hence, the economy rests on the public ownership of property. The land inhabited and worked by the kibbutz is not owned by any individual or by any family, nor even by the kibbutz itself. It is owned, rather, by the entire nation, having been acquired by a national agency, the *Keren Kayemet* (Jewish National Fund), by funds raised through voluntary contributions. The Keren Kayemet rents the land to the kibbutz on a ninety-nine year renewable lease, for which the latter pays an annual rent (starting only after its fifth year) of 2 percent of the original cost of the land, plus improvements. National ownership of land is an ethical imperative, it is believed, because it precludes such "evils" as land speculation, absentee ownership, and "unearned" income through rent. Moreover, it prevents the rise of a society composed of a landed gentry and a disinherited peasantry.

Although its land is owned by the nation, all other property in Kiryat Yedidim is owned collectively by the members of the kibbutz. Ideally, the individual owns nothing with the exception of small personal gifts and those personal

---

perience on another field trip. In a study of a Micronesian culture—also highly cooperative—the author spent full time at research, and though the people furnished him with food and other necessities, he did not pay them, nor did he work in the economy. It nevertheless did not occur to him to feel guilty, since leisure is important and labor is at a minimum in this society.

effects which he may buy with his annual "vacation allowance" of nine Israeli pounds (approximately nine dollars). Hence, the house in which he lives, the trucks and tractors he operates, the cattle he cares for, the clothes he wears, and the food he eats are owned by the kibbutz. Since private property has been abolished, the individual receives no wages for his work; since he lives in a house owned by the kibbutz, he pays no rent; and since he eats in the kibbutz dining room, he has no food bills. Moreover, he receives his clothes, like everyone else, from the kibbutz clothing room; smaller articles, like combs, toothbrushes, etc., he obtains at the kibbutz "store." Should he be ill, his medical and hospital bills are taken care of by the kibbutz. In short, the individual has no money, nor does he need any, because his economic needs are satisfied by the kibbutz.

The principle of public ownership derives, of course, from the emphasis placed on the moral value of equality. Private property, it is felt, together with the profit motive and the competitiveness that accompany it, destroy the bonds of brotherhood. The kibbutz insists that only in the absence of private property is it possible to establish an economic system in which economic classes and economic inequalities are abolished and, consequently, in which greater brotherhood can be achieved.

Communal ownership, then, is related to another moral principle underlying kibbutz culture: the principle of social and economic *equality*. In the event that Kiryat Yedidim does not have enough goods or services to supply all its members equally, distribution is regulated according to seniority of arrival in the country. For example, the new housing development, consisting of two-room, instead of the usual one-room apartments, is open only to those persons who have been in the country for at least thirty years. Except for such special cases, however, economic distribution is formally equal. In the distribution of clothes, for example, all women receive one good dress every two years, and a plain dress on alternate years. Men receive three pairs of *shabbat* (sabbath) pants and four shirts every year.[12]

In the past the emphasis on formal economic equality was taken much more literally than it is today. Clothes, for example, were not marked in the laundry, on the principle that all clothes were publicly owned. Hence, a person did not receive from the laundry the same clean clothes that he had previously worn. Instead, he was given the first pair of pants, dress, or socks that happened to be on top of the laundry pile. This, of course, created highly ludicrous situations, such as tall persons having to wear short pants, or slender persons being forced to wear large dresses. This system, known as *kommuna alef* (first commune), was soon modified at the insistence of the women, who demanded that they be fitted for dresses. The sizes of the clothes were marked, so that a chaver, when he came for his weekly laundry, would not necessarily receive the same clothes he had worn the week before, but he would, at least, receive his own size.

In the middle 1930's *kommuna bet* (second commune) was instituted. It was becoming apparent that the chaverim were not entirely careful with the clothes they wore, and there was a high percentage of torn and soiled clothes. It was felt that if the clothes were marked, and if each chaver were to receive the same clothes from the laundry, he could

---

[12] Dress clothes are called shabbat clothes, which, when they become worn, are used as work clothes.

then be held responsible for their care. This is the system that is still in operation. All clothing, like everything else, is technically owned by the kibbutz. But each chaver receives his clothing allowance for the year, and the clothes he receives are "his," in the sense that they are marked with his name, he wears them, and he is responsible for them.[13]

Despite this formal equality in the basic necessities, certain inequalities in luxuries have arisen due to conditions not provided for in the formal structure of the kibbutz. Some people receive presents of food, clothing, furniture, etc., from relatives who do not reside in Kiryat Yedidim, while others do not. Some individuals, moreover, work outside the kibbutz during their vacations, and purchase what they please with the money they earn. Some have relatives or friends outside the kibbutz with whom they can stay when they go to the cities, which enables them to save from their annual "vacation money" what others must pay in hotel and restaurant bills. This saving enables them to purchase small personal objects. As a result of all these factors, the complete economic equality that once characterized the kibbutz has been slightly qualified.

It may be stated as a general rule, however, that all individuals receive the same clothing allotment, eat the same food in the communal dining room, and enjoy the same (approximately) housing conditions, regardless of their economic skill, their economic importance to the kibbutz, their prestige, or their power. For, despite its awareness that persons differ greatly in ability or in skill—though it seems that it denied it, or at least ignored it, in its early

---

[13] It is of interest to note that the negligence that was discovered in the care of clothing under kommuna *alef* was not discovered in the care of land, houses, or other capital goods.

history—the kibbutz insists that such differences should not be used as a basis for differences in privileges. All individuals have an equal right to the good things of the community, although they do not contribute to it equally.

This observation serves to remind us that the equality principle of kibbutz culture is qualified by another ethical consideration—that of need. The kibbutz believes in the principle of "from each according to his ability, to each according to his need," a principle, which conflicts at times with its principle of equality. In resolving this conflict, it is usually the "need," rather than the equality, that prevails. A field hand, whose relative productivity is great, eats the common austerity fare of the dining room,[14] though he has worked strenuously in the hot Israeli sun; but an office worker (of low prestige in the kibbutz value hierarchy), whose productivity is low, may receive a special diet, comparatively sumptuous, because of some physical condition. A man with children works no harder than a man without children; but the kibbutz provides not only for his wants, but also for the care of his children. In effect, those with no children, or with few children, subsidize those who do have children.

Not so obvious upon first arrival in Kiryat Yedidim, but just as important for an understanding of kibbutz culture, is the social equality which exists, and of which one becomes acutely aware whenever he leaves the kibbutz for even a short time. There is no class structure in Kiryat

[14] Because of the mass immigration to Israel that accompanied the founding of the State, food was scarce before and during the period of this study. Hence the scarcity that characterized Kiryat Yedidim was a national, rather than a kibbutz, phenomenon. The author has been informed that the national, and presumably the kibbutz, situation has been considerably improved since that period.

Yedidim, and there is no differential reward system for different kinds of labor based on some ranking technique. Some kinds of work, as has already been observed, are valued more highly than others; but those who occupy the more highly valued jobs receive no greater reward than the others. The important psychological fact about kibbutz culture is that everyone, regardless of his work, is viewed as a worker, with the same privileges and responsibilities as anyone else. Menial work, which in capitalist society might mark one as a social inferior, does not carry that stigma in Kiryat Yedidim. The general manager—the highest elective officer in the kibbutz—is not the social superior of the cleaner of the latrines. Hence, there is no work which a person is ashamed to accept because it would demean him socially. There is, thus, little if any subordination of one group of individuals to another; there is no polarization of society into those who command and those who obey, those who are respected and those who respect. There is no need for some to be subservient before others, or to be "nice" to them, for fear of losing their jobs. In short, many of the social inequalities existing in a stratified society do not exist in Kiryat Yedidim.[15]

This achievement can be illustrated by two examples. The recently arrived European physician, not a member of the kibbutz, asked one of the women for the name of the "maid" in the clinic. She did not understand to whom he was referring until he explained that he meant the woman who regularly cleaned the clinic. The woman then explained to him that there were no "maids" in Kiryat Yedidim, that

[15] Those kibbutzim that have introduced industry into their economy have, thereby, made possible the rise of a class system. See Rosenfeld, pp. 766–774.

this woman would probably be sitting next to him at dinner that evening, and, moreover, that this "maid" was an important official in the kibbutz. While making a survey of the various types of kibbutzim, we arrived at a certain kibbutz in order to interview a member of the Israeli Parliament. We were told, on our arrival, that he was to be found in the cemetery—for his job, when Parliament was not in session, consisted in caring for the graveyard. He came to greet us in his work clothes and kindly consented to grant us an interview in the meadow, for his wife, who worked nights in the dairy, was sleeping in their room.

It should be emphasized that the absence of social classes as conventionally conceived, does not imply the absence of either some type of ranking system in Kiryat Yedidim or of "horizontal" social groupings. The kibbutz is *not* a homogeneous concentration of persons, all of whom enjoy equal prestige and power, and each of whom interacts with all others with equal frequency. On the contrary, differential prestige and power as well as social cliques are to be found in Kiryat Yedidim; and it may be well to delineate their broad outlines at the very beginning.

Although the various kibbutz offices are held on a temporary and a rotation basis, those who happen to hold these offices do enjoy considerable power. Moreover, as is noted below, though the tenure of office is limited to two or three years, only a small number of chaverim possess the necessary skills required to cope with the complexities of such offices as general manager, secretary, treasurer, etc., so that in effect these offices rotate among a small core of twelve to fifteen persons.[16] Hence, power within the kibbutz is not

[16] For a discussion of these offices and of the problem of tenure, see below pp. 78–83, 94–96.

equally distributed; it is, rather, concentrated within this small core. It should nevertheless be emphasized that those who occupy these offices enjoy no special privileges and receive no material rewards.[17] Their power, moreover, is limited by the fact that major decisions are made, not by them, but by the town meeting; and that they are under the constant surveillance of the town meeting, and subject to its power of recall. At the same time this core is not a united group, but is comprised of individuals and of sub-groups who disagree, and are often in conflict, with each other. Finally, this is neither a closed nor a self-appointed group. Rather, it is a group whose members are elected by the kibbutz on the basis of ability and demonstrated performance, and one which is always open to recruits chosen by the town meeting should it deem them capable of holding office.

Many of these same considerations apply to those who enjoy prestige. With one possible exception, prestige in Kiryat Yedidim is a function of achieved, rather than of ascribed, status; and the persons of prestige constitute a social category rather than a social group. Prestige is achieved by being a productive and devoted worker, by implementing kibbutz ideals in one's daily life, by being a "synthetic personality,"[18] and by being a vattik, a founder of the kibbutz. The first three qualifications are, of course, attained only through achievement and they are open to all. The fourth, though not open to present achievement, was attained through past achievement. Moreover, it is not sufficient merely to *be* a vattik; to merit prestige, the vattik must constantly validate his status by his daily behavior

17 See below, pp. 96–97.
18 See below, p. 153.

rather than by resting on the glories of his past. Nor, it should be noted, is the prestige of the vattikim inherited by their children. The latter must achieve their own prestige through the same avenues that are open to children of other chaverim, and the status of their parents confers upon them no competitive advantage.

But Kiryat Yedidim is not only stratified by power and prestige. It may be subdivided into "horizontal" groups, as well; that is, into friendship groups or cliques, based on at least four factors: age, occupation, residential contiguity, and interests. Usually these criteria overlap, for friendship groups—as measured by social visiting in the evening—usually consist of individuals of the same generation; the latter, in turn, usually share the same interests; and, as a result of the kibbutz system of distributing housing,[19] they usually live in the same living area. The kibbutz itself recognizes what it calls, four age "layers,"[20] and it is rare that a clique consists of individuals from overlapping "layers." Not all members of the same layer, however, comprise a single clique. Within the layers cliques are formed on the basis of common interests—intellectual, political, discontent, etc.

This combination of age and residential contiguity does not account for all cliques, for it is sometimes overruled by occupational interests and by power position. Those who comprise the small core which holds power are not neces-

[19] Housing in Kiryat Yedidim expands by the addition of whole new developments, rather than by the addition of single units. Since the new developments usually represent considerable improvements over their predecessors, they are allocated according to a priority system, usually based on seniority. The vattikim, for example, are now living in the newly constructed housing project while their married children are living—on the other side of the village—in the wooden houses which have been successively occupied by the vattikim, by a later group of settlers, and now by the adult children.

[20] See below, pp. 60–64.

sarily a friendship group, but they are, nevertheless, characterized by a high frequency of interaction, since it is they who must meet—frequently over a cup of tea in the evening—to solve the many problems that are constantly arising in the kibbutz; and they are not always of the same generation, nor do they live in spatial proximity.

Similarly, workers in some economic branches—the shepherds, for example—establish a strong *esprit de corps* which may carry over to their non-working hours. Hence, though not of the same generation and though they do not share a common living area, they constitute a clique based on personal friendship which had its origin in a common occupational interest. It should be noted, moreover, that to the extent that some economic branches are unisexual in character—as the shepherds—membership in the cliques is also unisexual, so that sex becomes a criterion for social grouping.

Another principle underlying the culture of Kiryat Yedidim is that of individual liberty; indeed, the kibbutz prides itself on being the freest society in the world. In the early history of Kiryat Yedidim, emphasis on freedom meant primarily freedom from the "artificial conventions" of an urban civilization. Once it was settled on its own land, however, and the necessity for some kind of social organization and authority arose, this earlier notion of freedom was expanded to include opposition to any system of authority. The kibbutz, it was assumed, was an "organic community," and its work would somehow get accomplished without the necessity of investing any individual or individuals with power over their fellows. Hence, Kiryat Yedidim had no officers, and all decisions were made in informal group discussions that included neither a chairman nor an agenda. As it grew larger, however, and as its economy expanded, it became evident that some kind of formal organization was required and that it was necessary to delegate power. But in order to prevent any individual from acquiring personal power and/or to prevent the rise of an entrenched bureaucracy, it was decided that all offices—from the most menial to that of the general manager—should be held for a maximum of two or three years. This tenure limitation, it was hoped, would lead to a rotation of individuals in the various power positions, and would, therefore, ensure the maximum liberty of the kibbutz members.

This emphasis on freedom, it should be noted, is manifested not only in its formal structure, but in its freedom of expression as well. Any curtailment of freedom of speech or of reading is abhorrent to its members, and no censorship of any kind exists.

Finally, a discussion of the moral postulates of this culture must include the principle which might be termed the moral value of the group. The group, in kibbutz culture, is not only a means to the happiness of the individual; the group and group processes are moral ends in their own right. This has three aspects. It means, first, that the interests of the individual must be subordinate to the interests of the group. When the needs of the individual and those of the group come into conflict, the individual is expected to abdicate his needs in favor of the group's. This applies to vocational interests, as well as to ideological convictions. A person's vocational preferences are usually considered in deciding his work assignment; but if the kibbutz requires his labor or skill in some special branch, he is expected to recognize the paramount needs of the group. The same logic applies to ideological matters. An individual is permitted complete freedom in the process of arriving at political decisions and in attempting to convince others of his point of view. But once a formal decision is reached by the kibbutz, he is expected to acquiesce in its decision and to support it, however much it conflicts with his personal views.[21]

A second aspect of the emphasis on the ethical value of the group involves the assumption that the individual's motivations will always be directed to the promotion of the group's interests, as well as of his own. Behavior is expected to be characterized by *ezra hadadit*, or mutual aid. This means that every member of the kibbutz is responsible for the welfare of every other member and for the welfare of the kibbutz as a whole, just as the kibbutz is responsible for the welfare of each individual. The consequence of this principle is that no one is to suffer for lack of medical care, education for his children, food, shelter, clothing, or any other need, as long as the kibbutz can provide him with these requirements.

The emphasis on the moral value of the group means, finally, that group living and group experiences are valued more highly than their individual counterparts. Indeed, so important is the value of group experience that those chaverim who seek a great degree of privacy are viewed as "queer." The kibbutz is interested in creating a *chevra*. The ultimate criterion of either a good kibbutz, a good high school, or a good kindergarten, is whether or not it has become a chevra. The term, chevra, literally, denotes a society; but its connotation—and its meaning for Kiryat Yedidim—is a group which is characterized by intimacy of

---

[21] This entire paragraph serves to indicate that the individual's freedom is restricted in many ways, despite the kibbutz emphasis of liberty.

interaction, and by mutual concern, if not by love. A chevra, in short, is a *gemeinschaft* or, to use their term, an "organic community." It is apparent, therefore, that the individualist, the person who cherishes his own privacy more than a group experience, constitutes a threat to the group. His desire for privacy either prevents the group from becoming a chevra, or symbolizes the fact that it is not a chevra, for if it were, he would prefer to be with the group than to be alone.[22]

In this respect, the kibbutz shows its kinship with the

[22] The belief in the primacy of the group has many ramifications. In the realm of art, for example, a teacher criticized *Tobacco Road* because it is "pornographic," and because it represents the feeling of the author alone, and not of the group. A chaver criticized the novel, *Young Hearts*, because it is "not true." When the writer protested that the author may have presented the "truth" as he saw it, he retorted, "Literature must express the feeling of the entire group, and not of one individual, or it is not literature." A kibbutz intellectual criticized Chagall as being "unrealistic," in the sense that he evades the important *social* problems and becomes absorbed in his *private* fantasies.

Moreover, this emphasis on the group explains why The Federation is entirely opposed to what it calls, "careerism." In speeches and articles attempting to encourage the city youth to join the kibbutz movement, opposition to the pursuit of a personal career is a constant theme. In the present world, with its oppressions and inequities, it is argued it is indecent to pursue a personal career, to seek one's personal pleasure, or to satisfy selfish ambition. The morally sensitive person eschews personal ambition and a desire for a better personal life in order to work for a better world.

This emphasis on the group and its welfare, moreover, probably accounts for the almost complete absence of concern with psychiatric values in the kibbutz. At no time during this study did the writer hear any conversation dealing with such topics as "peace of mind," "personality adjustment," "freedom from anxiety," and the host of other psychological concerns that are endemic in contemporary American culture. At times, one hears talk concerning an individual's lack of integration into the kibbutz, a problem which is of serious concern to the chaverim; but one seldom hears discussions of intra-personal adjustment. The elimination of *social* conflicts and of *international* tensions, and the achievement of *world* peace—these are the goals to be achieved, not their individual counterparts.

shtetl. The following description of the shtetl applies, without qualification, to Kiryat Yedidim.

> To insist on privacy if you are not sinning is a serious misdemeanor . . . One of the worst things you can say of a man is, "he keeps it for himself" or "he hides it from others" whether "it" is money or wisdom, clothes or news.
>
> Locked doors, isolation, avoidance of community control, arouse suspicion . . . "Home people," *heymisheh mentschen* . . . are free to come in whenever they like at any time of the day . . .
>
> Withdrawal is felt as attack, whether physical or psychological, and isolation is intolerable. "Life is with people" . . .
>
> Everywhere people cluster to talk, at home, in the market place, on the street. Everyone wants to pick up the latest news, the newest gossip . . .
>
> The freedom to observe and to pass judgment on one's fellows, the need to communicate and share events and emotions is inseparable from a strong feeling that individuals are responsible to and for each other.[23]

These moral postulates constitute the social ethics of Kiryat Yedidim and represent, for them, the basic tenets of socialism. But socialism is only one of the twin principles on which kibbutz culture rests; the other principle is Zionism. For Kiryat Yedidim, the kibbutz is not only a means to social and personal liberation, it is a means to national liberation, as well. Socialism, as defined by the tenets described in this chapter, represents the universalistic principle of kibbutz culture; Zionism represents its particularistic, Jewish principle. It is no accident, therefore, that Kiryat Yedidim was founded in Palestine rather than in Eastern Europe, the birthplace of the founders.

The Zionist convictions of Kiryat Yedidim which, for

---

[23] Zborowski and Herzog, pp. 225–227.

the most part, they share with the entire Zionist movement, may be simply stated. The Jews constitute a Nation, however dispersed they may have been in the last 1900 years of their history, and however lacking they may have been in the external *accoutrement* of nationhood. Every Nation has not only a right, but a duty to survive and to perpetuate its national culture. The physical survival of the Jewish Nation is under a constant threat as long as the Jews remain a national minority living among other political Nations. Only in their own "historical homeland" is it possible for them to escape antisemitism and to escape their anomalous minority status. But this minority status has not only made the Jews an easy target for antisemitism, it has distorted their psychological and cultural complexion. Being deprived of numerous channels for economic activity, the Jews have been forced into a narrow range of economic outlets—they have become "middlemen." Middlemen are not only economic parasites, but they become distorted by the very nature of their work. They have no appreciation for nature and, hence, strike no roots in the soil; they have no understanding of the essential dignity and creativity of physical labor; they develop a sterile intellectualism, a scholasticism which has no basis in real life.

Zionism can change all these characteristics. By living in their own "homeland," Jews are no longer economic parasites, for they are not only middlemen, but they also work the land and run the factories. Having "normalized," that is, broadened, their economic base to include the entire range of economic activities, the cultural and intellectual life of the Jews will become "normalized" as well, since it will have its roots in the creative life of the people. And this economic and cultural normalization, in conjunction with its national normalization—escape from a minority status and, hence, from antisemitism—will enable the Jews to take their rightful and normal place among the nations of the world. In short, Zionism, for Kiryat Yedidim, although a particularistic movement, has as its ultimate aim a universalistic and humanistic goal. This goal is not the geographic segregation of Jews, with the intention of developing specific Jewish characteristics that will separate the Jews from the non-Jewish world. Its aim, rather, is the concentration of Jews in their homeland so that they may develop a "normal" national life which, in turn, will enable them to interact with the rest of the world as normal human beings, rather than as members of a dependent, parasitic, fearful minority. For Kiryat Yedidim, then, national liberation is not only as important as social and personal liberation, it is a necessary condition for their existence.

This is not to say, however, that its conception of Zionism does not contain much of the ethnocentrism that characterizes other nationalist philosophies. Like other Israelis, the chaverim polarize their world into *Aretz*, whose literal meaning is "country," but which is used to refer to *the* country, Israel; and *chutz la-aretz*, which refers to the rest of the world (literally, "outside the country"). So, too, they polarize the peoples of the world into *Yehudim*, a term which includes Israeli and non-Israeli Jews alike, and *Goyim* (literally, nations), the rest of mankind. This distinction is rhetorical, inherited from an epoch in which the world was polarized into friend (Jews) and foe (the rest of mankind). Nevertheless, it does not take long for one to realize that this rhetoric expresses an important contemporary psychological attitude. The ethnocentrism of the chaverim is expressed, moreover, in their insistence that all

Jews ought to settle in Israel, and in their expressed amazement that any Jew who has visited Israel should want to return to his native country.

The Zionist philosophy of Kiryat Yedidim serves to explain some of its important characteristics and behavior. Its emphasis on physical labor and its choice of rural, rather than urban living, stems not only from its general social philosophy, but from its Zionist convictions: the "normalization" of Jewish national life requires that Jews return to physical labor and that they strike roots in the soil. Moreover, the very geographic location of the kibbutz was dictated by its Zionist conviction. Kiryat Yedidim was founded on what was then swampland, in an area which was remote from Jewish settlement. This was part of deliberate Zionist settlement policy, whose aim was to drain the Palestinian swampland so that more acreage could be brought under cultivation, and to continuously extend the frontiers of Jewish colonization so that all of mandated Palestine would be dotted with Jewish settlements.

It is this same Zionist philosophy that today motivates Kiryat Yedidim, together with other kibbutzim, to devote so much of its manpower and energies to non-kibbutz, nationalist goals. During, and immediately following, World War II kibbutz members were to be found in Europe in the vanguard of those who risked their lives in order to smuggle Jewish refugees out of Europe and into Palestine. Since the war, the kibbutzim have lent some of their members for work in the refugee camps that are scattered throughout Israel. Finally, since Kiryat Yedidim views itself as a Zionist agency, it has opened its doors for the settlement and rehabilitation of refugee youth. When children from Hitler's Europe and, more recently, from Moslem countries arrived in Israel, the country was faced with the problem of how to provide for their care. The kibbutzim, in an agreement with the Jewish Agency, agreed to accept groups of adolescents who would live and be educated in a kibbutz until they were prepared to take their place in the life of the country. And when one group leaves, another takes its place. The kibbutzim provide them with food, shelter, and their entire education. This is not to say that their motivations were entirely altruistic. Kiryat Yedidim, for example, derives some benefit from this arrangement in the stipend it receives from the Agency for each child it accepts and in the work performed by the youths in the kibbutz economy. The fact is, however, that the financial gain is small, and is more than offset by the great inconveniences which this arrangement causes the kibbutz, all of whose facilities are already strained.

These, then, are the moral postulates of Kiryat Yedidim and, indeed, of all kibbutzim. They are important, not only because they constitute the basis for the social structure of the kibbutz, but because they provide a clue to an important premise of its living: the premise that life is serious. It is serious because the realization of these values, rather than immediate pleasure or self-seeking, is taken to be the purpose of living.

The feeling that life's primary meaning is to be sought in the realization of values that transcend one's own personal importance was best expressed by a chavera who had recently returned from a visit to the United States. When asked by the author how long it had taken her to become lonesome for Israel, she replied that she missed it almost at once. In America, she said,

. . . they have no values. Of course, in Israel we have austerity, but we have values: we are absorbing immigrants, building a new society. Hence, you feel that your life has meaning. But what meaning does it have in America?

The consciousness of the seriousness of existence which is characteristic not only of Kiryat Yedidim, but of the kibbutz movement as a whole, is emphasized at every opportunity, including festive occasions. The annual nation-wide dance festival, for example, is held at Kibbutz Dahlia, and is staged by various groups throughout the country, including the kibbutzim. The year of the author's attendance, the audience numbered more than 50,000 and the theme of the festival was the cultural contribution of each of the groups of immigrants to Israel; the dances and songs of the various countries of origin were presented by these groups which had migrated from every part of the world. But, amidst the spectacle of the colors and music of many cultures, arose the feature tableau of the evening, wherein was depicted the tragedy of Jewish life throughout the Diaspora and the struggle and eventual success of the return to the Homeland. The audience was reminded that there were still many Jews suffering in the Diaspora, and that the task of all was to work for their redemption and return. It seems that even an evening of folk art cannot be enjoyed simply and for itself without some message of social significance.

Our problem, now, is to discover how it was that the founders of Kiryat Yedidim—young Jews from the shtetls of Eastern Europe—left their middle-class homes and emigrated to Palestine in order to found a community based on the principles just described.

CHAPTER 3

We have always been extreme. We were extreme in demanding *hagshama* (self-realization by immigration to Palestine), rather than remaining Zionists in the Diaspora. In Palestine we were extreme in demanding return to the land and to agriculture. In agriculture we were extreme in demanding kibbutz. In kibbutz we were extreme in demanding (geographical) border kibbutzim. Hence, there are deep psychological roots for our political extremism. We are always on the border.

Statement by a chaver

THE SOCIAL HISTORY OF KIRYAT YEDIDIM

The European Background

THE FOUNDERS of Kiryat Yedidim were predominantly of Polish origin, and although they migrated to Palestine at an early age—in their late teens or early twenties—their European experience has left its indelible influence on the kind of community they established. This European experience can be analyzed under five aspects, as far as its influence on the vattikim is concerned: (1) the status of Jewry in Poland, (2) the broader culture of the shtetl, (3) parent-child relationships in the shtetl, (4) the Zionist movement, and (5) Jewish and other European youth movements.

THE STATUS OF POLISH JEWRY. Eastern European Jews had long been the victims of a tradition of antisemitism,[1] an antisemitism which included not only social discrimination, but also physical attacks and pogroms. Nevertheless, in the early years of the twentieth century, many Jews in Poland were beginning to think that Western Enlightenment and liberalism, which were slowly permeating Eastern Europe, would bring them the emancipation they were seeking. Some looked forward to eventual assimilation and identified themselves with Polish nationalism and with the Polish cultural renaissance. Their hopes were strengthened when Polish schools were opened to Jews, because they saw in this secular, national education the road to their eventual integration within the larger Polish society.

It soon became apparent, however, that these hopes were to be frustrated. Even after the schools were opened to Jews, "the Jewish students were made to feel at every point that they were strangers, and that they were not acceptable in the eyes of their Polish classmates."[2] And even those who sought acceptance by complete assimilation were told that they "were not wanted in the Renaissance of the Polish national society."[3] The realization that they were not wanted, in spite of their feelings of genuine Polish patriotism, came as a severe blow to many of these Jewish young people, and it served as a potent influence in their determination to seek their salvation in other ways. The crucial importance of this rejection is evident from the spontaneous references to specific rejection experiences on the part of the vattikim in the course of conversation. The Polish

[1] See Dubnow, *The History of the Jews in Russia and Poland.*
[2] From a book published by a Veteran Settler of Kiryat Yedidim.
[3] *Ibid.*

schools, remarked one vattika, "were very patriotic in emphasis, and the Jewish students shared this Polish patriotism." The latter considered themselves to be Poles, and were Jewish only in their homes; "otherwise we forgot that we were Jews." But in the experience of this woman there occurred an event "which I shall never forget," although she was only ten years old at the time; this experience was shared by many others. It was Polish Independence Day (May 3), and she was very excited as she prepared to go to school, because there was to be a celebration in her class. When the class was assembled the teacher announced that all the Jewish children could return home, because "this is our holiday, not yours." This was a "terrible blow" to her, and it served as a psychological preparation for her entry into The Movement.[4] This disillusionment with Polish education and with the possibilities of acceptance by Polish society was exacerbated by the outbreak of anti-semitic pogroms after World War I, in which Jews were killed and their houses pillaged by Polish peasants, often with the active assistance of the Polish police and army. This proved to be the final blow for the educated youth, and The Movement organized a mass exodus from the Polish schools, and in their stead established Jewish *gymnasia*. "It became apparent," said a vattik, "at least to the members of The Movement, that there was no solution to the 'Jewish problem' within Poland."

[4] The Movement exists today in two forms. It is the name of the youth movement, both in Israel and abroad, which prepares young people for kibbutz living. Even the children who are reared in the kibbutz become members of this youth movement before they become members of the kibbutz. But The Movement is also the name of the political party which was founded by the members of the European youth movement when they arrived in Israel. This party has since joined with two other small parties to form a new political alliance, but the members of the former party remain a faction within the larger group, known as The Movement.

THE CULTURE OF THE SHTETL. Most of the vattikim lived either in shtetls or in city ghettos whose culture was that of the shtetl, or they were born of orthodox parents who continued to adhere to the culture of the shtetl. This culture, whatever may have been its objective merits,[5] was viewed unfavorably by the new generation of Jewish youth. For them, the shtetl was a "poor and gloomy Galician village" in which people lived in "narrow alleys,"[6] in both a physical and a psychological sense. It produced people who were but "caricatures" of what true human beings could become. The shtetl Jew, we read in an official publication of The Movement,

... is a caricature of a natural and normal man, both physically and spiritually. As an individual in the group he shirks responsibility, and does not know organization and discipline. It appears to him that he is wiser than all men, and they must discard their ideas for his. He especially excels in argumentation and "pilpul" (casuistry), that for him become ends in themselves.[7]

The antagonism of the youth to traditional Jewish culture and to the personality type it had created, was extended to a dislike for the so-called Jewish physical type. Even today, adults in the kibbutz often point to their young, blonde *sabras* (native-born Israelis), and ask with pride, "would you ever guess that they are Jewish?" Or, to cite a typical reaction, a vattika commented that two young American Jews who were visiting the kibbutz were "so nice-looking you would never know that they were Jewish." When the

[5] For an ethnography of the shtetl, see Zborowski and Herzog.
[6] Veteran Settler, *op. cit.*
[7] From "Our Program," published in 1917. This characterization of the Jew, points to an important aspect of Zionism which has seldom been commented upon—its antisemitic component. But compare Kaufman, "Anti-Semitic Stereotypes in Zionism."

author pointed out the antisemitism implicit in her remark, she admitted that this was so, adding that she has always "hated" the "typical" Jewish physical characteristics.

This youth, then, although spurned by the non-Jewish world, could not find comfort in their Jewish world. They rejected the one, and were rejected by the other.

PARENT-CHILD INTERACTION. Of considerable psychological importance for the understanding both of their opposition to the shtetl and of the system of "collective education" which they were later to establish in Kiryat Yedidim was the opposition of this youth to its parents. "We were always opposed to the life of our parents," was the comment of one vattika. "We always," said a vattik, "stressed the necessity for rebellion against parents and the parental way of life." A constant refrain which one hears in any discussion concerning kibbutz education is the importance of preventing the parent-child conflict that had characterized their own childhood and adolescence. This conflict between parents and children in the shtetl is summed up by a chaver:

Not even in the midst of his family life did the Jewish youth find consolation or stimulation. The split between fathers and sons widened. The sons stood, as it were, at the crossroads. They had escaped from the world of yesterday, in which their fathers were still immersed, but the world of the future was still enveloped in fog.[8]

[8] Veteran Settler, *op. cit.* It is of no small theoretical consequence to point out that many values and forms of their fathers' lives are retained by the chaverim, many of which are indicated throughout this monograph. The most general and perhaps most significant continuity is in the degree to which the daily routine is regulated. The lives of their fathers were regulated in even their minutiae by the compendium of rabbinic law, known as the *Shulchan Aruch*. The daily lives of the chaverim are regulated to almost the same degree by the rules of The Federation. These rules govern such diverse aspects of their lives as the number of children permitted within a dormitory, the nurse-child ratio, the number

YOUTH MOVEMENT. Having rebelled against the "world" in both its Jewish and general manifestations, these youths sought their outlet in The Movement, an organization which represented the confluence of two historical streams —the European youth movement and the Zionist movement. Zionism, as a secular political movement, had been a potent force in Eastern Europe from the time of the first international Zionist Congress, held in Basel in 1897.[9] A number of Zionist parties and youth organizations had soon sprung up, and The Movement was among the latter. Originally, this was a scouting movement with Zionist sympathies but which neither emphasized nor encouraged migration to Palestine. Its main emphasis was on the scouting aspect of its program, as its original ten principles indicate. A member of The Movement is:

1. A man of truth
2. Loyal to his people
3. A brother to his fellows
4. A helpful and dependable brother
5. A lover of nature
6. Obedient to the orders of his leaders
7. Joyful and gay
8. Economical and generous
9. A man of courage
10. Pure in thoughts, words, and deeds[10]

---

of hours to be worked in a day, the length of the annual vacations, the minimum housing facilities, the minimum amount of furniture for each room, the leisure time to be provided a pregnant woman or nursing mother, and a host of others.

[9] For the history of the Zionist movement, *see* Levensohn, *Outline of Zionist History*.

[10] From "Our Principles," published in 1917. The last principle was interpreted to mean opposition to drinking, smoking, and sexual relationships.

This scouting emphasis was strengthened when a number of young Polish Jews who had fled to Vienna were exposed to the German youth movement immediately after World War I. This German youth movement left an indelible impression on them, for in their eyes

... the bright and modern images of the German youth were like magic. We, who had yearned for freedom and emancipation, saw in these young men and women, the prototype of emancipated youth. For many this vision was like a revelation, and they devoured the literature of this youth movement, and drank its words with great thirst; they were impressed and influenced by all its notions.[11]

The "notions" of these groups—particularly those of the Wandervögel, whose program most influenced The Movement—were simple. They included a revolt against tradition; love of nature; a love of nation, which seemed to consist of a vague *mystique* of the "folk"; self-expression; emphasis on the emotional aspect of life; the gospel of "joy in work." This was a program which stressed the regeneration of the individual, and his emancipation from the bonds of urban mores and artificial convention. This meant, in both practical and psychological terms, a break with parents and the parental generation. As Becker puts it, they "... loathed and hated the world of their elders, and were ready to follow any Pied Piper whose mystery and power held promise of a new realm where longings found fruition."[12]

Like other "primitivistic" movements in history—and this was a "primitivistic" movement, *par excellence*—the members of the German youth movement believed that all the pettiness and sordidness of human behavior were a func-

[11] Veteran Settler, *op. cit.*, p. 13.

[12] Becker, p. 73. This book, particularly chapter 5, is a valuable description and analysis of the German youth movement.

tion of city living and its concomitant luxuries and false conventions.[13] Once emancipated from these evils of civilization, human nature would realize its full potentiality, and joy and camaraderie would characterize human social life. For this youth, then, The Movement represented

. . . the visible embodiment of rebellion against flabby school routine, insincere church attendance, flatulent concerts, boring parties designed for display and climbing, nauseous student jollifications laden with the sluggish ceremonial and spurious heartiness of the paternal *stammtisch*, well-meant but repellant counsel about ways of getting on in the world . . .[14]

This rebellion, however, did not take the form of political activity. The Movement did not develop a program for the destruction of these "false" values, nor, for that matter, any other political programs. Instead of advocating a change in contemporary society, it prescribed an escape from society into the world of nature, where "adventure was still possible."

Trudging along with the beloved leader, came the new way of life: wandering at will through fields, forests, and hills, pitching camp in a ruined castle or under the lindens fringing a little cluster of peasant houses where the shams of the city were absent.[15]

For the Jewish youth, this escape into nature was particularly captivating. As a vattika, describing her experience in

[13] "Primitivism" is used here in the meaning attributed to it in that excellent book by Lovejoy and Boas, *A Documentary History of Primitivism and Related Ideas*. It refers to the notion that man's true excellence is to be found in those social conditions which correspond most exactly to a "state of nature." This concept is, of course, closely related to the "Noble Savage" idea of the eighteenth century, and to certain aspects of nineteenth-century romanticism.

[14] Becker, p. 75.

[15] *Ibid.*

these outings, put it, "Jews don't know what nature is, what a tree is." Their hikes in the youth movement, she said, gave them "the peace of nature," which impelled them to settle on the land when they left for Palestine.

The "primitivism" of these groups was expressed not only in a return to nature, but in their emphasis on the ascetic life. At the very beginning

. . . there was rejection of comfort in favor of hard primitivism and later . . . abstinence from alcohol and tobacco, refusal to participate in ballroom dancing, avoidance of motion pictures, and a host of other self-imposed inhibitions. These lent an ascetic quality to even the less rigorous contingents of the youth movement and helped to make the break with the adult world really evident to even the most obtuse parent, school teacher, or pastor.[16]

Some of the other more important "self-imposed inhibitions" which The Movement accepted included simple housing, simple clothing, and the avoidance of any make-up by women. This ascetic tradition is still very much alive in Kiryat Yedidim.[17] At the same time one of the important factors contributing to the "crisis" in the kibbutz movement is the tension between this historic tradition of asceticism and the desire for luxury and comfort which has become a strong motive in the lives of many chaverim.[18]

Though the German youth movement stressed the importance of individual freedom, self-expression, and emancipation from the group, it was not long before the group—that is, their *own* group—began to assume great importance. The group served two functions in the lives of German youth, and there is little question but that it served the same func-

[16] *Ibid.*, p. 98.
[17] See below, pp. 67–70 ff.
[18] See Chapter 6.

tions in the lives of those Jewish youths who founded Kiryat Yedidim. In the first place, the "sense of belonging to a band of dissenters, to a conventicle of the elect, had a peculiar thrill for you."[19] A vattika remembers that The Movement gave "substance to our lives, for we felt that we were different from others, better than they, for we were going to start a new life."

The crucial significance of this feeling of being "different" and "better" than others because of a determination to build a "new life," cannot be underestimated. It is this feeling, together with its social and psychological consequences, which served—and continues to serve—to transform a nebulous and romantic scouting movement into a cohesive and integrated sect and, later, into a self-conscious political community.[20]

The other function served by the group was to provide its members with precisely those emotional experiences which would give them the sense of joy and freedom they sought. "Their cherished selves," writes Becker, "would expand and deepen in and through the surging emotions called forth by banding together with the like-minded and by undergoing the experiences of the 'expedition' and the 'nest.'"[21] That these experiences were profound and deep-

[19] Becker, p. 75.

[20] The sect-like character of the kibbutz, which will be discussed below (see Chapter V), is one of the first impressions the author had of the kibbutz. It is of some interest to note that Becker, in his analysis of the German youth movements, can characterize them by no other term than by "sect." "Identification with the group . . . ," he writes, "came to be the way in which the initially random conventicles of dissenters were fused into sects of the like-minded and consciously elect." (Ibid., p. 83)

[21] Ibid., p. 77. The "expedition" refers to the periodic hiking trips, and the "nest" was the meeting place of each local chapter. The latter (in Hebrew, ken) was adopted by The Movement while still in Europe. Today, however, the term refers to each chapter, rather than to its meeting place. Thus there is a ken Tel Aviv, a ken Kiryat Yedidim, etc.

seated is attested to by the spontaneous references to them on the part of the vattikim thirty years later. Indeed, they were so important that they served, according to a kibbutz leader, as the model for the communal form of living that they were to create in Palestine. "The ideology of work," he said, "came from Russian Zionism and the early kibbutzim; communal living came from the hikes in The Movement."

Since The Movement emphasized the regeneration of the individual and, consequently, the ultimate regeneration of society, it devoted much of its energies to the formulation of the "ideal" educational system. This, said a vattik, "was our main interest; it became an *idée fixe* with us. For three or four years thousands of our people struggled with this problem. It was then that the educational philosophy and structure which is found in the kibbutz today was formulated."

ZIONISM. It can be observed from the foregoing discussion, as well as from the principles of The Movement, that the latter was primarily a continental youth movement, in which Zionism played a minor role. As late as 1917, in the article describing "Our Program," nothing is said about Zionism as being integral to it. The three major emphases of this "program" were, with one exception, the three emphases of the German youth movements. The first emphasis was that of *changing* Jewish life, rather than of escaping from it. The change did not involve migration to Palestine, however, but a change in accordance with the values of the youth movement. The other emphases included the living in groups, the eschewal of formal education, and the turning to nature for instruction.

The important turning point in the Zionist career of

The Movement came with the pogroms in Poland and the Ukraine after the war, to which reference has already been made. Many of the members of The Movement experienced these pogroms personally, and were deeply affected by them. At least one of their members committed suicide in despair. "This was the final event in the decision to go to Palestine; we could not remain in Poland," was the conclusion of one vattik. Post-war Polish antisemitism was merely one item, said a vattik, in a long Jewish indictment of Western culture and of the "bourgeois ideology of the French Revolution." Thus, when these young Jews who were to found Kiryat Yedidim realized that that ideology—including rationalism, liberalism, emancipation—was "one big lie," they decided to emigrate.

Their Zionist decision, it should be noted, was not based on any "positive" Zionist ideals, but on a negative reaction to European society. And this attitude toward Zionism and, ultimately, to their own Jewishness, has had important psychological consequences for the chaverim, as well as for their children. Like the other nationalistic movements of the nineteenth century, Zionism was part of a romantic tradition which looked for a renaissance of an indigenous national culture. Like these other nationalisms, Jewish nationalism stressed the glories of its People's cultural past, and prophesied a recrudescence of these glories once it achieved national independence in its own land. But this *mystique* of nationhood was foreign to the original ideology of The Movement. Far from being an expression of Judaism, Zionism was viewed by them as an escape from Judaism—the culture of the shtetl—as well as an escape from the grim realities of Jewish life in the Diaspora, with its persecutions and its pogroms. In short, Zionism, they believed, would enable the Jews to achieve a "normal" existence.[22]

Whatever their Zionist motivations, it is significant that, once the decision was made, it involved more than official affiliation with the Zionist movement or explicit endorsement of the Zionist cause. It involved, rather, the decision to migrate to Palestine. Only in Palestine, they believed, could they find self-realization. As a chaver has written, The Movement:

. . . was not satisfied with an analysis of the national situation, and with establishing the correct diagnosis, but it obliged its members to action, in order to turn the disaster into the road to emancipation. And from this followed its active attitude to the national problem, namely, acceptance of responsibility in the development of the history of the nation.[23]

Their decision to migrate, like so many other aspects of their history, becomes more intelligible within the general framework of the European youth movement. In general youth movement experience it was discovered that, when no explicit membership criteria were required, any one with "tensions" could, and did, join. Eventually, this situation:

. . . becomes intolerable for those of more intense persuasion, and they begin to look for the outward sign of inward grace among their fellows—and these signs were not always evident . . . (This sign came to be) . . . the continuing sense of fusion acquired in and through the supreme test of the expedition.[24]

The Jewish movement was confronted with the same problem; but since its problems were more extreme than

[22] Whether one can achieve a "normal" national existence without some pride in one's national past is questionable, and the ambivalence that marks the attitude of the sabras toward their Jewishness indicates that "normalcy" is not quite so simple as the early settlers had originally assumed.

[23] Veteran Settler, *op. cit.*

[24] Becker, p. 84.

those of its German counterpart, the "sign" it demanded was correspondingly more extreme. Instead of demanding an "expedition" into the country, it demanded one outside the country—*aliya*—to Palestine. The insistence on aliya, or migration, claims a very perceptive vattik,

> . . . was the real solution for us, since it was the final outlet, the culmination of the youth movement. Instead of collapsing like other youth movements, (ours) succeeded because it offered a final realization or culmination in Palestine. If it weren't for Zionism, (The Movement) would have become just another episode in the life of those who did not want to continue the life of their fathers.[25]

In 1920, they left for Palestine.

Aliya

In perspective this migration seems like an absurd adventure. The ninety or so immigrants who arrived in Palestine and who, one year later, were to found Kiryat Yedidim were still in their teens—eighteen and nineteen years old—with little conception of what the land or people were like. Their ignorance of the then current situation in Palestine was so marked that they did not know of the few existing

---

[25] It should be noted, however, that their very rebellion against "the life of their fathers" included an important value of the latter's life—Zionism. The Zionism of their fathers, to be sure, was of a different quality from their own. It was primarily a religious Zionism which looked to the Messiah for the Restoration of God's People to His Holy Land, or it was a passive political Zionism which involved the support of Zionism without their own migration to Palestine. In both cases the parents objected to the emigration of their children. Nevertheless, this ultimate rejection of their fathers (physical separation) and of their way of life led, in an interesing psychological paradox, to a closing of the circle rather than to a widening of the gap. Indeed, one might speculate whether the choice of Palestine rather than Uganda, for example, was not motivated by an unconscious desire to identify with their fathers in the very process of rebelling against them.

collectives, such as Degania, which had been founded in 1909. They knew little, if anything, of the economic conditions of the country, and they were not even sure that they would be able to find employment. They knew neither where they would live nor how they would live. These middle-class, urban youths, whose only rural experience had been with "hikes" in the youth movement, had no plans, except for the nebulous one of working on the land. However fantastic and quixotic this adventure may seem to us, it is partially explicable in terms of their youth movement background. The youth movements were opposed to order, plans, goals, specified objectives. "It would be hard to find a 'purer' type of irrational social action in any society," writes Becker of the Wandervögel.[26]

Wilhelm Stählin, a Wandervögel leader, stated the position most dramatically:

Where lively people are together no one needs a programme. Our happiest hours were those in which there was nothing planned beforehand, argued out, and finally fixed. Instead, words and songs quelled out of the living present and out of the deep bonds which wove every participant into an internalized unity. There is nothing more wonderful and fruitful than communion in a small group of confidants where no plan and no "order of the day" hems in spontaneous vitality and the spirit that "blowing where it listeth," unites and enthralls us. Every day is begun with eagerness and hope, and every hour brings forth our wandering gratitude for rich, over-flowing experience. Poor in soul are those persons who because they always have "something laid out" and always know what must be done at this moment and talked about at (sic) that never get around to the joys of simply living and being together with friends—without *any* program.[27]

[26] Becker, p. 96–97.
[27] *Ibid.*, p. 97.

The physical conditions in Palestine met by these new arrivals were so harsh that many found it impossible to adjust to the new environment and returned to Poland. At first they could not find work, and they had practically nothing to eat. Moreover, since they were not yet adapted to the physical environment, many became seriously ill. In one place all eighty contracted malaria and were hospitalized. Some of them, although not willing to return to Europe, left the group to try to make their own way in the cities. Those who remained with the group finally founded the kibbutz.

It was at this time that this small band of immigrants had an intense group experience that was to leave its mark on their future course, an experience which is remembered today as their "Golden Age." They were living in Nevei Gila, a spot in some then isolated mountains, and it was there that they first experienced the meaning of an important youth movement concept—the "organic community"—that is, a small community whose solidarity and integration are based on intimate personal relations. "Organic community," which connotes many of the same sentiments as the *Bunderlebnis* of the German youth movement, constituted one of the major goals of the European youth movements. Carl Blüher, the German youth movement theoretician whose thought was one of the important influences on the vattikim, taught that the Bunderlebnis was the important consequence of the "expedition."

Then began to come into being something that we had long felt but had never translated into living experience: we were an inseparably united fellowship. When at long last we found the right path into the valley there was aroused a feeling of intense joy which grew out of the dangers we had triumphantly endured, yes, but still more because we had stood a test proving that we were finally bound by friendly and comradely ties.[28]

The period which the vattikim spent in Nevei Gila not only bound them together in "friendly and comradely ties," but it represented a uniquely "creative moment" in their history, as one of them put it. "It was as if the best we were capable of found its expression there." He compared their intense emotional experiences, and their successful attempts to create an "organic community," to the creativity of Jesus in those same mountains two thousand years before.

Since this period was to serve, as it were, as the prototype of the ideal kibbutz, it is important to understand the nature of this "creative moment." These, it must be remembered, were a group of youngsters—"spoiled children," as one chaver put it—who had left their homes and their families and had come to a strange country whose landscape was gaunt and forbidding, whose physical environment was difficult, and whose climate was harsh. They were alone, isolated, and friendless. Within this socio-psychological setting, they were, so to speak, thrown back on their psychological heels; and their strength and consolation—if they were to experience these at all—had to come from within their own group. The psychological bonds induced by this mutual dependency-security relationship were established in a physical environment of wild but beautiful mountains, and in a social environment free from conventional ties and responsibilities. These factors, combined with their freedom in sexual behavior and their consequent romantic-erotic attachments, conspired to create what one vattik termed, "a state of hysteria." Given this psychological setting, it is

[28] *Ibid.*, pp. 82–83.

little wonder that they experienced a sense of "organic community."

The importance of this experience for the vattikim lay in the fact that it provided these young people with a vision of what their ideal society could be, and it was this vision that motivated the establishment of the kibbutz. But few of them realized then (as few realize even today) that this experience could probably not be recaptured. Nevertheless, this utopian vision serves today as the standard by which the chaverim evaluate the contemporary kibbutz. The resulting contrast has only served to create that tragic tension which is the inevitable result of the discrepancy between the real and the ideal.[29]

Having captured this common vision, these pioneers realized that they must translate their vision into action, for, commented a chaver, if they did not "begin to create something, the vision would disappear or become fatuous." Hence, he continued, they "went down to the valley to create." They settled near a city, where they lived in a tent camp and attempted to eke out a living by road construction. This, too, was a period of intense emotional experience, as well as one of great hardship. For six months they had been unemployed, and had had little to eat. When they at last began to work on the highway, they soon realized how poorly equipped they were for manual labor. The transition from their life in Europe—a life of comfort and relative prosperity—to a life of strenuous physical labor and poverty—a life which provided them with scant rations and with mattresses of cardboard on which to sleep—was extremely difficult. "We were unprepared for it," said a

[29] See Chapter 6 for the role played by this "tension" in the current "crisis."

vattik. "We had no idea it would be that hard." But hardship was the badge of a chalutz. "When I complained about the lack of mattresses," recalled a vattika, "my husband said, 'you are not a chalutza.' And when I protested about the clothes which never fit me, he said, 'you are not a chalutza!'" Then, half-sheepishly, she added, "the fact is, it was very hard for me." "It was very romantic," commented another vattika, "but it was very hard." She added, as an afterthought, "but if one wants to live for an ideal, he can overcome hardships."

Without depreciating the importance of this "ideal," it should be emphasized that other factors, as well, enabled these pioneers to overcome their hardships. For them, as for their counterparts in the German youth movement, the ability to withstand and to transcend physical hardship—even to transmute it into an important spiritual experience—was a source of great ego satisfaction. Nature was not only to be enjoyed, but, like work, it was something to be conquered. The battle cry of these pioneers, it will be recalled, was kibbush ha-avodah, the conquest of labor, which implied the conquest of nature. Hence, it is probably not inaccurate to apply to them what has been written of the Wandervögel. They

. . . found a peculiar beauty and thrill in slogging through a rain-drenched countryside, laughing at torn and sodden clothing until they arrived at a shelter where they could slump and dry out before a roaring fire. Promethean defiance of nature because of success in becoming one with it was the essence of such elated experience.[30]

If the hard labor and the difficult conditions gave to the pioneers intense ego-gratification, the group experience—

[30] Becker, p. 82.

such as the one in Nevei Gila—continued to provide them with deep-seated emotional satisfactions. Again, as in the latter case, the term, "hysteria" was used by a vattik to characterize the intensity of this emotion. To those conditions that had given rise to "hysteria" in Nevei Gila, and that obtained here as well, there was added one important new influence: *Chassidism*.[31] Chassidism, according to the Veteran Settler, served to link these young Jews with their past.

We did not want to remain uprooted. We sought some bond to a cultural heritage of previous generations, and we found the treasure of Chassidic song and lore. In the evenings the kibbutz would assemble in the center of the camp and sing—an echo of the songs of generations concerning *shechinta b'galuta* and *kisufei geula*.[32]

The choice of Chassidism was not accidental. Both the Chassidim and the chalutzim, observed a vattik, had "broken the chains of the forms of traditional Judaism," and both had "rebelled against their fathers." Hence, "we found an intimate relationship between our lives and the Chassidic lives." This relationship was so meaningful that, despite their meager physical sustenance, they found the energy to produce some Chassidic plays, which, writes the Veteran Settler, gave them "spiritual sustenance." For, despite the intellectual and social chasm that separated the chalutzim from

[31] Chassidism, a religious folk movement which had its origin among Eastern European Jews in the eighteenth century, stressed the mystical and emotional aspects of the religious life. The Chassidic emphasis on nature, joy, and dancing, would naturally appeal to these youths, despite their own indifference to religion.

[32] Veteran Settler. The two Hebrew concepts may be translated respectively as "the exile of God (from the Holy Land)" and the "longing for redemption."

the characters in these plays, the latter, says a vattik, "expressed much that was close to our hearts."

They not only sang Chassidic songs and produced Chassidic plays, but they also danced in the manner of Chassidim; that is, they danced with *kavvana*, or "devotion." "For months we had nothing to eat, but we danced all night," recalls a vattik. This statement—for one who has seen the *hora*, their favorite folk dance, and who can visualize it danced with kavvana—expresses with supreme eloquence the intense emotionality of their group experience. Danced with kavvana, the hora can be both the cause and the expression of the group emotion which seems to have characterized that period. This is a group dance in which the participants, who are linked to one another arm-on-shoulder, are united in a large circle. The group thus becomes a unity, in which each individual faces the center and can see every other individual. The unity of the group is expressed not only spatially and physically, but kinesthetically, as well, for the momentum of the dance creates a centrifugal force which threatens to thrust the individual from the circle; but his centrifugality is conterbalanced by the centripetal force emanating from the entire group, and he is drawn again towards the center by the entwined arms of his fellows on either side. Thus the dancer experiences a sense of freedom and abandon, but it is a freedom checked at every step by the pressure of the group, whose sense of unity is enhanced all the more by the rhythmic beat of the feet and by the monotony of the never-ceasing repetition of the song. Thus can the group both create and express the hysteria of its individuals.

In addition to Chassidism, the vattikim came under another important influence: the ideas of Sigmund Freud. In looking for a "theory that could explain our feelings, our stress, and our turmoil," explained a vattik, "we came upon psychoanalysis, and it was as if Freud had written especially for us." This early emphasis on Freud is now a source of considerable regret for some of the vattikim. For as one of them put it: "Freud ruled in our society, and this postponed the acceptance of Marxism." Psychoanalysis, however, did more than "explain" their own personal lives. Its theories contributed much to the educational system which they were later to establish.

This period was important not only for its psychological effects on the chaverim, however, but for the experience it gave them in the organization of communal living. It was at this time that most of the important institutions of the present kibbutz, such as public ownership, the town meeting, the committee system, and many others, were developed. It was at this time, too, that they decided to form a kibbutz, a community which would emphasize the primary value of labor. Because of this decision, many of the chaverim who did not share this labor orientation left the group. On the other hand, their lack of a truly crystallized philosophy and, more particularly, their lack of a political program, alienated those who demanded political activity; and they too left the group. Because of these defections, however, they had become an integrated group, with a strong sense of *esprit de corps*, and with confidence in their ability to create a new society. Hence, when they were invited by the Jewish Agency to settle on their own land, they were eager to begin.

CHAPTER 4

[The kibbutz] is the foundation cell of the future society that is already in process of realization today . . . The *kibbutz* society has carried out a complete revolution of life, and has changed the ancient order of human social living. The property system, method of production, division of labor, foundation of the family, the character of human relations, the status of women, the foundation of education—all have changed in their fundamentals and are in the process of a permanent change.

Speech by a kibbutz leader

THE KIBBUTZ AS A COMMUNAL SOCIETY, I

The People and their Setting

THE POPULATION of Kiryat Yedidim numbers approximately five hundred persons and comprises three generations. There are approximately two hundred and fifty adult members of the kibbutz, most of whom migrated to Palestine from Europe, more specifically, from Eastern Europe. This immigration, however, did not occur at one time, so that the adults can be stratified into age groups, depending upon their year of immigration and their eventual arrival in the kibbutz. The remaining chaverim are native-born Israelis who came to the kibbutz from the cities or who were born in Kiryat Yedidim and joined it as adults.

These age groups represent an informal age grading system and, indeed, they are referred to as *shichvot*, or "layers,"
by the kibbutz. The oldest layer consists of the founders of
Kiryat Yedidim, about eighty strong, who are roughly fifty
years old. In most respects this is the most important layer
in the kibbutz. The latter's social structure was designed to
implement its values; the leadership within the kibbutz,
both formal and informal, stems primarily from its ranks;
kibbutz representation in the national kibbutz movement,
in the labor movement, and in national politics is comprised
primarily of members of this layer; and the intellectuals of
Kiryat Yedidim are, in the main, members of this group.

The second layer also consists of immigrants from Eastern
Europe who joined Kiryat Yedidim from ten to twenty
years after its founding. All had been trained in The Movement and, therefore, had acquired the values of the kibbutz
and had received extensive preparation for kibbutz living
before their arrival. This is the largest layer, numerically
speaking, consisting of about one hundred and twenty chaverim. Although some of its members are highly cultured,
this is the least intellectual layer in Kiryat Yedidim and it
has the least amount of formal education. Many of the officials of Kiryat Yedidim, committee chairmen, and economic
foremen come from its ranks. At the same time much of the
pressure for innovation—that is, for retreat from the original
values of the kibbutz—is exerted by members of this layer.

The third layer, comprising individuals in their late
twenties, consists of about forty chaverim who, for the most
part, are either sabras[1] or European immigrants who arrived

[1] A sabra is, in current Israeli usage, any native-born Jewish Israeli.
In general the term will be used in this monograph to refer to those
individuals, children or adults, born in Kiryat Yedidim.

in Israel at a very young age. A small number of this group consists of children of Kiryat Yedidim who are now members of the kibbutz. The great majority, however, consists of former members of The Movement in Tel Aviv and other cities in Israel, who were invited to join Kiryat Yedidim (about ten years before the inception of this study) so as to provide the kibbutz youth with a larger peer group. This is the group from which the kibbutz youth has chosen its marriage partners. This layer, and particularly those of its members who were trained in The Movement in Tel Aviv, is highly gifted intellectually; in it are to be found at least one composer, painter, dancer, dramatist, actor, and ideologue. It is beginning to assume greater and greater responsibility in the economy and is becoming more articulate in the various councils of the kibbutz. Moreover, much of the pressure against innovation and the insistence that the kibbutz remain faithful to its original values arises from within its membership.

The youngest layer consists of about twenty chaverim in their early twenties, who are recent graduates of the high school. About half of them are children of Kiryat Yedidim, the other half consisting of city children who studied in the kibbutz high school and who, upon graduation, chose to become members of the kibbutz. More than half of this layer are still serving in the army, however, and return to Kiryat Yedidim on Saturdays or holidays. This group occupies important economic positions and some of its members have even been elected as foremen of their economic branch. It is still a highly inarticulate layer, however, seldom expressing its opinions in kibbutz councils.

In addition to the chaverim and their children, who also number somewhat more than two hundred and fifty, there are other groups living in the village. These include the parents of some of the chaverim, who were brought to Israel by the kibbutz from their European homes, and two youth groups sent by the Jewish Agency to study and work in the kibbutz. One of these groups is composed of immigrant children and the other of urban children from economically depressed families. At the time of the writer's visit, there was also an Army group stationed at Kiryat Yedidim (both males and females in Israel may serve part of their term of compulsory military service by working in agricultural settlements). We shall not be concerned with the latter four groups.

The physical environment in which the chaverim live is quite different today from the swampland first inhabited by the founders of the kibbutz. At the foot of a mountain range famous in Biblical history, Kiryat Yedidim is now part of a fertile valley. On the other side of the mountain lies an enemy country, and the night guard patrols with a loaded rifle.

The climate alternates between the hot, dry heat of summer and the cold rain of winter. The burning heat of the summer day makes labor between the hours of noon and 2:00 P.M. prohibitive, and a *siesta* is generally taken at that time. Even the morning hours are intensely hot at the peak of the summer, so that during the grape harvest, for example, the workers rise at the first hint of daylight—3:00 or 4:00 A.M.—to pick grapes until 10:00 A.M., at which time the harvest ceases lest the heat of the sun ruin the grapes in the harvesters' baskets. During this season, the earth is parched, gardens are shriveled, and the mountain looms a dead brown, bereft of shrub or flower. The winters, on the other hand, are marked by steady rains and cold winds, although snow is a rarity to be regarded with wonder by the children. The rooms, which remain damp throughout this winter season, and the clothes, which never seem quite dry, are probably responsible for much of the "rheumatism" which afflicts many of the vattikim. The general unpleasantness of winter is exacerbated by the morass of mud, making walking a clumsy effort, and necessitating the constant wearing of knee-length boots.

The short spring and fall seasons, however, are welcomed by the chaverim as times of great beauty. The weather is mild, and—in spring—the emergence of a mountain in bloom and of gardens riotous with color creates a perceptible change in the general temper of the people.

The kibbutz and the land it works cover an area of approximately 11,000 *dunam*.[2] Like the typical European agricultural village, the village proper is situated in a hub, as it were, from which radiate the various fields and orchards. Those members who work in the remote fields leave the village in the morning and return in the evening, although many whose work is closer to the village return at noon for their noonday meal.

The houses are laid out in parallel rows on either side of the communal dining hall, which is the physical and social center of the kibbutz. Surrounding the dining room is a large landscaped lawn, which serves to set it apart from other structures and to emphasize its centrality. The houses themselves are built in the form of ranch-house apartments with, as a rule, four individual living units in each apartment. Each unit consists of one room and, in some cases, a small porch which serves in summer as a second room. Generally, each apartment is separated from the others, as well as from

[2] A dunam is approximately one-fourth of an acre.

the network of sidewalks traversing the village, by large lawns surrounded by high shrubs. Much attention is devoted to the care of these lawns, and almost every chaver has a flower garden, which he tenderly nurses in the evenings after work. Because of the individual's pride in his garden, and because there is at least one full time gardener in the kibbutz and one on the high school campus, Kiryat Yedidim has the reputation of being one of the loveliest villages in Israel.

Not all dwellings follow the pattern above, however; as Kiryat Yedidim has undergone considerable expansion, its architecture has changed. The growing wealth of the kibbutz has permitted each successive housing project to be better than its predecessor. The vattikim lived in tents when they first settled on the land, and some of the younger chaverim, who have only recently graduated from high school, do so today. The first permanent housing to be constructed consisted of wooden houses, which are still in use today, and are inhabited generally by the young married couples. The next construction period witnessed the erection of brick houses, stuccoed on the outside, with a small porchway at the entrance. All entrances faced in the same direction, as is the case with the wooden houses, providing a minimum of privacy. In the next period, the buildings were constructed so that half the entrances faced in one direction, and half the other—thus affording greater privacy—and each unit was provided with a sitting porch with an overhanging roof. The last building project, in process of completion during the writer's study, was luxury housing by kibbutz standards. The units comprise a room and a half, a large porch, and private bathroom.

Each room is inhabited by one couple, and serves as a

combination bedroom-living room—the minimum housing required, since cooking is done in the communal kitchen, meals are eaten in the communal dining room, and children sleep in the children's dormitories. Communal toilets and showers, separate for men and women, take the place of private bathrooms.

The typical room is simply, but attractively, furnished with products made in the kibbutz. Basic furnishings comprise a bed, writing table, combination clothes closet and chest, chairs, bookcases, and lamps. Bedspreads and rugs, of subdued colors and simple, skillful designs, are woven in the kibbutz and are reminiscent of the more subdued Mexican products. In addition, each room may have a radio, supplied either by the individual or the kibbutz, books acquired by the individual, and one or more good prints, either borrowed from the kibbutz or acquired by the individual. Thus, each room is provided with approximately the same furnishings, but each couple uses its own ingenuity and skill in arranging the colors and furnishings, so that rooms express the inhabitants' individuality.

In addition, the village includes a laundry, sewing room, clothing storehouse, kosher kitchen and dining room for the elderly parents of the chaverim, dispensary, office, store, library, reading room, and the children's dormitories and school. In construction during the author's stay was a *bet tarbut* (literally, "culture house"), which was to house the library and to provide an auditorium for concerts, lectures, and plays. On the periphery of the dwelling area are the sheds and barns for cattle, horses, sheep, and goats; chicken coops; garage; tractor sheds; warehouse; produce storeroom; packing plant; and carpentry shop. Separated from the village by the main highway is the high school, with its classrooms, dormitories, and dining room.

Many aspects of kibbutz living are a reflection of the ascetic philosophy which characterized the youth movement from which most of the chaverim entered the kibbutz. The Movement was (and is) opposed to pre-marital sexual behavior, smoking, drinking, fancy clothes, and "fast" living. At first many of these behavior patterns, as well as those associated with luxurious living, were viewed as synonymous with the decadent life of the cities. Later, they became symbolic of the hated *bourgeoisie*. In the early history of Kiryat Yedidim, therefore, the combination of poverty and an ascetic philosophy conspired to make for a primitive existence. Tents served as houses, food was scarce, and clothing was limited. As the economic condition of the kibbutz improved, the chaverim moved from tents into wooden houses, but little attempt was made to provide anything beyond the barest essentials. For many years, for example, the typical room included only a bed and a chair. Only recently has the kibbutz deemed it necessary to provide the chaver with such amenities as a table, clothes closet, curtains, rugs, and bookcases. The reason for this tardiness, said one vattika, was not economic, but moral. "Our ideal was to live like Spartans. The founders thought there were more important things to think about than comfort. So for the first twenty years the kibbutz did nothing for the comfort of the chaverim."

And this is still true. Kiryat Yedidim, though an old kibbutz, lags behind some of the younger kibbutzim in its "health and welfare" benefits. It did not erect permanent housing until relatively late; its sanitation system is old and grossly inadequate; its showers are dingy and overcrowded; its dining hall and kitchen facilities are a constant source of irritation. "There were more important things to think about."

The introduction of each additional comfort or amenity has been fought by the "die-hards" as a compromise with the original ideals of the kibbutz. The first radio to appear in Kiryat Yedidim was received by a chaver as a present, and he presented it to the kibbutz, which placed it in the dining room. No one needed a private radio at that time, since most people spent their evenings in the dining room, which served as a community center. As the people grew older, however, and as they began to spend less time in the dining room and more time in their private rooms, it was pleasant to have a radio in one's room. But the few people who acquired private radios were looked upon most unfavorably. Not only were they introducing private property into the kibbutz, but they were also introducing unnecessary luxuries. Gradually, however, others began to acquire radios, and soon the kibbutz began to assume responsibility for providing its members with radios. Today, it distributes from ten to twelve radios a year, and almost every chaver has one in his room.

In view of the intense summer heat, it would be a welcome relief after a hot day in the fields to return to a room cooled by a fan. Some of the chaverim have obtained fans as gifts, or have acquired them through their annual cash allowance, but the kibbutz has refused to supply the chaverim with fans. They, too, are viewed as an unnecessary luxury and a compromise with its ideals. The kibbutz has gone so far, however, as to buy fans for such public accommodations as the dining room and the office.

In spite of the opposition to fans for the summer, there has been some willingness to do something about the damp and cold winters. Since the houses have no heating systems, it is often necessary to wear coats in the winter evenings or to crawl into bed. Some chaverim acquired electric heaters, but the kibbutz decided that they consumed too much electricity, and it exchanged them for oil stoves. Since then, the kibbutz has been distributing a few such stoves every year, and eventually there will be one in every room.

This influence of the original ascetic pattern extends to food and drink, as well. The typical chaver rarely drinks wine or hard liquor, and many return the bottle of wine that each member receives on Passover, with the wine still in the bottle. Drinking to excess is never practiced, and drunkenness is unheard of. Food, of course, is scarce, since the entire country is on a rationing system. Little effort, however, is made to improve the preparation of the food that is available; hence, it is often monotonous, bland, and tasteless. Combined with this lack of variety in preparation is the absence of "graciousness" in its eating. People eat hurriedly, with no lingering over their food, and with little conversation. The objective situation precludes the possibility of gracious eating. The morning and afternoon meals are eaten hurriedly, as it is necessary to get to work. The evening meal entails no such obligation, but the small dining room is crowded and noisy, and it must serve not only the chaverim, but the many youth groups which are receiving their training in the kibbutz, as well. What is required, therefore, is a new dining room which would enable the chaverim to enjoy a leisurely evening meal. But its construction is always delayed, because "there are more important things to think about."

There is strong evidence, however, that people are beginning to oppose this ascetic tradition. The very fact that they are demanding many comforts which in the past would have been viewed with complete disdain, is indicative of this new trend. An extreme example of this trend was expressed by a chaver, while passing by the home of the veterinarian, who was not a kibbutz member. It is a small, four-room house, and the chaver was rhapsodic in describing its merits. He then said, in a half-whimsical, half-guilty voice, "and what if we were all to have a house like that? Would it be so evil? Do you think it would destroy our collectivism? Why shouldn't we each have a house?"

This trend away from the older value expresses itself in two forms: the beginnings of private property in luxury goods, which will be discussed in another connection, and the frequency of private "parties." Shepherds, poultry workers, and fishermen, respectively, sometimes have parties at which they eat products of their branches with their friends. Some men hunt wild boar and ducks which also constitute the basis for welcome private parties. Some people go into the fields in order to obtain agricultural products which are generally not served in the dining room. Corn, for example, is never served as part of a meal, although it is raised in large quantities for the cattle. But many people may be seen in the evening, eating corn which they have picked and roasted. These events occur infrequently, to be sure, and often evoke guilt feelings in the participants, but they are indicative of a trend which the kibbutz will eventually be compelled to recognize officially.

Despite this new trend, the primitivistic philosophy of the youth movement is still a potent force in the kibbutz, particularly among the vattikim. When a young chaver extolled the merits of a "Parker 51" fountain pen, a vattik exclaimed angrily, "This is the height of snobbery! Isn't an ordinary pen good enough? Even in America, they are not so snobbish!"

Economy

Extending out from the living quarters of the village is the kibbutz farm, in all its diversity. When it was founded, Kiryat Yedidim received from the Jewish National Fund 100 dunam of land per couple, making a total of approximately 800 dunam. Today it is working 11,000 dunam, though not all of it is in the immediate area of the kibbutz proper. Unlike some kibbutzim, Kiryat Yedidim has resisted the introduction of industry, so that its sole source of income is agricultural, with the exception of the small amount it receives from the wages of those few chaverim who work outside the kibbutz in non-agricultural jobs. For the most part, however, even these jobs are undertaken, not for their income-value, but for the contributions they make to the kibbutz agricultural economy. Hence, these men work in an olive press, a bus line, a trucking line, or a garage—all regional cooperatives which serve to promote the agricultural interests of the kibbutz.

The agriculture of Kiryat Yedidim is divided into the following eight branches.

(1) *Dairy:* The dairy produces a half-million *liter* of milk a year, but its income is the lowest of all the agricultural branches.

(2) *Field crops:* This branch harvests five or six thousand tons every year. In a good year, the net income is high, yielding 6–8 *lira*[3] per man-day.

(3) *Vegetable gardens:* This branch yields 400–500 tons of produce for the local market per year.

---

[3] In 1951, the lira, or Israeli pound, was worth $2.80 at the official rate of exchange. The black market rate, however, was $1.00 or less, and this latter figure is the more accurate, as far as the buying power of the lira is concerned.

(4) *Fishery:* The kibbutz has constructed artificial fish ponds, which yield 70 tons of fish annually. The net income is high—6–8 lira per man-day.

(5) *Fruit orchards:* Eighty tons of grapes, 7000 boxes of grapefruit, and 20 tons of olives are harvested annually for the market, but the net income is only about three lira per man-day.

(6) *Flocks:* The kibbutz raises both goats and sheep. The former are milked, and the latter are raised for their wool.

(7) *Poultry:* The kibbutz chickens lay about a million eggs per year, yielding a net income of 6–8 lira per man-day.

(8) *Fodder:* This branch harvests about 25,000 tons annually of clover, alfalfa, and silage (corn, sorghum, and sugar beets).

The total gross income of the kibbutz economy is about 250,000 lira. This, it is apparent, is big business. Agriculture is completely mechanized in Kiryat Yedidim, which owns ten tractors, three combines, and three trucks.

Since the economy of Kiryat Yedidim is socialist, its accounting system demands a brief explanation. It is based on the man-day income (*yom avodah*) of each economic branch—that is, the total income of a branch, divided by its total number of workers. In Kiryat Yedidim, about two-thirds of the labor is performed by chaverim and the remaining third by temporary workers (youth groups, Army, etc.). Labor is divided into two categories for accounting purposes: productive labor (*avodah productivit*), that is, labor which produces a profit, or which increases the capital investment of the kibbutz; and non-productive labor (*avodah lo machnisa*, literally, labor which does not produce an income). Each of these categories of labor is broken down into certain broad categories which may be outlined as follows:

A. Productive work (*avodah productivit*): This category includes about half the manpower.
   1. Work which yields a cash return (avodah machnisa):
      a. work in the *meshek*, or the agricultural branches of the kibbutz (listed above).
      b. hired labor outside the kibbutz, that is, members who are employed outside the kibbutz (listed above).
      c. construction work.
   2. Capital improvement (*avodah bitruma*): any work in the kibbutz that serves to increase the capital value of its economic investment, such as repair of machinery, building, etc.
   3. Managerial work: labor performed by the treasurer, purchasing agent, general manager, etc.
   4. Youth leadership: the kibbutz receives a small cash income for providing leaders and teachers for the various youth groups stationed in the kibbutz.
B. Work which yields no income (avodah lo machnisa)
   1. "Service" (*sherut*) for adults: this includes
      a. tailor shop
      b. laundry
      c. kitchen and dining room
      d. night watch, maintained every night, in the event of military attack or of marauding from across the border.
      e. sanitation, which includes the cleaning of toilets and showers, spraying of mosquito-breeding ponds, etc.

2. "Service" for children: this includes nurses, teachers, cooks, etc.
3. Unemployment, including members on annual vacations, nursing mothers, etc.
4. Sickness
5. Inclement weather
6. Service in the army reserve
7. Work in the youth movement

Since about 50 per cent of the total manpower of the kibbutz is involved in "non-productive" work, the half which is engaged in productive work must produce enough to provide for the entire kibbutz. It costs an average of 90 *grush* (9/10 of a lira) to maintain a member for one day (*yom kiyyum*); the average man-day productivity (*yom avodah*) of each member, including those engaged in non-productive as well as productive labor, is about two lira. Hence, the productivity of the average member is more than twice his maintenance cost.[4] This difference, however, does not represent profit. Kiryat Yedidim has many expenses in addition to those entailed by the maintenance of it members. It owns only about 20 per cent of its capital investment; the remainder represents borrowed money and a large mortgage. The interest rates on its loans and mortgage are high, and they consume much of its income. Nevertheless, the kibbutz is a going concern, economically speaking.

We may now turn to the division of labor in the kibbutz. With some few exceptions, the branch in which a person works is determined by his desires and skills. Since the profit motive is absent, and since, theoretically, all manual work

---

[4] Yom kiyyum is computed by dividing the total maintenance cost by the number of chaverim, just as yom avodah is computed by dividing the total productivity by the number of members.

enjoys equal prestige, a person's choice is determined primarily by the intrinsic satisfactions he obtains from his job. Ideally, the kibbutz attempts to satisfy the desire of the chaver, on the simple grounds that an unhappy worker is an unhappy kibbutz member. If a person not only has a strong desire to work in a certain branch, but also shows some skill in this work, it is most probable that he will be assigned as a permanent worker to the branch of his choice, and the work-assignment chairmen automatically assign him to that branch when they plan the daily work list. On rare occasions, however, when a particular branch is in desperate need of men for a special task, and there is a draft of personnel from other branches, he may be transferred for a few days.

There are situations, however, in which a person does not work in the branch of his choice. There are several reasons for this—all potential sources of kibbutz tension and conflict.

(1) The person does not have the requisite skill or knowledge. Often a person who does not have the requisite skill for a branch of his desire does possess certain skills enabling him to become a permanent worker in another branch. When this is the case, even though the latter is his second choice, the arrangement is usually satisfactory. There are instances, however, in which a person is generally unskilled, so that he can fit in nowhere—or, at any rate, he would not prove to be an asset in any branch. In such a case, the person may end up a *p'kak* (literally, a cork), a person who has no permanent assignment, but who is used as part of the floating manpower of the kibbutz, being assigned to any branch in need of temporary hands. One day he may substitute for a sick person in the carpentry shop; another

day he may take the place of a vacationing shepherd, and so on. The kibbutz tries to avoid relegating anyone to the position of p'kak because of its demoralizing effect on the chaver. In a society in which labor is the highest value, a person who is formally recognized as having little working ability enjoys little prestige, and work-prestige is one of the important motives in the dynamics of the kibbutz economy.

(2) The branch is already filled and does not need additional workers. In this case, the worker may be assigned to another branch with the understanding that when a vacancy occurs in the branch of his choice, he will be permitted to fill the post. Often, however, as he works in his job, he grows to like it, and has no desire to be transferred.

(3) Certain jobs are generally disliked or require special training which most people do not have or from which they would not benefit. In such cases, the position is filled either by exerting pressure on some individual to take the job, or by a formal draft voted by the town meeting. When pressure is exerted on an individual, it is likely to be moral pressure. For example, the kibbutz needed a baker, as its hired baker was retiring. It was decided to have a member of the kibbutz serve in this post, but few wanted the job, as it is hard, hot, and dirty work. The "Committee on Economic policy" decided that the best person for the job would be *chaver x*, a mild man. When he refused to acquiese in this decision, the secretary spoke to him privately, pointing out that he would save the kibbutz much money if he would learn the trade. The next day, the general manager spoke to him, and stressed the fact that he was the logical man for the job, as he did not have a regular work assignment; and to choose someone regularly assigned would have a disruptive effect on the kibbutz economy. The following day,

chaver x announced to the author that he would probably take the job—as a matter of conscience.

If a draft is resorted to, it is not compulsory, so that a person who shows good cause for not being drafted will be exempt from serving. If he shows no cause, however, and if the kibbutz insists on asserting the principle of the individual's subordination to the welfare of the group, it can threaten to expel the chaver for refusal to accept its discipline. Workers must sometimes be drafted for the dairy because the work hours are staggered, so that the day is broken up and evenings are not free; hence, few are eager to work in that branch of the economy. High school teaching is another job which most men, in a community which emphasizes manual labor, do not like, and for which many are not suited. Again, it is often necessary to draft someone for this work, although it is usually understood that a person may resign after serving a minimum period of, say, five years, if he so desires. Work in the Youth Movement in the cities is disliked by many persons, since it takes them away from the kibbutz and their families for the entire week. Here, again, it is often necessary to draft a worker.

(4) Certain jobs are regarded as so distasteful, that they are filled by a permanent rotation system in which almost everyone serves his turn; the most notable instance is work in the kitchen and dining room, such as cooking, dishwashing, and serving—the women serving for a one-year period and the men for a two- or three-month period. The only exemptions from this rotation are the ill, the aged, and teachers. An inconvenient job such as that of night watchman is also filled by a rotation system, the period of service being for two weeks.

(5) The person is ill, and cannot engage in strenuous

physical work. Such an individual—as well as nursing
mothers who because of their maternal responsibilities cannot work in permanent positions—is assigned to a suitable
job not necessarily to his liking.

(6) There is, finally, the problem of the woman who has
worked in a permanent job, and who has to retire because
of pregnancy, childbirth, and the period of nursing. If her
job has been satisfactorily filled during her absence, she may
be unable to return to it until there is another vacancy. In
the meantime she must take another job, which she may not
particularly desire. This is one of the important sources of
dissatisfaction among the women, and it will be examined
again in the discussion of the "problem of the woman."[5]

Kiryat Yedidim has always been suspicious of formal
authority, and it has been as reluctant to introduce formal
leadership patterns into its economic system as it has been
to introduce such patterns into any other aspect of its social
structure. Nevertheless, as the economy increased in complexity, patterns of authority also gradually increased, so
that today Kiryat Yedidim has a relatively complex system
of committees, officials, and foremen who are charged with
the determination and execution of its economic policies.
At first it was assumed that any chaver could, with proper
experience, occupy a managerial position. Hence it was
believed that all offices would rotate among the entire membership, and that this restriction on the tenure of office, in
addition to the restriction on the rewards of office, would
preclude the rise of bureaucratic power. It was discovered
through experience, however, that this assumption was untenable, and that if the kibbutz were to achieve and to retain
its economic solvency, it could not afford to permit any but
the most skilled and the most efficient to assume positions of

[5] See Chapter 6.

responsibility. Hence, though the important offices do rotate, so that no individual holds a job for more than two or three consecutive years, they rotate within a small group of twelve to fifteen men whose abilities are recognized by the others.

Committee members and office holders are elected in town meeting on the basis, generally, of recommendations from the nominating committee. Committees serve for one year, and officials for two or three years. The various committees include the following:

1. *Committee on Economic Policy (vaadah mishkit).* This committee, which consists of fifteen members, initiates policy on all economic matters affecting the kibbutz, and makes most of the important long-range economic decisions. Most of its membership is elected directly in town meeting, each member representing a different branch of the economy. In addition to those elected members, this committee includes the two work-assignment chairmen, the treasurer, secretary, and general economic manager of the kibbutz.

2. *Executive Committee (vaadat hanhala).* The six members of this committee include the general economic manager, treasurer, and the accountant, as well as three members of the Committee on Economic Policy. This is the executive committee of the latter, and makes the day-to-day decisions on economic matters on the basis of the broad policies laid down by it.

3. *Planning Committee (vaadat tochnit).* This committee has a restricted life, serving only at the beginning of the year. It projects an over-all annual plan for the kibbutz, but has little power. Some chaverim would like to see it become a standing committee, empowered to institute long-range plans.

4. *Work Assignment Committee (vaadat avodah).* This

committee, which consists of the general economic manager, the general secretary, and the work assignment chairmen, meets every month or two to draw up a general plan for the most efficient and probable allocation of man-power for the succeeding period.

5. *Construction Committee (vaadat binyan)*. The plans for the construction of new living houses, dormitories, school buildings, etc., are the functions of this committee.

It will be noted that these committees, whose authority derives from the town meeting, have policymaking rather than executive functions. The latter functions are exercised by economic "officials." The general economic manager (*merakkez meshek*) holds the most important economic office in the kibbutz as he is the official in charge of the entire productive sector of its economy. It is he who is responsible for the execution of all agricultural policy, and his is the ultimate authority concerning the allocation and supervision of manpower and resources. Because of the strenuous nature of his office, the general manager is freed from all other work. Furthermore, since the technical knowledge required for this job is extensive, he usually holds office for a period of two to four years.

The task of the treasurer (*gizbar*) is not so much concerned with the money the kibbutz already has, as it is with the attempt to find new sources of money. This is a major undertaking in present-day Israel, and it requires his absence from the kibbutz for the greater part of the week. As in the case of the general manager, the technical requirements and responsibilities of this office are so great, that the treasurer usually holds his office for three years, and he is relieved of all other work.

Since all manufactured goods, as well as processed foods,

are bought outside the kibbutz, Kiryat Yedidim elects a purchasing agent (*merakkez keniyot*) who travels daily to the various cities to obtain the goods required by the kibbutz. This is, therefore, a full-time job, and the person who holds it is relieved of other economic functions.

Perhaps the most difficult of the managerial positions is that of the work-assignment chairman (*sadran avodah*). The population of Kiryat Yedidim has not expanded as rapidly as its economy, so that it suffers today from a serious labor shortage. Moreover the economic demand for water and pipes for irrigation, as well as for such heavy machinery as tractors and combines, is much greater than their supply. The resulting competition among the various economic branches for these scarce commodities—both human and mechanical—is often acute, and it is the function of the work-assignment chairmen, in conjunction with the general manager, to allocate them equitably.

Since the majority of men are in "productive" work, and since most of the women are in "service" work, a man is elected work-assignment chairman for the former category, and a woman for the latter. These chairmen meet every evening with the foremen of the various economic branches —often for long hours—to decide where each chaver, as well as the other available manpower, is to work. They then organize a work schedule for the following day, which is posted that evening on the bulletin board in the dining room. Although this is a strenuous job, it does not require unduly great skill or technical ability (although it does require considerable tact and diplomacy), and the members serve a one-year term. Moreover, although this office is time consuming, the chairmen are not regularly relieved of their normal economic responsibilities.

In addition to these various committees and officials, who are responsible for the economy as a whole, each branch of the economy has a foreman who is directly responsible for the administration of his branch. The position of foreman, like the other managerial positions in the kibbutz, is elective; but the manner of election depends upon the nature of the branch. In those branches in which the workers are permanent, the foreman is elected by his fellow workers in the branch. Where the workers of a branch are temporary, however (because of the distasteful nature of the work, so that its membership rotates) the foreman is elected by the town meeting. The foreman is an administrative, rather than a policy-determining, official. He makes the daily decisions concerning the number of workers, in addition to his permanent crew, he requires; where and how they are to be allocated; what machinery he will require. Since almost all permanent workers in a branch are experts in their work, the foreman is merely a temporary *primus inter pares;* temporary, because this responsibility rotates among the members of the branch. Policy decisions concerning the branch are made, therefore, by the entire branch, and not by the foreman alone.

The foremen of the following branches are elected by the town meeting: the yard, warehouse, laundry, kitchen, clothing room. The latter three positions are so intensely disliked, however, that it is more accurate to describe their method of recruitment by the term, "draft," rather than by "election." The latter two positions are, in the kibbutz division of labor, "women's work," while the foremanship of the laundry may be filled by either male or female.

The tenure for the foremanship of the laundry is indefinite, although the occupant is expected to serve a minimum of one year. Seldom is this position held for more than two years because it is a difficult one, physically speaking. The foreman of the clothing room is responsible for the distribution of new clothing, and decides the priority according to which the dressmaking shop sews new dresses. Although her tenure of office is not stipulated, she seldom serves more than a few years because of the tensions engendered between her clientele and her.

The foreman of the kitchen and dining room has what is considered to be the most difficult job in the kibbutz. Working conditions in the kitchen are poor, facilities are inadequate, and food is scarce—as it is throughout Israel. Hence, this position rotates among the women, and each is expected to serve for a period of two to three years.

We must now attempt to describe what is, perhaps, the most interesting and the most crucial aspect of the kibbutz economic system: economic motivation. In the absence of private property, and of money, it is obvious that the profit motive does not operate in this society. Moreover, this is not a stratified society in which persons in authority compel their subordinates to carry out their responsibilities. Kiryat Yedidim has no supreme political authority—other than the group itself—and its economic executives and managers serve, as has already been noted, at the pleasure of the people. Nevertheless, despite the absence of those economic motives that have become conventional in other western societies, the chaverim successfully operate an economy of no small proportions.

It should be noted in the first place that the absence of the profit motive does not imply that other conventional motives are absent from kibbutz economic behavior. The chaver has at least four personal motives for not shirking his economic responsibilities and for working hard and efficiently. As is the case in capitalist society, the harder he works, the greater the economic returns he receives. It is true that the returns from his labor do not accrue to him directly, so that he does not see the immediate effects of his productivity. Nevertheless, his own standard of living is dependent upon that of the group which, in turn, depends upon the productive capacity of its members. Everyone is aware of the fact that if he were to "take it easy," and, that if others were to do the same, then he, along with the rest, would suffer. Hence, one important source of work-motivation in Kiryat Yedidim is the motive of personal economic improvement.

It should be remembered, moreover, that most chaverim have deliberately chosen to live a rural life and to work in an agricultural economy. Furthermore, the chaver, in most cases, works in a branch which interests him the most. Consequently, the average person enjoys his work, deriving pleasure from its actual performance, as well as from its end product. What Veblen termed, "the instinct of workmanship," or what is called "mode pleasure"—in contrast to "end pleasure"—are as applicable to the average chaver as they are to anyone else. In short, a second personal motive for economic behavior consists in the fact that the average chaver derives intrinsic satisfactions from his work.

Competitive pride is a third source of economic motivation. The average chaver is a permanent member of a particular economic branch—the orchard, the wheat fields, the dairy, etc.—and his immediate attachment and identification is with his branch, taking pride in its success, and becoming depressed by its failures. And though he wishes to see the entire kibbutz prosper, he derives great satisfaction from knowing that his branch contributed its share—or more—to this prosperity. Hence, he is motivated to work hard in order for his branch to receive a favorable rating in this informal competition. To note but one example: normally the most productive branch in the kibbutz is field crops, and the workers in this branch generally show a perceptible superiority over those in other branches. The year in which the author's research was conducted, however, was a drought year, and the yield from the grain harvests was low. Thanks to artificial irrigation, however, the vegetable gardens had a highly successful year. The pride of the garden workers in this fact was apparent to all.

A final personal motive for efficient and productive economic behavior is prestige. It will be remembered that labor is one of the paramount values in the culture of Kiryat Yedidim, and that hard, efficient labor is a necessary, if not sufficient, determinant of prestige. In the absence of the profit motive, the respect of one's fellows has become an important motive in this society. Few are willing to jeopardize this respect by shirking on the job, and since most work is performed in cooperative work groups, shirking would be spotted immediately. Given the importance of labor in the kibbutz hierarchy of values, public opinion—or *daat haka-hal*, as it is known—is a highly important factor in work motivation.

These personal motives for work, important though they are, are not sufficient to explain the economic behavior of the chaverim. The economic skills of most of them would assure psychological satisfactions—prestige, pride, etc.—at least as great outside as inside the kibbutz. Moreover, for many chaverim the economic motive of an improved standard of living would yield higher returns in a competitive market than the return which the kibbutz provides them. It follows that economic behavior in Kiryat Yedidim includes satisfactions and motivations that are not found outside. This inference is confirmed by the evidence. We shall first examine the unique economic satisfactions offered by the kibbutz.

The economic system of Kiryat Yedidim offers the average chaver a sense of security which is difficult, if not impossible, to obtain outside the kibbutz. This function of the economy arises from its comprehensive system of social security and from the absence of prestige functions of wealth in the kibbutz. The social security system is so comprehensive that the individual has few, if any, economic worries. As long as the kibbutz as a whole enjoys economic well being, his economic welfare is assured. As long as there is any food at all, no one will go without food; as long as there is any clothing, no one will be without clothes. The chaver may worry about the economic condition of the kibbutz, as a whole, but he is not obsessed with how he will pay his own rent, his personal medical bills, the cost of his children's education, etc. These are the concern of the kibbutz. If, for example, a couple has a baby, they have no cause for financial worry. The medical and hospital bills are assumed by the kibbutz, as are the baby's future clothing, education, and food bills. Nor does a new baby present a problem so far as housing is concerned, since he lives in the Infants House.

The same absence of worry characterizes the ill and the aged. If a chaver is ill, he is sent to a hospital or receives medical attention at home, and the kibbutz assumes the expenses. When he returns from the hospital, he may have to be on a special diet, which the kibbutz provides. If he is unable to return to work for a number of months, or even years, he need not worry about the economic welfare of his family. Nor does the chaver have to worry lest he remain unemployed when he recovers, for he is immediately re-employed. If permanently disabled or too old to work, his standard of living suffers no change. He continues to live exactly as he had lived when he was working. In fact, if his condition calls for a special diet or special housing, his standard of living may actually be improved because of his illness or age.

Equally as important as its material security is the psychological security to be found in the kibbutz economic system. What is important in this connection is not so much the positive aspect of security, such as the profound sense of belonging which the chaver feels as a member of a communal society, but rather the freedom from that psychological insecurity which stems from economic competitiveness. The kibbutz, for example, is free from the entire complex of "conspicuous consumption." Since all property is owned in common, the drive to accumulate property in order to achieve prestige, power, or ego-gratification is absent. Such anxieties as are elicited by the fear that one's clothes are in the wrong style, or that one's house and furniture are outmoded, or that one's residential area is unfashionable, are unknown in Kiryat Yedidim. Thus, a basic source of anxiety in our own culture—anxiety arising from the prestige functions of property and wealth—is not to be found in the kibbutz. The reaction of Kiryat Yedidim to a performance of *Death of a Salesman* is highly revealing in this connection. In discussing this play with a number of chaverim, it became apparent that the average chaver either could not appreciate the profound tragedy of Willy Loman, since he did not understand the nature of his frustrations, or else that he understood these frustrations full well, and drew invidious comparisons between his own culture and the culture of Willy Loman.

Although the desire of the average chaver to work in the kibbutz economy is explicable in terms of the security this economy offers him, this ego function does not suffice as an explanation for the devotion, zeal, and responsibility which he displays in his work. The latter can be explained only in terms of that superego function which the kibbutz terms, *hakkara*. This term, literally, may be defined as "consciousness"; but hakkara connotes more than consciousness, as that term is generally understood. This is an ethical-ideological concept, connoting a conscious awareness of one's moral responsibilities to the kibbutz in the latter's political, as well as in its economic, meaning. If I work because of hakkara, it is because I recognize that the economic welfare of the kibbutz depends upon every chaver's working as efficiently as possible; and because I further recognize that the political future of the kibbutz, its ability to win others to its cause and, eventually, its ability to change the structure of the entire Israeli society in accordance with its ideals, depends, among other things, upon the economic success of the kibbutz. It is not suggested, of course, that hakkara is constantly present in the consciousness of the chaver, any more than any other superego function is, or that it operates with equal force in every individual. Nevertheless hakkara is a very important motive in the economic behavior of the average chaver.[6] Indeed, without this concept, the daily economic life of the chaver would remain inexplicable. His work is not supervised by any supervisor, foreman, or overseer; he punches no clock when he comes

[6] It is important in other aspects of his life as well. See below, pp. 97–98.

to work or when he leaves, and there is no one to check on his punctuality or his efficiency. Yet, when the morning bell rings at 5:30, he arises; and at 6:00, when the workers start for the fields, he is prompt. He may work alone at some task, or he may work with a work-detail; but in either case he does not leave his task until the lunch hour, when he returns at 11:30 to the dining room or, if his work is far from the dining room, when he quits to eat lunch in the fields. Again, he returns to his work promptly after the noon siesta, and returns to his room only after the end of the workday at 5:30. If he is in the midst of some work, he may remain after the end of the working day, although there is no one to compel him to do so, and he does not receive time-and-a-half for overtime. All these activities are performed, not only because by so doing he is benefiting himself, or because the group expects this kind of responsibility from its members, but because of his hakkara.

It is probably no exaggeration to say, therefore, that the average chaver, despite the absence of a "profit motive," is more responsible in his work than is the worker whose motive is private gain. His job, performed with hakkara, becomes more than a job and more than a way of making a living. It becomes a *sacred task*, a calling, in the religious sense of that term, dedicated, not to the greater glory of God, but to the welfare of his group. It is this latter aspect of kibbutz responsibility that serves to distinguish it from the responsibility which a private farmer may experience. The latter works for himself and, should he make a mistake, only he will suffer. In the kibbutz, a mistake by one person will not only cause him to suffer, but will bring suffering to the entire group. As a result, he is much more careful, as no one wishes to experience the guilt of having caused the group to suffer. One of the chaverim, for example, used the wrong chemical when spraying fruit trees; instead of saving the trees, it killed them. When the chaver discovered his mistake, he fell into a deep depression, although no one reprimanded him for a mistake which others could have made just as easily. Nevertheless, although most chaverim were highly sympathetic, he told a chavera that he wanted to kill himself, and in discussing the economic consequences of his error with the secretary, he asked for a rope with which to hang himself.

Kibbutz economic behavior, to sum up, is motivated by security and hakkara, as well as by the more conventional material and psychological satisfactions found in other societies.

Authority and Social Control

In order to understand the dynamics of social control in Kiryat Yedidim, which has few patterns of *formal* authority, it is necessary to grasp an essential psychological feature of this community. Kiryat Yedidim is not like an ordinary Western village whose inhabitants may be united by the sheer fact of physical proximity. Nor are the chaverim united by bonds of kinship, so characteristic of the folk society. Nevertheless, the kibbutz is a *gemeinschaft*, not only because of its small size and the opportunity this affords for the frequency and intimacy of interaction. It is a *gemeinschaft*, rather, because it functions *as if* it were united by bonds of kinship, *as if* it were a lineage or a large extended family. In their own eyes, as well as in the eyes of the outside observer, the chaverim constitute a family, psychologically speaking, bound by ties of common residence, common experiences, a common past and a common fate, and mutual aid—all the ties which bind a family—as well as a common ideology.[7] The kibbutz, like the shtetl, presents a "picture (which) is less of the family as a segment of the community than of the community as an extension of the family."[8]

Since the chaverim view each other as psychological kin, conformity to group mores—even mores as exacting as those found in Kiryat Yedidim—poses no special problems. The chaverim, like the members of any family, take it for granted that he who is sick shall be given the best care; that the individual's needs, not his contribution to the economic welfare, determine what he shall receive; that a person's superior economic position does not entitle him to better food, or finer clothes, or a nicer room. The discussion of kibbutz authority and social control must be perceived, therefore, within this socio-psychological context.

The sovereign body of Kiryat Yedidim is the town meeting (sichah kellalit), which includes every chaver of the kibbutz. As the ultimate authority on all intra-kibbutz matters, the town meeting is very jealous of its powers. The chaverim still retain much of the distrust of authority that characterized their youth movement days, and they are reluctant to delegate authority. Most important decisions, and sometimes those less important, are made in the town meeting. The annual budget, a new building program, the expansion of an agricultural branch, the election of officers and committees—all are debated in the town meeting. The

---

[7] This familial aspect of the kibbutz is manifested on the biological level, as well. In all instances, children who have been born and reared in Kiryat Yedidim, have obtained their mates from outside the kibbutz. This voluntary exogamy is entirely explicable by the statements of the sabras that endogamous marriages are viewed by them as incestuous.

[8] Joffe, p. 239.

stand to be taken on a political issue, the amount of activity to be devoted to a political campaign, the decision to admit an American anthropologist to the kibbutz to do research, the problem of the intellectual level of the children, the complaint of the women concerning kitchen facilities— these and countless other problems, large and small, are the domain of the town meeting.

Town meetings are regularly held twice a week. There are at least three reasons for the frequency of such meetings. In their opposition to bureaucracy, the chaverim are reluctant to entrust decisions to executive responsibility, and in their desire to remain a "pure democracy" they have not created a representative legislative body. Hence, most matters which in other societies would be delegated to administrative officials, or which would come within the jurisdiction of the legislative body, remain the responsibility of the entire community. Secondly, since the kibbutz is similar in many respects to a large family, many decisions that in most societies are made within the family are made in Kiryat Yedidim by the town meeting. Should a student be sent to study in the city? Should a disturbed child be sent to a psychiatrist? These, and similar "familial" questions, must be decided by the entire community. Finally, the kibbutz is a religio-political community, and many problems which are not viewed as subjects for community discussion in other societies are frequently part of the agenda of the town meeting. The problem of the women in the community, the participation of the younger people in community life, the meaning of a recent political event for the future of the kibbutz, the proper role of the Arabs in the national life of Israel—all are subjects for town meeting.

Underlying all these town meetings is the implicit belief

that proper decisions—proper, in the sense of just and efficient—can be made only after intensive group discussion. These are often heated and long, and many meetings do not adjourn until after midnight. Even after the formal adjournment, groups of chaverim may remain in the dining room to continue the discussions informally.

Informal discussions are as important, as heated, and even more frequent than are the formal ones. In the fields, in the dining room, in the showers, there is constant discussion—a current book, American politics, a bill in the Israeli Parliament (*Knesset*), the desire of a couple to leave the kibbutz, an art exhibit, the prospects of a good crop, the advantages of a new tractor, a recent lecture on existentialism—these and countless others are debated interminably. Long in advance of town meetings, most people have made up their minds on issues to be presented; on the basis of these informal discussions, lines are drawn and partisans are prepared with arguments. And long after the meetings have been held, the discussions continue unabated.

The importance which Kiryat Yedidim ascribes to discussion is of particular historical interest. In a book describing the culture of the shtetl, the authors write that every problem in both the family and the community,

... is subject to lengthy discussion, with full probing of every possible side of every question ... Life would be dull without constant discussion, and that is impossible without constant disagreement.[9]

Apparently, this is another aspect of shtetl culture that its descendants in the kibbutz have retained; for this quotation accurately describes the situation in Kiryat Yedidim.

[9] Zborowski and Herzog, p. 301.

The expansion of the kibbutz made it impossible to operate with any degree of efficiency on the basis of a town meeting alone, and it became necessary to institute a system of formal leadership and authority, comprising "offices" and committees. When they found it necessary, however, to institute this system of formal leadership, they attempted to preclude the possibility of any one individual assuming too much power by restricting the tenure of office to a few years. This was accomplished by instituting a system of office rotation, and by the restriction of the "rewards" of office, so that no one could, or would, remain in office beyond his allotted time.

Since many of the committees and offices have already been discussed in the section on the kibbutz economy, this section will be devoted exclusively to the other committees and offices.

The general secretary (*mazkir*) is the general factotum of the kibbutz; he prepares the agenda for, and is the chairman of, the town meeting; he is in charge of all official correspondence; he serves as liaison between the kibbutz and the kibbutz Federation; and, in general, plays the same role in the social life of the kibbutz that is played by the general economic manager in its economic life. Because his duties are heavy, the secretary is relieved of at least one-half his normal work-load in his regular work assignment.

Assisting the Secretary in his supervision of the kibbutz social life are a number of elected committees.

1. *Secretariat (mazkirut)*. This committee deals with all matters affecting the kibbutz society, with the exception of economic matters. It is a six-member committee, comprised of the general economic manager, the two work-assignment chairmen, the General Secretary, and two other elected members.

2. *Nominating Committee (vaadat minuyim)*. This committee nominates the officials and committee members for the following year, so that its tenure is brief. Some chaverim object to the existence of a nominating committee as constituting a retreat from pure democracy.

3. *Education Committee (vaadat chinuch)*. This committee deals with all matters concerning the communal education and socialization of children from infancy until they enter the high school. Membership is divided equally between laymen and educators.

4. *The High School Committee (vaadat mosad)*. This is the education committee for matters of concern to the high school and its program.

5. *Cultural Committee (vaadat tarbut)*. The cultural committee is in charge of the entire cultural program of the kibbutz. It arranges for lectures and concerts, plans holiday celebrations, arranges courses on various subjects, and supervises the library and reading room.

6. *Welfare Committee (vaadat chaverim)*. The function of this committee is to deal with the personal and interpersonal problems of the chaverim, including such matters as the provision and distribution of housing and furniture, the arrangement of annual vacations, the distribution of the annual "vacation" money, all matters dealing with health and illness, and the assistance of relatives who live abroad.

7. *Security Committee (vaadat bitachon)*. The security committee has charge of all problems of military preparedness in event of an enemy attack.

8. *Landscape Committee (vaadat shippur)*. The members of this committee are in charge of the entire landscaping program of the kibbutz.

In a very important sense, these various committees and the others already described constitute the building blocks of the society, for every aspect of kibbutz life is entrusted to them. If a committee should not function well in any given year, that aspect of kibbutz life in its charge is neglected and damage caused by this neglect sometimes continues for considerable time.

Although few people serve in the most responsible positions, it is clear from the brief description of the committees, offices, and foremen, that every chaver will eventually have to serve on some committee or assume some position of authority. The nominating committee has sixty to seventy positions to fill every year. Add to this another twenty positions, such as branch foremen, which are filled in other ways, and it is apparent that almost every member of the kibbutz must be active in one position or another. One of the major difficulties confronting the kibbutz is to persuade people to accept these positions of responsibility and authority. Some positions, such as the supervision of the kitchen, are so intrinsically onerous, that it is understandable why people should seek to avoid them. But it is difficult to understand, at first glance, why this attitude should prevail in regard to other positions of responsibility.

The fact is, that the rewards of authority are not commensurate with the responsibilities entailed. There is no financial remuneration; there is little formal prestige; and there is not a great deal of power attached to these positions. In addition, many of these jobs are extremely time-consuming and, in many cases, persons who hold them are not relieved of other responsibilities—so that most of the work must be done in the evenings, after they have already devoted a full day to their regular jobs. This means not only that they are tired, but also that they seldom get to be with their families, a serious misfortune to the average chaver. Hence the kibbutz cartoon depicts a candidate for office in the city running after people asking them to vote for him, in contrast with the "candidate" in the kibbutz, shown fleeing his fellow-members, begging them *not* to vote for him.

Nevertheless, people do run for office, and they do accept positions of responsibility, and one sometimes wonders if their reluctance to do so is entirely genuine. It seems apparent that part of the refusal to accept an official position has become a pose. The office-hating chaver has become a part of kibbutz folklore, and is an integral part of its self-image. The kibbutz would be suspicious of a chaver who agreed to run for office as soon as he was approached by the nominating committee. The first answer is always, "I don't want it"; this is the answer one is expected to give. Nevertheless, the reluctance to accept committee assignments, as well as the minor executive positions, is probably quite genuine, and constitutes an important social problem.

No individual or group of individuals hold punitive power. All authority is vested in the town meeting, and although the norms of the kibbutz are followed almost without exception, there are no policemen, judges, or courts in this society. In short, social control in Kiryat Yedidim has been achieved with a minimum of formalized patterns of authority. Hence, the dynamics of kibbutz social control demands some description.

The most important form of social control in Kiryat Yedidim is that exercised by the individual himself because of his hakkara. This superego phenomenon has already been examined in another connection[10] as constituting an important motive in economic behavior, so that it need not detain

[10] See above, pp. 88–90.

us here. It is sufficient to point out that a person who chooses
to live in a kibbutz does so voluntarily because he believes
that kibbutz life is superior to life in "the world." To violate
the norms of his chosen society constitutes a gross contradiction, for it represents, as it were, a denial of the very
motives that impelled him to join the kibbutz—the recognition of the superiority of kibbutz culture to the culture
outside.

For those to whom these original motives are no longer
as compelling as they formerly had been, there are public
forms of social control, both informal and formal. The most
effective informal technique of social control in any *gemeinschaft* is public opinion. In the kibbutz, public opinion is
of even greater importance because of the almost complete
absence of privacy to be found in this society. The simple
fact of communal living itself places a premium on privacy.
It is rare that one has the opportunity to be alone during
the day—one works in a work gang, eats in a communal
dining room, showers in a public shower, etc. It is even
difficult to find privacy in one's room. During the summer
months, the windows are open, and one can never escape
the noises from outside the room. In the winter months,
children must be entertained inside, rather than on the
lawn, as is customary in the summer, making privacy impossible. Even after the children leave, it is difficult to find
complete privacy in only one room with a spouse always
present.

Evenings yield little more privacy than days. The average
chaver participates in some group activity almost every
evening. The intensive kibbutz schedule includes holidays,
celebrations, committee meetings, classes, lectures, movies,
and the bi-weekly town meeting. "Our lives," say the

chaverim in a tone of both pride and complaint, "are too full." It is little wonder that a chavera who was studying English in her spare time complained that she had only one free evening a week in which to study. Hence, the sheer frequency of interaction, brought into being by the nature of communal living, as well as by the intensive kibbutz schedule, keeps one constantly exposed to the public eye.

Communication, moreover, is rapid in a small society, so that few activities can long remain concealed. As in any small society, activities are reported and conversations are repeated, so that secrecy is all but impossible. Moreover, with some few exceptions, the chaverim are exceptionally straightforward in their relations with their fellows. Just as they do not attempt to conceal their own thoughts or be-havior—because of the futility of attempting such conceal-ment—so they do not attempt to conceal their opinions of their fellows. It is expected that people will treat others with candor, and with little evasion or circumlocution. Indeed, the chaver who does not employ such candor is not trusted. One person, for example, has been given posi-tions of responsibility in the kibbutz because of his excep-tional talents. Nevertheless, the chaverim generally dislike him because he is not *yashar*, literally, straightforward. Should a chaver violate the group norms, it would not only be known in a short time, but he would be openly criticized for his behavior. Such group censure, informal though it is, is highly effective in a small community, and would render his existence in the kibbutz untenable. It is not surprising, then, to be told that:

Everyone is concerned about public opinion. Here you can't escape it. Everyone in the kibbutz knows about everyone else. Sometimes it is too much so.

But public opinion operates in semiformal and formal ways, as well as on an informal basis. Two semiformal techniques employed during this study may be reported here; one dealt with a relatively unimportant problem, the other with two serious problems. One of the vexing problems that confronts the kibbutz is the general reluctance on the part of chaverim to accept a work assignment in the dairy. Attempts had been made to induce certain of the young men to accept such an assignment, but these attempts had met with failure. At no time, however, were these young men publicly censured for their refusal. Another grave problem for the kibbutz is the slow but steady increase in private property. The acquiring of a small refrigerator by one couple aroused much private comment, but there was no official reaction. Although the kibbutz views this situation with grave concern, it has not yet devised any formal techniques for coping with it. Both these problems, however, were prominent in two skits that were presented as part of the celebrations of the Jewish festivals of *Purim* and *Succot*. In the Purim skit, there was a pointedly witty scene devoted to the unnamed, but easily identifiable, young men who refused to accept an assignment in the dairy. And in the Succot skit, there was a prominent reference to the "refrigerator." The author does not know the reaction of the couple who owned the refrigerator, but the reaction to the "dairy" skit was immediate. The following day when the author was working in the fields with one of the young men, the latter spontaneously referred to the skit and voluntarily admitted that he had been seriously affected by it.

Another problem, not so serious, but one which demanded immediate attention, was handled in still another way. Kiryat Yedidim celebrates the festival of Passover with an annual public *Seder*, or Passover ceremony, to which friends and relatives outside the kibbutz are invited. Its choir usually plays a prominent part in this celebration, but it had not been diligent in rehearsal attendance this year, and there was a strong possibility that it would not be prepared by Passover eve. Three days before the celebration, a notice signed by the Holiday Committee appeared on the bulletin board. The notice stated that only three days remained till Passover, and the choir was not yet prepared because its members had not attended rehearsals. If the choir did not meet the following three nights for rehearsals, the Holiday Committee would recommend to the Secretariat that the festival be cancelled. Beneath this announcement appeared the names of the choir members, and the sections in which they sang. The notice had its desired effect. Rehearsals were held with full attendance each night, and the choir sang at the Seder.

When the pressure of public opinion, exerted in informal and in semiformal ways, is not effective, the kibbutz has recourse to more formal procedures. These procedures are resorted to when a serious breach of kibbutz norms has occurred—such as a refusal to abide by an official decision of the kibbutz, or a violation of some part of its moral code. The first procedure is to bring the person's dereliction to the official attention of the kibbutz at a town meeting. This is a powerful sanction, and the very threat to use it is usually efficacious in this community where people are so sensitive to public opinion. A young man, for example, who had been asked by The Federation to accept the leadership of its national Youth Movement, refused to comply with the request. The Secretariat informed him that they would bring the matter before a town meeting, whereupon he agreed to accept the invitation.

On the other hand, when the mere threat to bring the

matter to the attention of the town meeting is not sufficient to change the person's behavior, it then becomes necessary to carry out the threat. A woman who was working in the dairy, for example, was assigned by the Work Committee to the kitchen detail, as her turn in the rotation system had come up. She refused, and her case was brought before the town meeting. The entire meeting was devoted to this problem, but before it could be resolved, other and more pressing business occupied the agenda at succeeding meetings, and the author does not know the outcome. In another case, a person who had access to the kibbutz "store" was accused by another member of utilizing some of the goods for his private use. This charge evoked a heated debate, and the Secretariat appointed a committee to investigate the charge. After completing its investigation, the committee reported that the accused was innocent of the charge, although they did note some irregularities in his behavior. The town meeting which was called to hear the evidence was stormy, and did not adjourn until 2:00 in the morning. The accused was finally exonerated.

The ultimate sanction that Kiryat Yedidim has at its disposal is expulsion. If a member is brought before the town meeting and is found guilty of a crime, or if a member refuses to acquiesce in a kibbutz decision, it may vote to expel him. Some time before our arrival in Kiryat Yedidim, a man had been accused of stealing, had been found guilty at a town meeting, and was expelled from the kibbutz. His family, of course, were not expelled and they chose to remain.[11]

---

[11] About six months later, this man wrote the kibbutz that he viewed it as his home, that he could not live happily anywhere else, and that it was his intention to return. He did so, and there has been no attempt to

During the writer's stay in the kibbutz, a couple asked for leave of absence, and a town meeting refused to grant it. The couple announced their intention to take a leave, whether it was granted or not. This deliberate challenge could not be ignored, and they were threatened with expulsion. They persisted in their plans, and were expelled.

This ultimate sanction of expulsion, however, is seldom employed. The chaver who would be so offensive as to merit expulsion is a person who is discontent with kibbutz life and who would probably leave eventually anyway.

Although there are few instances of the violation of kibbutz values in Kiryat Yedidim, this society, like any other, is confronted with the problem of aggression. It is highly doubtful if any society, no matter what its culture, can abolish the existence of aggressive impulses in its members, and it is equally doubtful if any society can prohibit all external expressions of those aggressive impulses which their members experience. Indeed, far from prohibiting all manifestations of aggressions, societies sanction certain expressions of aggression by providing for their institutionalization. Kiryat Yedidim is no exception to any of these generalizations. One could well postulate, however, that in a small and cooperative community—such as Kiryat Yedidim—aggression will not find an expression in economic competition of the kind that characterizes our own society, and that its interpersonal expression within the society must be minimal if the latter is to maintain its cooperative culture. These assumptions are, to a great extent, borne out by the

---

force him to leave, particularly since the evidence had not been conclusive.

To the author's knowledge, this is the only incident of stealing on the part of a kibbutz member. In a village where doors were never locked, stealing was unknown until the arrival of the "oriental" youth groups.

data. It is instructive, nevertheless, to examine the competitiveness and interpersonal aggression that does exist, before turning to its institutional canalization.

Interpersonal aggression is found, in the first place, in the form of gossip and petty criticism. An important social function of the communal shower room, for example, is the opportunity it affords for gossip, and the importance of this gossip may be gauged by the joking complaints of the older women as they moved into their new living quarters: since these new quarters had private plumbing, where would they gossip? In addition to gossip, there is much petty criticism and "back-biting." This seems to be particularly true of the women. It is not long before a woman being interviewed begins to point out the faults in others—in Chavera A, for the way she takes care of children; in Chavera B, for her authoritarianism; in Chavera C, for her sham meekness; in Chavera D, for her inconsiderateness, etc. Their criticisms are directed not only toward specific individuals, but toward other persons in general. Almost everyone, in the course of conversation, finds something to criticize about the kibbutz—people don't respect kibbutz property; they are not active in kibbutz activities; they don't assume a proper attitude of responsibility; they are beginning to introduce private property, etc. Almost always, it is others who are guilty of these characteristics, not themselves. The implication is clear: if other chaverim were like them, Kiryat Yedidim would be an ideal place in which to live. This criticism may be viewed, from one vantage, as a generalized hostility towards others.

Quarreling and complaining are another form in which aggression is expressed. Strong outbursts of criticism are frequent occurrences at town meetings. Most quarrels observed in the course of this study were precipitated by problems arising in the course of work—the allocation of workers to different branches, or the allocation of horses or tractors or water. Foremen of different branches quarrel among themselves or with the work-assignment chairmen. Conflict arising from economic problems, however, is not restricted to the daily meeting of the work assignment chairmen and the foremen. The shower room, already mentioned as the center for gossip, is also the center for many arguments, and the conflicts over the distribution of manpower or machinery often occur in the men's shower room. These arguments may assume serious proportions, and the author not infrequently saw chaverim burst into rages and become blue with anger in the course of such conflicts. These arguments remain on a verbal level, however, and never break out into physical clashes—at least, the author never observed any.

Interpersonal aggression is often expressed in skits. That skits are used as a technique of social control has already been discussed, but they also serve as a vehicle for the expression of aggression. One of the kibbutz officials, for example, a person highly respected for his abilities, was disliked for some of his personal qualities. Within a period of three months, he was satirized in three skits, and the uproarious reaction of the chaverim indicated quite clearly that their aggression towards this person was released by this dramatic technique.

Competition, like aggression, finds interpersonal expressions in Kiryat Yedidim. Where goods and services are scarce, or where values are important, there is competition in the kibbutz. And, as in other societies, the degree of competitiveness varies from individual to individual. One source of competition is children. Parents are very proud of their children, brag about them to others, and compete with other parents in praising their merits. A mother tells others about the words her infant is speaking, and other mothers immediately give examples from their own children to show that they are even more advanced in this regard. A girl is praised for her ability in climbing olive trees, and a father says that his daughter is even better.

Competition in economic behavior is often apparent. Children's "nurses," in particular, tend to praise their own abilities and criticize those of other "nurses." In the fields certain women consciously compete with each other to see who accomplishes the most work, or who will be the first to complete her work. In short, there is competition within an economic branch for prestige. This is not surprising when it is remembered that work is the highest value in this culture, and that prestige in work is, at once, one's only private possession and one of the few measures of one's worth. This competition for prestige, one chaver remarked, "is often very harsh." In one of the agricultural branches, for example, there are two experts, both of whom enjoy a national reputation. Their relationship is strained, and they avoid each other. During the hot summer months, when certain kinds of food were not to be found in the kibbutz, some of the people complained that were it not for the rivalry that existed between the experts, there would have been no shortage. Neither had attempted to remedy the situation, so it was claimed, lest the other receive the credit for it.

At times interpersonal competition for economic goods becomes bitter. Often there is wrangling over the assignment of rooms and of furniture, and complaints may be heard against both the welfare committee for its unjust assignments, as well as against the chaverim who have received "unmerited" better rooms or better furniture. Particularly bitter is the competition between the women over the limited supply of material and of skilled help for the making of dresses. The bitterness aroused by this competition is generally channeled against the manager of this branch, and it is usually so keen that her tenure of office is of limited duration.

It is apparent, therefore, that the chaverim have aggressive impulses, and that some of their aggression finds expression in their interpersonal relations. Nevertheless, it is probably accurate to say that much of their aggression is displaced from their fellows, and is channeled rather into other, and for the most part, acceptable directions. These canalizations consist of work, politics, and (recently) "race" prejudice.

There is little doubt but that a crucial latent function of work and politics in the kibbutz is the opportunity they afford for the release of aggressive impulses. Politics is probably the most important psychological outlet for the expression of aggression in the kibbutz. In its attempt to create a better world, the kibbutz has found that it faces considerable opposition, and it has come to view this opposition with an intense hatred. Indeed, it is not unfair to say that the kibbutz hates almost everybody since it views almost everybody as an opponent. Outside of Israel, all the "bourgeois" countries are hated, and only the Soviet Union and the "People's Democracies" are "loved." Inside Israel, the Socialist "reformists" are hated even more intensely than the *bourgeoisie*. And within its own political party, the "right wing" is at times attacked with a bitterness generally reserved for opposition parties. This hatred finds a daily release through reading the Party's daily newspaper. Here the chaverim are told repeatedly that most of the world consists of evil men who are intent on making war, invading the Soviet Union, dismembering Israel, and destroying both the working class and the kibbutz movement.[12]

If politics provides the chaverim with a psychological outlet for aggression, work provides them with its most important physical outlet. Because the hours of work are long, because the sun is hot, and because the soil demands continuous care, it is apparent that work consumes most of their physical energies. The intensity and compulsivity with which they approach (attack, would perhaps be a more appropriate verb) this work indicates that the conquest of nature provides an important canalization for their aggressions.

But aggression is not only released through politics and physical labor, it is also expressed in interpersonal relations —but against non-chaverim. Although the ideology of the kibbutz stresses international and inter-racial brotherhood, the attitudes of some of the chaverim as expressed in their interpersonal relations with non-Jews and non-Israelis betray much prejudice. The wife of the newly arrived doctor, for example, was a Gentile, and the chaverim neither liked her nor attempted to accept her. A typical response to questions concerning their attitude towards her was, "she's a *goya* (Gentile woman), and the Jews like the *goyim* no more than the *goyim* like the Jews." The prejudice against the "oriental" Jews has "racist" overtones. The youths from Morocco and Iraq, who were living in the kibbutz, were often referred to contemptuously as "*hashechorim*," the

[12] For a detailed description of kibbutz ideology, see Chapter 5.

dark ones; and snobbish reference was often made to both their oriental origin and their "primitive" behavior. The following remark of one chaver may not be typical, but it is indicative of a general attitude. One day, when the work in the kitchen was particularly slow and inefficient, he exclaimed, "What can you expect? The only ones working there now are Africans, Asiatics, and Americans!"

CHAPTER 5

THE KIBBUTZ AS A
COMMUNAL SOCIETY, II

Parents and Children

IT IS DIFFICULT to decide whether the family or even marriage, in their conventional forms, exist in Kiryat Yedidim. From its very inception, Kiryat Yedidim has stressed two polar entities—the individual and the community—and it has attempted to minimize, if not to eliminate, any intermediate groups between the two. In its conventional sense, not even the "nuclear" family exists in the kibbutz, except in a highly attenuated form. In a broader sense, however, one might say that the whole kibbutz is a family—a large extended family. In either case, it is premature to evaluate the kibbutz family, for Kiryat Yedidim is in a state of transition, and it is difficult to predict what structures might yet emerge. It is apparent, for example, from an examination of the history of Kiryat Yedidim, and from conversations with the vattikim, that it had originally expected to destroy both marriage and the family in their conventional meanings. The changing attitudes of the vattikim, however, as well as the attitudes of the sabras toward marriage and the family, and the changing social conditions in the kibbutz—brought about by the existence of children and grandchildren—have served to create a structural fluidity in these kibbutz groupings.

It will be remembered that the vattikim, when members of the Youth Movement, were in rebellion against the Jewish culture of the shtetl, as well as against the bourgeois culture of the European city. And among the many aspects of these cultures that they wished to change were the "false" sexual morality of the city, the "patriarchal" authority of the male, the "dependence" of the child on his father, and the "subjection" of women. Their rebellion against the first two traditions led them to a radical revision of the marriage relationship; their opposition to the latter two led to a serious modification of the traditional family.

We shall first consider the marriage relationship. The Youth Movement had a strong "puritanical" tinge, and its general emphasis on "purity" in living extended to its attitude toward sexual relations. Love, for the sixteen-year-olds in the movement, was a serious matter, not to be taken lightly, as it was by the "decadent" *bourgeoisie*. "We were serious; we were too serious," said one vattika, critically. They were opposed to even mild flirtations; and one vattika recalls, as an historic curiosity, a weekend trip they had taken to the mountains in Europe, in which there was "not even a kiss." "We thought," she commented, "that we were supermen. In this sense, the young sabras are healthier than we were; we were confused."

When these people, in their late teens and early twenties, arrived in Palestine, they were confronted with the problem of establishing their own sexual morality, and this task was not easy. "It was difficult," commented this vattika, "from an erotic point of view." The sex ratio was 2:1—sixty males and thirty females—which was difficult enough. In addition, they were supposed to live together in one community, but not as couples. "It is little wonder that we were all," as she put it, "concerned with sex." This was the period in their history when Freud was studied seriously, not so much for intellectual stimulation, as for practical guidance. But Freud "only created greater confusion."

After some initial soul-searching, the pioneers attempted to arrive at a satisfactory relationship between the sexes by trial-and-error. They were convinced that it was possible to create a relationship between the sexes on a sounder and more natural foundation than that which characterized "bourgeois" marriage, and they experimented with many substitutes including informal polygyny and polyandry. They attempted to break down the traditional attitude of sexual shame in which they had been reared by instituting a mixed shower, but that experiment was soon abandoned— "Our previous training was too strong." As for marriage, they believed—and still believe—that a union between a man and a woman was their own affair, to be entered into on the basis of love and to be broken at the termination of love; neither the union nor the separation were to require the permission or the sanction of the community. Today, for example, if a couple wishes to marry, the partners merely ask for a joint room; if they wish a divorce, they return to separate rooms. It should be added, however, that since the kibbutz is not an autonomous society, it must take account of the laws of the land, according to which illegitimate children have no civil rights. Hence, when a woman becomes pregnant, the couple becomes legally married.

It is in this same spirit that kibbutz children have received their sexual education. Children are discouraged from engaging in sexual experimentation, but they are taught in school about sexual matters in an objective way. The high school youth are also discouraged from engaging in sexual experiences, as well as from forming romantic attachments, not for reasons of sexual morality, but because it is felt that such experiences divert their energies and interests from their intellectual and social activities. On the other hand, the sexes share common rooms in the dormitories from infancy through high school graduation and they share a common shower until they enter high school. In the not too distant past, showers were shared in the high school as well, but this practice was abandoned by the children themselves.

Upon entering the kibbutz as full-fledged members, the recent high school graduates may enter into sexual relationships with impunity. Sexual affairs are viewed as the exclusive concern of the couples involved until they fall in love and decide to get married. When that occurs they apply to the housing committee for a common room, and the granting of this request constitutes the official community recognition and sanction of the marriage.

From the very beginning the terms, "marriage," "husband," "wife," were abandoned because of their invidious connotations. A man and woman do not get "married"; they become a "pair" (*zug*). A woman does not acquire a "husband," she acquires a "young man" (*bachur*) or a "companion" (*chaver*). By the same token, a man acquires not a "wife," but a "young woman" (*bachura*) or a "companion" (*chavera*). Divorces were frequent in the past, but they created few hardships, since there were no legal problems involved, and few of the couples had as yet had children. For there seemed to have been a common understanding when they were still living in work camps, that they would delay having children until a permanent settlement had been acquired. Even after they settled in Kiryat Yedidim, however, the chaverim felt that they should not raise children until the geographic and economic conditions

of the *kibbutz* were improved. (They were living in swampland, and suffered a serious shortage of food.)

In the past when two persons fell in love and became
united as a "couple," they attempted to deny their relationship, as it were, by seldom being seen together in public,
or by acting casually towards each other if they were to
meet in a public place. Partners were even "ashamed" to
enter the dining room together; they would enter separately
and eat at different tables. One chavera tells how embarrassed she was when her husband not only insisted on
entering the dining room with her, but went so far as to
put his arm around her in public. During our stay in Kiryat
Yedidim, a number of chaverim went on a trip which
marked an important occasion in their history, because it
was the first times that mates accompanied each other on
a trip. In the past, this was unheard of; each would go his
separate way and, returning, would greet everyone in the
kibbutz except his mate.

The reason for this public "denial" of a strong bond
between partners seems to have been twofold. In the first
place, to have acted otherwise would have been "bourgeois,"
and the kibbutz viewed bourgeois behavior as a stigma. Secondly, Kiryat Yedidim, it will be recalled, emphasized group
living as an end in itself, so that the individual's strongest
tie was supposed to be with the entire community. It was,
therefore, important for a person who had acquired a "companion" to emphasize the fact that he had not divorced himself from the group life, and that he was not creating a
private life or developing private interests that would sever
his ties with the group.[1]

---

[1] On another "level," the denial of sexual relationships may be viewed
as part of the sexual puritanism that characterized the philosophy of the
youth movement. This puritanism is still an integral part of kibbutz life.
One seldom, if ever, hears sexual references in a mixed group, and even

But the opposition of the kibbutz to bourgeois marriage rested not only on its antagonism to the "false" and "hypocritical" sexual morality of this marriage; it was based also on the strong feminist philosophy of the Youth Movement. The bourgeois woman, as viewed by the chaverim, is little better than a chattel servant. She has few legal rights or political privileges, and she is economically and socially dependent upon her husband. Her "place" is in the home, and her main task is to serve her husband and her children. In their new society, women were to be the equals of men in all matters—their subjection to men in bourgeois society being a result of the social system rather than of natural inferiority. But if the traditional marriage arrangements were to be perpetuated, women could not become men's equals. They would again be legally dependent upon their husbands, since their legal status would be that of Mrs. So-and-so. They would be socially dependent upon their husbands, since their social status would depend upon the latter's social status. And they would be economically dependent upon their husbands, for they would again be relegated to housework, while their husbands remained the providers. If this "patriarchal authority" of the husband was to be destroyed, it was necessary to change the legal, social, and economic status of women. This, the kibbutz feels, has been achieved.

The abolition of the marriage ceremony, the chaverim assert, has abolished the woman's legal subjection to the man. She does not assume his name, and her legal status in the community is not that of his wife, but that of a chavera of

---

in an all-male work detail, for example, the conversation seldom includes sexual jokes or references. The author encountered not a single incident of the above.

the kibbutz. Hence, both are chaverim of the kibbutz, equal in all respects. Though living in the same room, they remain legally distinct as far as the kibbutz is concerned. Nor is the woman's social status dependent upon that of her husband. A woman's prestige is not enhanced by the fact that her husband is recognized as a leader, as a skilled worker, or as a person of great knowledge; nor is it lowered because he is stupid, irresponsible, or highly inefficient. Moreover, the absence of private ownership in property and of differential wealth makes it impossible for a woman to enjoy prestige because of her husband's economic fortunes. Finally, her economic dependence upon her husband has been destroyed by making men and women co-equals in the economic life of the kibbutz. Since the woman, like the man, works in the kibbutz economy rather than in her own home, she earns her own living and is not dependent upon her husband for her support. A woman satisfies her economic needs, there-fore, not as a dependent of her husband whose labor pro-vides for her, but as an independent worker in her own right whose contribution to the economic welfare of the community equals that of her husband. Should she desire to divorce him, she need have no fear of losing her source of economic support. Moreover, woman's inferior position in the economy was abolished, it is believed, by destroying the traditional division of labor based on sex. In the early days of the kibbutz, sexual division of labor was minimal. Both men and women shared the work in the kitchen and other traditional "female" occupations, and they both shared the work on the roads, on the tractors, and in other traditional "male" occupations. Today, this is no longer the case although some women still work in the fields, and men take their turn at kitchen work. When the "problem of the women" is examined[2] it will be observed that much of the original feminist philosophy, and even more of its practice, has undergone a considerable change. Nevertheless, the basic structure of the marriage relationship remains today as it was in the past, with but two changes. Divorce, which was relatively frequent in the past, has become infrequent. This increase in marriage stability probably is due to the fact that the vattikim are no longer the hot-blooded young rebels they were in their youth, and that their married children seem to be opposed to divorce on principle. Actually, the entire attitude of the kibbutz towards sex seems to have undergone a great change. Sexual promiscuity is viewed with suspicion, and extramarital affairs, although not censured, are no longer approved. The one extramarital affair which occurred during the writer's stay (of which he was aware, that is) was viewed by many chaverim as "adultery," though the word was never used.

The second important change has been the public recognition and the admission of a "couple" relationship. Spouses go on trips together, take their vacations together, and eat their evening meals together, as a matter of course, without shame and embarrassment. Moreover, one occasionally hears a woman referring to her mate as "my husband" (baali), an idiom that would have been taboo in the past. When the author chided one of the women for using this term, she remarked "what's the difference? In the past, these things meant a lot to us; but now that we're older, they don't mean very much."

Some sabras go so far as to have a public celebration when they become a "couple," something that would have been shocking in their parents' generation. But an even

2 See Chapter 6.

greater deviation on the part of the sabras, and one which some viewed as a serious breach of kibbutz morality, occurred during our stay. Two sabras, who had been a "couple" for two years, decided to become legally married in order to preclude the criticism they would encounter in Jerusalem, where they were to study. The night of the ceremony, the bride's father arranged for a festive celebration of the *Chatuna* (religious marriage) of his daughter. The criticism of this by kibbutz members was on two counts—the reference to the marriage in religious terms, and the celebration of the occasion as if the marriage ceremony really marked the beginning of their marriage, when, from the point of view of the kibbutz, they had been officially married two years earlier.

With this description, the question still remains as to whether "marriage," as that term has been cross-culturally defined, exists in the kibbutz. According to Murdock, marriage entails two distinct but interlocking culture patterns: a relatively permanent sexual relationship, and economic cooperation between at least two persons of opposite sex.

> Sexual unions without economic cooperation are common, and there are relationships between men and women involving a division of labor without sexual gratification . . . but marriage exists only when the economic and the sexual are united into one relationship . . .[3]

It is apparent from the description of the kibbutz "couple" that its relationship involves neither economic cooperation nor a division of labor. There is, to be sure, a division of labor based on sex in the kibbutz as a whole, and it should be stressed that this division is an important expression of "economic cooperation." But, since men and women alike

[3] Murdock, p. 8.

perform their economic functions within the community rather than within the home, and, since the fruits of their labor are channeled into the public rather than into their own private treasury, it is apparent that the sexual division of labor is a division that obtains between the males as a group and the females as a group, rather than between a specific sexual pair.

Since the kibbutz "couple" does not satisfy Murdock's "marriage" criteria, we may either state that marriage, by definition, does not exist in the kibbutz, or we may set up other criteria. The problem, however, is not germane to this study, and we shall not be detained by it. It is important, however, to discern what function is served by the institution of the "couple," in lieu of the functions served by the traditional institution of marriage. It may be suggested that the "couple" has one generic and crucial function—the satisfaction of a need for intimacy. This need may be divided into a physical and a psychological dimension; that is, the partners receive sexual satisfaction and psychological security (friendship, comradeship, succor, etc.) from their relationship. It is this second aspect of the relationship that distinguishes two persons who are having an affair from a "couple," and this is the distinction which is made by the kibbutz itself. Lovers do not ask to share a common room, nor would they be given one were they to request it. When two persons ask to share a room, it is assumed that they are not only lovers, but that they are in love.[4]

---

[4] Kiryat Yedidim views marriage as both a natural and a desirable state. The attitude of the chaverim toward the unmarried is represented by the comment of one woman in referring to an unmarried chavera: "She's such a good woman; it is a pity she has no bachur." Nevertheless, fifteen of the 200 adults in the kibbutz (exclusive of the young generation) are either bachelors, widows or widowers, and divorced persons who have not remarried. In general they have the same privileges and responsibili-

The identification of the family in Kiryat Yedidim is even more elusive than is the identification of its marriage. The family, according to Murdock's cross-cultural study,

. . . is a social group characterized by common residence, economic cooperation, and reproduction. It includes adults of both sexes, at least two of whom maintain a socially approved sexual relationship, and one or more children, own or adopted, of the sexually cohabiting adults.[5]

In describing the relationship between the adults and the children in the family, Murdock states that the "physical care" and "social rearing" of the children are the most important responsibilities of the adults. And as for the latter responsibility, he writes:

The burden of education and socialization everywhere falls primarily upon the nuclear family . . . Perhaps more than any other single factor, collective responsibility for education and socialization welds the various relationships of the family firmly together.[6]

The kibbutz "family" includes two adults of opposite sex who "maintain a socially approved sexual relationship" and their "own or adopted" children. As we have already observed, however, it does not include economic cooperation, nor does it include common residence, since the children live in separate children's dormitories. This "family," moreover, does not have the function of education and socializa-

---

ties as married persons. There are instances, however, in which they are at a disadvantage. In constructing the new housing development for the vattikim, the kibbutz decided that the unmarried would not be entitled to the new housing since they did not require a room and a half. The one unmarried woman in this group was quite bitter about this. "I suppose I'll have to get married in order to earn my pension," was her comment.

[5] *Ibid.*, p. 1.
[6] *Ibid.*, p. 10.

tion, since this function is fulfilled by the "nurses" and teachers in the communal dormitories as part of the system of "collective education," a system which arose as a function of the kibbutz protest against the "patriarchal" father and the "subjection" of women.

One way in which the "dependence" of the child upon the "patriarchal" father could be eliminated was to remove the child physically from the father, and to entrust him to the care of some other person. This was done by instituting children's dormitories, in which specialized "nurses" and teachers, rather than the father (and/or the mother) raise the children. As the education journal of The Federation puts it,

The changes in the family, whose economic foundations have been uprooted, have brought about a change in the status of the man and woman in the kibbutz society, and with that a change of the status of the father and mother in the family. This is most pronounced with respect to the function of the father, for all his ruling privileges, the source of his formal authority, are destroyed.

The father not only does not rear the child, but he also has no specific responsibility for him. The child is provided for by the kibbutz as a whole; he receives his food in the dormitory dining room, his clothes from the dormitory storeroom, his medical care from the dispensary, and his housing in the dormitories. This is a deliberate policy, the aim of which is to prevent the child from feeling economically dependent upon the father which, according to kibbutz analysis, is the greatest source of the father's authority in bourgeois society. The official book on education, published by The Federation, puts it clearly: one of the results of the system of collective education has been that:

. . . the child is emancipated from the rule of the father of the family . . . In the patriarchal family the child is dependent economically and legally on the father as provider, on the "master of the household," which is not true in the kibbutz. The child is not dependent, in any objective sense, except on the kibbutz as a whole.

Again, we read that:

. . . related to the economic structure of the family in the kibbutz (is the fact that) the kibbutz has put an end to the patriarchate . . . The father does not enjoy the superior position that was the privilege of the "economic provider" in the ordinary society.

The aim of the kibbutz, then, was to weaken the traditional family by destroying the seat of the father's authority. In this it has succeeded.

But the kibbutz also attempted to change the woman's role in the family. It has already been pointed out that the vattikim were feminists, and one facet of their feminism has been examined above—the desire to abrogate the traditional dependence of the female on the male, of the wife on her husband. But there is another aspect of their feminism which relates more specifically to the family—the desire to abolish the consequences of what is termed *ha-tragedia ha-biologit shel ha-isha*—"the biological tragedy of woman." Because woman must bear and rear children, she has had little opportunity for cultural, political, or artistic expressions. If she could only be freed from this time-consuming responsibility, as well as from such other domestic duties as cleaning, cooking, and laundry, she would have the time to devote to these other interests and would become the equal of men. In other words, the crux of the problem was to be found in *shichrur ha-isha meha-ol shel sherut*—"the emancipation of the woman from the yoke of domestic service." By instituting a system of communal socialization, it was believed, it would be possible to achieve part of this goal—the emancipation of woman from the burdens of child-rearing. And if her children were reared by professional nurses, the woman would not only be free from that responsibility, she would be spared the chores of housekeeping as well, since she and her husband would require little room.

Her complete "emancipation," however, included the abolition of all domestic chores. This was accomplished by the various communal institutions of the kibbutz: the communal laundry, kitchen, and dining room relieved her of the chores of laundry, cooking, and dish-washing. Thus, woman is relieved of the care of her children and of her traditional domestic chores.

In sum, the kibbutz has succeeded in eliminating most of the characteristics and functions of the traditional family. The parents have little responsibility for the physical care or for the socialization of their children; the relationship between mates does not include economic cooperation; and parents and children do not share a common residence. Taking these facts, alone, into consideration it may be concluded that the family, as characterized by Murdock, does not exist in the kibbutz. On the other hand, though the family does not exist in a structural-functional sense, it does exist in a psychological sense. Although parents and children do not share a common residence, they are deeply attached to each other and comprise a distinct and recognizable social group. Moreover, the chaverim themselves refer to this group as a *mishpacha*, or family.[7]

[7] For an extended discussion and attempted resolution of this entire problem, see Spiro, "Is the Family Universal?"

The one characteristic of all kibbutzim, on which all observers are in unanimous agreement is the attachment of parents for their children. Kiryat Yedidim, like other kibbutzim, is a child-centered society, par excellence. Children are prized above all else. In observing the kibbutz and from interviewing parents one receives the distinct impression that no sacrifice is too great to make for the children. Adults are willing to live in sub-standard housing as long as children may live in stuccoed brick dormitories. Adults share two shower rooms—one for males and one for females— and two toilets, but each children's dormitory has its own shower and toilets. Adults are content to eat dairy meals and few desserts, so that the children may enjoy meat and desserts at almost every meal. Adults work long hours in the fields with brief annual vacations, while their children receive a high school education, including many extracurricular activities, so that they work—even when high school seniors—only a few hours a day, and enjoy a three-month summer vacation. Finally, so that parents may devote the late afternoon to their children, the kibbutz works during the heat of the day even in the summer, instead of taking a long afternoon siesta and beginning the afternoon work after the hottest part of the day has passed.

This general attitude of Kiryat Yedidim toward all its children is a reflection, of course, of the attitude parents have toward their own children. These parents, to be sure, do not have the many responsibilities that parents in other societies have for their children. But, instead of weakening the parental tie, the kibbutz system of "collective education" has strengthened it. For most parents, the entire day is a prelude to the brief period in the late afternoon when they are joined by their children. Upon return from work—

4:30 in winter and 5:30 in summer—the parents shower, change their clothes, and hasten to the children's dormitories to greet their children, if the latter have not already arrived at the parental rooms. The next two hours are sacred; they are to be devoted exclusively to the children, and nothing is allowed to interfere. During this "children's hour" all activities in the kibbutz come to a standstill; one wit has observed that if the bordering Arab state were to attack the kibbutz at that time, it would win a handy victory, since the chaverim could not be induced to leave their children. In summer, parents and children spend their time romping on the grass, playing games, visiting the animals, strolling through the fields. In winter, they are confined to their rooms, and activities consist of playing, reading, listening to music, and talking. When it is time for the children to return to their dormitories, they are usually accompanied by their parents, and the final departure is sometimes difficult for both. Parents and children are together not only every afternoon, but on Saturdays and holidays as well.

The eagerness of parents to see their children is equalled only by the eagerness of the children to see their parents. This is not surprising. In the dormitories the children must not only share their nurse's love with many other children, but they are subjected to her discipline as well. Furthermore, they must conform to the regimen and routine which dormitory life demands. In their parental room, on the other hand, they can monopolize their parents—most children have no more than a couple of siblings—they are seldom disciplined, and they are indulged to the point where the chaverim say they are "spoiled." Hence it is, that children generally mean their parental room when they refer to "my room," and they brag about the abilities and accomplishments (real or imagined) of their parents, much as children in our own society.[8]

The intense parent-child relationship here described generally lasts until the children enter high school, at which time it diminishes considerably and in some cases almost disappears. This attenuation of erstwhile deep affectional bonds is almost always asymmetrical, however—it is not shared by the parents. Parents frequently complain that they seldom see their children now that they are in high school and that, when they do, they seem to have little in common. The reasons for this change are complex in nature, and will be analyzed in a forthcoming volume.

The kibbutz educational system, known as "collective education" (*chinuch me-shuttaf*), emerged from a number of considerations. The philosophy, if not the practice, of collective education had already been worked out by the Youth Movement in Europe under the influence of Carl

[8] For those scholars interested in the comparative study of kinship systems, Kiryat Yedidim is, at present, of little interest. There are too few relatives, other than those that fall within the nuclear family, to permit any generalizations concerning the patterning of kinship behavior. There are kinship terms, however, for the various relatives that are designated in the Western kinship system. They are, of course, terms which the kibbutz shares with the larger Israeli society. In Kiryat Yedidim some of these terms are used only as terms of address, others as terms of reference, and some are extended beyond their kinship reference. To be specific, the terms for father and mother (*abba, imma*) are used as terms of address, and apply specifically to biological or adoptive parents. At times, however, a young child addresses his nurse as "mother," in an unwitting extension of a kinship term. Both juvenile and adult sabras employ these parental terms in reference and address; in general, however, the adult sabras employ their parents' proper names when referring to them.

The terms for son and daughter (*ben, bat*) refer exclusively to biological or adopted children, when preceded by the personal possessive, and they are used exclusively as terms of reference. These terms are extended, however, to refer to all kibbutz children, when used without the personal possessive, or when used with the personal plural possessive.

The terms for uncle and aunt (*dod, dodda*) designate all the relatives

Blüher. This philosophy was joined to the kibbutz feminist ideology and to kibbutz opposition to the traditional family with its authoritarian father and husband. Philosophy and ideology were wedded to practical necessity when the vattikim first arrived in the country. It became apparent that if they were to survive economically it was imperative that they be able to devote most of their manpower to productive work. Collective education would enable those women who otherwise would remain at home to work in the fields. These, then, were the motives for instituting this novel system.

Once this educational system was created, the educational

---

that are conventionally designated by these terms in the Western kinship nomenclature, but they are seldom, if ever, used as either terms of address or of reference. Proper names are used, instead. On the other hand, the terms for "uncle" and "aunt" are frequently employed by the sabras to refer to any elderly stranger.

The terms for nephew and niece (*ben ach, ben achot; bat ach, bat achot*—"brother's son, sister's son"; "brother's daughter, sister's daughter") are never used in address, and rarely as reference, except for purposes of identification.

Sibling terms (*ach,* "brother"; *achot,* "sister") are never used in address, and are used as reference only for purposes of identification. Cousin terms (*ben dod,* "uncle's son"; *ben dodda,* "aunt's son"; *bat dod,* "uncle's daughter"; *bat dodda,* "aunt's daughter") are never used in any context.

Grandparental terms (*saba,* "grandfather"; *sabta,* "grandmother") designate biological grandparents, and are used—at least by young children—as terms of both reference and address. These terms may be extended beyond their kinship usage to refer to any old man or woman. Moreover, the parents of both the vattikim and of the middle-aged chaverim who joined the kibbutz at a later time are referred to by everyone with the term "grandfather" or "grandmother" preceding their proper names—such as, Saba Aryeh or Sabta Miryam, and they are so addressed by all the children.

Terms for grandchildren (*neched,* "grandson"; *nechda,* "granddaughter") are used in reference, but not in address. In general, everyone, including older children, addresses young children as *chamudi* ("my precious," "my adorable") rather than by their proper names.

leaders viewed its functions (as distinct from the motives for its creation) as crucial for the survival of the kibbutz and for the development of certain prized qualities in its children. "Collective education," writes an educational theorist of The Federation,

... is a necessary consequence of the collective society ... (It serves) as a link in the attempts of a revolutionary movement to change the behavior and the institutions of human civilization ... (Its) historical purpose (is) to establish the foundation for the transmission of the kibbutz ideology to the coming generations, and to cultivate a human type that will be prepared to implement it in life.

The "human type" which the system of collective education wishes to cultivate, according to the same theorist, is a person who will be:

... an active and conscious (*baal hakkarah*) member of his kibbutz ... possessed of a dialectical-materialistic *weltanschauung;* devoted to his People, and versed in its history; faithful to his homeland and prepared to defend it; devoted to the workers' movement, the socialist nations, and the concept of brotherhood among peoples; expert in the problems of the country and of the world, and alert to what is happening in them; at home in the concepts of the scientific world; and of cultivated esthetic taste.

A newborn infant enters the kibbutz educational system at the age of four days, that is, when he returns with his mother from the hospital. At that time he enters the Infants House (*bet tinokkot*), and becomes an official member, not of the kibbutz, but of the "Children's Society" (*chevrat yeladim*); and in this Society he remains until, upon graduation from high school, he is elected to membership in the kibbutz. Kiryat Yedidim is similar to a religious sect in that membership is not a right conferred upon an individual by birth. Rather, it is a privilege which the group confers upon an adult who, at the age of consent, knowingly and willingly accepts its values and its way of life. Hence, although the children live in Kiryat Yedidim and are raised by Kiryat Yedidim, they are not viewed as members of the kibbutz until their candidacy is announced and they are formally elected as chaverim.

The Infants House includes a maximum of sixteen infants ranging in age from four days to approximately one year, who are in the charge of a head "nurse" (*metappelet*, literally, "caretaker") and two full-time assistant "nurses." The children's "nurses" in Kiryat Yedidim are not professional, medical nurses, but female members of the kibbutz who have usually received formal training—educational, psychological, and in some instances, medical—in the care and rearing of children of the age group entrusted to their care.

In addition to their initial period of formal training, these "nurses" are sent periodically to the training center of The Federation for short courses and refresher courses. With the exception of two nurses in the Infants House, however, these women receive little, if any, medical training.

Since the infants may not be taken to their parental rooms until they are six months old, almost all their physical needs, with the exception of feeding, and most of their other needs as well, are satisfied primarily by the nurses. Weaning, which is a gradual process, is usually completed by the eighth month, but until that age infants are breast-fed by their mothers, who follow a pattern of scheduled feeding. Since this schedule at the beginning includes six feedings around the clock, and only gradually tapers off until the weaning is completed, the infant sees his mother at frequent intervals. Moreover, since the feeding takes about an hour, and since the mother usually plays with the infant before and after feeding, changes his diapers, and tucks him back into bed, it is not unlikely that the kibbutz infant has as much opportunity for interaction with his mother as have infants who are raised in private homes.

Since the father works during the day, his sole daily contact with the infant takes place during the late afternoon visiting hour. During this hour, as well as during the free visiting hours on Saturday when both parents visit their infant together, the Infants House, porch, and lawn are filled with numerous adults, romping and playing with their infants.

The first important change in the infant's life occurs at the age of six months, when he may be taken to his parents' room in the afternoon for one hour. The second important change occurs at the age of about one year, when he is moved from the Infants House to the Toddlers House (*bet peutot*). This change marks an important turning point in his life for he must become adjusted to a new physical environment, at least one new nurse, new (and slightly older) children, a new routine, and new disciplines. In the Toddlers House, which comprises two nurses and eight children, the infant is gradually toilet trained; he is taught to feed himself; and he learns to get along with his playmates. At this age the infant may remain in his parental room for two hours in the evening. This two-hour period is not a rigidly determined limit; it represents the approximate interval between the parents' return from work and the child's departure for bed. Moreover he may be taken to their room not only on Saturdays, but on other days on which they may be free.

Like the other children's dormitories, the Toddlers House is designed for the convenience of children of that age: beds, tables, chairs, utensils, wash bowls are all in miniature. Again, as in the case of the other dormitories, it is designed to meet all their needs. The children not only sleep, but also eat and play in the dormitories. Hence, each building for children under school age is modeled on the general scheme of one or more bedrooms, a combination dining and playroom, and a shower and dressing-room. Each dormitory has a play yard with play objects appropriate to the age of the group. The toddlers' yard is enclosed with a fence, since the nurse is not always readily available and the children might easily stray into such dangers readily found on any farm.

In some instances the group of eight children in the Toddlers House remain with the same nurse until they enter the kindergarten (*gan*), at which time they not only change buildings, but nurses as well. In most instances, however, the group remain with their nurses until they reach nursery age—between the years of two and three—at which time a nursery teacher (*gannenet*) generally replaces one of the nurses. The nurse continues to care for the physical and emotional needs of the children, but the specially trained nursery teacher is in charge of their social and intellectual development. Sometime between their four and fifth birthdays, the children encounter another important change. At this time the group passes into the Kindergarten. This not only involves a new building and, sometimes, a new nurse and kindergarten teacher, but it also involves the enlargement of their original group to include sixteen members. This is brought about by the merging of two nursery groups into one kindergarten. This merger is an important event in the lives of the children, for this enlarged group, or *kevutza*, will remain together as a unit until its members reach high school age. This kevutza is, in many ways, the child's most important social group, not only because of its long duration, but because of the frequency and intensity of interaction within it.

Although the emotional and intellectual levels of the children differ considerably as they pass from the Toddlers House to the Kindergarten, the institutional aspects of their lives, with which we are concerned here, are quite similar. Since the children live in groups it is necessary that their lives be routinized to a considerable extent, and the various children's dormitories have similar schedules.

The children all rise in the morning at the same time and have a free play period before breakfast. After breakfast, there is usually an organized group activity supervised by the nurse or the nursery teacher, its nature depending upon the age of the children. These activities are diverse, including games, art (drawing, dancing, singing, sculpting, etc.), listening to stories told or read by the nursery teacher, hikes into the fields, tours through the animal barns, etc. The morning is broken up by a mid-morning snack, after which there is either a free play period or a continuation of the organized activity. After lunch all the children must nap or rest for approximately two hours. When they waken from their naps they change into their "good clothes," are given a snack, and spend the rest of the afternoon in either free or organized play. As in the case of the other two meals, supper is a communal meal, and after supper the parents arrive to take their children to their rooms. Children spend approximately two hours with their parents, who accompany them to their dormitories when it is time to return.

Before going to bed the children almost invariably receive a shower—in addition to showers they may receive during the day—after which they are tucked into bed by their nurse, who usually tells them a story or sings a song before turning out the lights. The children are then left alone until the following morning, except for a periodic check during the night by the night watchman for the children's dormitories.

It should be indicated that boys and girls experience few differences based on sex in their daily routine of living. They sleep in the same room, and use the same showers and toilets. Moreover few, if any, differences are to be discerned in their games.

It is apparent that the significant persons in the child's life, in addition to his parents whose roles have already been discussed, are his nurses, nursery and kindergarten teachers, and his kevutza. If only because he spends most of his time with them, a child's nurses and teachers are parental surrogates in almost every sense of the term. They care for almost all his physical desires and needs—they feed, bathe and clothe him, and nurse him when he is ill. They rear him and, hence, care for many of his social needs. Most of the child's knowledge of his physical environment, his skills, and his knowledge of his own (kibbutz) culture, including its values, behavior patterns, and techniques, are taught him by these women. Finally, since they are for him psychologically significant persons, they are of great importance for his emotional development. The nurses and nursery teachers institute most of his disciplines, impose upon him most of his restrictions, teach him—or encourage him to use—most of his techniques for need satisfaction and drive-reduction, and all the while reward and punish him, express approval and disapproval, give affection and withhold affection.

The other group of significant persons in the child's life is his kevutza. Almost all the child's daily activities, his experiences, and his belongings are shared either voluntarily or under compulsion with these age-peers. It is little wonder, therefore, that the children are obviously ambivalent towards each other. It is exciting to share experiences, but it is frustrating to share one's beloved nurse or the only toy auto in the dormitory, or the only blue book trimmed in yellow. The sharing of the latter objects is usually motivated only by adult compulsion or persuasion, and leads to frequent and intense fighting and quarreling within the kevutza. This in turn intensifies the child's relationship to his parent—the only object he need not share (unless he has a sibling). But it is the sharing of experience that accounts for the desire of the children to return to the dormitory in the evening, and the great enthusiasm with which they greet their fellows as they enter. Parents are fine for so long, but after that one wants one's friends: this seems to be the attitude of the children.

Between the ages of five and six the children in the kindergarten pass into a new dormitory, where they receive their first formal intellectual instruction, including the study of reading and writing; and when they complete a year in this *kitat maavar*, or "transitional class," they are ready to enter the primary school. The school is a large building, including both dormitory and classroom facilities. For the first time children live in a building that includes not only their own (approximately) age-peers, but other children whose ages span a wide range—from seven to twelve. Each kevutza, or group of sixteen children, remains distinct in that it has its own teacher, classroom, and bedroom. But the entire student body eats together, plays together, and participates in the same extracurricular activities. Hence, the functional "children's society" for these children includes not only their kevutza, but the entire school population, known as their chevra.

This passage into the school is an important event in the lives of the children, not only because it marks the commencement of their serious formal education and expands their interactional group, but also because it introduces them into social responsibility and work. Until they enter the school the children have no chores. Their dormitory may "own" a few chickens or a duck which they, together with their nursery teacher, feed. But once they enter the school, each child has specific responsibilities which require about an hour a day to fulfill. These responsibilities include, among other things, making beds, cleaning their bedrooms and classrooms, setting the tables in the dining room, and working in the school's vegetable garden or in its poultry run.

Behavior in the classroom is informal. Instruction is by the project method, the students having a choice in the selection of the project to be studied. Teachers, like nurses, are called by their first names—as was the case before the children entered the school, and will be throughout their educational careers. This informality includes not only an egalitarian social milieu, but also an informality in the method of instruction. There are neither exams nor marks, hence the process of passing from one grade to the next is entirely automatic. The curriculum itself is little different from the curriculum of an American grade school.

The completion of the sixth grade, when the children are about twelve years old, marks another important turning point in their lives—entry into high school. This is important for a number of reasons. In the first place, the children move from the small area in which the various children's dormitories are located to an entirely different location, one which is relatively remote from the kibbutz living area. Their kevutza, which has remained together for seven or eight years, is now split up, its members uniting with children from other kibbutzim and from the cities, to form two or three new groups. Moreover, for the first time in their socialization-education, males become significant figures in their lives, and females become relatively unimportant. In the grade school not only are all the teachers and nurses women, but the nurses still retain their importance as mother-surrogates, with whom the children retain an intimate and confidential relationship. In the high school, however, the nurses are little more than chambermaids and, furthermore, most of the teachers are men. Instead of the nurse, the significant person in the child's life is his "educator" (*mechannech*). The "educator" is the homeroom teacher of a kevutza, who teaches one of the main subjects, and who generally remains with the kevutza until its graduation from high school. He is not only responsible for the intellectual growth of the members of his kevutza, but for their social and emotional welfare as well. He discusses their problems, calls them to task for some misbehavior, and in general serves *in loco parentis*.

A fourth important change, initiated by their entry into the high school, occurs in the work activity of the children. In addition to working in the high school campus in such jobs as landscape gardening, vegetable gardening, and kitchen detail, they also work daily in almost every branch of the kibbutz economy. The students ride into the fields in the afternoon with the adult members of the branch to which they are assigned, and work under their supervision. Since their work assignments change at regular intervals, each student has an opportunity to work in almost every branch of the kibbutz economy before he graduates from high school. As a result of this broad experience the student usually knows in which branch of the economy he wishes to work when he becomes a member of the kibbutz. Time spent in work ranges from one and one-half hours, in the case of the seventh graders, to three hours, in the case of the twelfth graders. As is the case with respect to almost all their other activities in the high school, the students are in complete charge of the work assignments. A work-assignment committee, modeled after its kibbutz counterpart, posts the daily work assignments of all students in the high school dining room.

A fifth important change initiated by the high school is the entry of the students into the Youth Movement of The Federation, the same movement which their parents had organized in Europe. Previously, to be sure, the children are made aware of the fact that they are not the children of "mere farmers." In classroom discussions, in dramatic presentations, in school celebrations, and in the observance of Israeli and Workers' Festivals, the socialist and Zionist ideology of the kibbutz is impressed upon them. Now, however, they are not only taught the ideology, but they become official members of The Movement which is dedicated to the realization of the kibbutz ideology.

Finally, this is the period in which the children find that most of their interests and needs can be satisfied in the diverse life of the high school, and they visit their parental rooms less and less frequently.

The social structure of the high school is a miniature of the kibbutz itself. Student government, including a council and a number of committees, is responsible for almost all the non-academic life of the students, including disciplinary problems. The students have considerable power, including the power of expulsion—a prerogative which was exercised in the case of one girl a few years ago.

Extracurricular activities are vast and varied, including band, orchestra, glee club, sports, study groups, The Movement, and assemblies. As has already been noted, sexual affairs are frowned upon in the high school, as are other bisexual activities that tend to isolate a couple from group activities. Nevertheless, boys and girls do pair off, and love-making occurs; but such activities take place in the kibbutz itself, or on camping and hiking trips. "Dating," in the sense of taking a girl to a dance, a movie, a party, etc., does not exist. Social dancing, indeed, is not found in any form, although folk-dancing is a favorite activity. Related to this non-dating pattern is the absence of make-up on the part of the girls, and of fancy clothing on the part of both girls and boys. The typical dress for either sex for any occasion —classroom, work, celebration, or any other—consists of shorts and blouse. In colder weather girls wear skirts, and boys wear khaki trousers.

The high school curriculum is very intensive, and in this respect, it is more nearly like that of the European *gymnasium* than of the American public high school. Although the students will eventually become farmers and workers, there are relatively few "technical" subjects, and no "home economics." The emphasis is rather on a broad liberal education, with special emphasis on the humanities—particularly history, literature, and the arts—including music and painting.

Upon graduation from high school the students do not automatically take up their lives in the kibbutz. Since Kiryat Yedidim is a voluntaristic community, membership is elective. Hence, it is felt that even the children of chaverim should have the experience of living in a non-kibbutz society before announcing their candidacy for admission. Before the State was declared, the children worked for a year in the city; but since the declaration of the State, all children upon graduation from high school must serve for two years in the army, after which they announce their candidacy. In its entire history not one child has elected to live outside the kibbutz, and in no case did the kibbutz refuse membership to one of its own children. Not only have all the children elected to become chaverim, but in most of the instances in which adults have resigned from Kiryat Yedidim, their adolescent children chose to remain in the high school, and later became members.

After election to membership these young people have the same rights and responsibilities as their elders.

Ceremonial Life

Celebrations in Kiryat Yedidim may be divided into informal social gatherings or parties (*mesibbot;* singular, *mesibba*), and formal group celebrations (*chagim;* singular, *chag*). The function of the former class is to honor a specific person or a special group. During the writer's stay in the kibbutz, for example, there were parties in honor of a chaver who was about to depart for a two-year absence in the United States, for a youth group which was leaving Kiryat Yedidim to establish its own kibbutz, for the army group that had been working in Kiryat Yedidim and was about to complete its service, for the recent high school graduates who were being admitted into the kibbutz as members, and for our own departure for the United States.

Formal group celebrations, on the other hand, involve the ceremonial expression of group values and of traditions, including the celebration of the anniversary of the founding of Kiryat Yedidim, and of holidays of national, political, and agricultural significance. All these, of course, are in addition to the observance of the Sabbath.

Kiryat Yedidim is anti-religious in the conventional meaning of "religion." Its Zionist motivations are national and social, not religious, and it has consistently attempted to remove any "religious" aspects of Judaism from its culture. Hence, though it celebrates many of the traditional festivals and holidays of Judaism, including the Sabbath, it has reinterpreted their meaning in accordance with its secular outlook.

The Sabbath (*shabbat*) is observed as the weekly day of rest, rather than as a Holy Day. Except for work which must be performed, such as the milking of the cows or the care of the animals, work ceases on Friday evening, and does not commence again until Sunday morning. Although the Sabbath has been deprived of its religious meaning, it still retains its traditional festive touch. The Friday evening meal is usually more elaborate than the weekly evening meal. The tables in the dining room are covered, unlike the rest of the week, when meals are eaten off bare tables. The dining room is filled to capacity because of the addition of city friends, of chaverim who work in the city and return on the Sabbath, and of kibbutz youths who are serving in the army and have received weekend passes. There is a perceptible change in the spirit of the group at the Friday evening meal.

Friday evening is frequently the occasion for a lecture or a concert. Since there is no need to rise early the next day, this is also the favorite evening for social visiting, at which time the tea pot is brought out, and a rare piece of cake or cookie—and perhaps even some candy—is served.

Saturday is spent leisurely—reading, resting, and, if one has small children, spending the day with them, showing them the animals, walking through the orchards, playing. As the traditional Sabbath invariably ended with a religious service (*Havdalah*), so the kibbutz Sabbath ends with the weekly town meeting, which serves to bring the chaverim back to the more tangible realities of living.

But Saturday is not always shabbat. Although most chaverim have a rest day on Saturday, many, for a variety of reasons, have their shabbat on some other day of the week. Since certain kinds of work must be performed on Saturday —cows milked, a harvest completed, children cared for, meals cooked—those who perform these tasks have their shabbat on a weekday. In most cases, however, a rotation system operates so that persons working in such branches may sometimes have their shabbat on Saturday. There are other reasons, however, for not having shabbat on Saturday. If, for example, a person wishes to go to the city, it is almost impossible for him to travel on Saturday, since Israel permits no public transportation on that day. His solution is to work on Saturday, and to take his shabbat during the week.

In addition to the Sabbath, Kiryat Yedidim celebrates the following holidays of the Jewish religious calendar: *Rosh Hashana*, the New Year; *Chanuka*, the Feast of the Maccabees; *Purim*, the Feast of Esther; *Pesach*, or Passover; *Shavuot*, or Pentecost. All these holidays have been reinterpreted, however, in national, social, and agricultural terms.

Rosh Hashana, the New Year, occurs in September; in traditional Judaism[9] it is one of the High Holidays. Religious services in the synagogue involve the reading of prayers which stress contrition and forgiveness of past transgressions. It is believed that, on this day, God decides a person's fate for the coming year. In keeping with its secularist philosophy, Kiryat Yedidim celebrates Rosh Hashana as its New Year, but without the religious significance. On the eve of the New Year, the dining room is decorated with paintings, greenery, and designs; banners hung on the walls greet the diner with a "Happy New Year!" The tables, covered with white cloths, are heavy with food (one of the few times of the year when food is abundant) and with beer, a rare beverage. In the evening there is a celebration (*mesiba*). The one witnessed by the author included a brief piano recital by the kibbutz composer; a long and detailed report on the economic condition of the kibbutz by its economic manager; a program of songs by one of the youth groups; and some humorous sketches, performed by one of the talented chaverim. This program was an observable failure—most of the audience, particularly the young people, left in the middle of the program, and those who remained did so from courtesy, rather than from enjoyment. The reaction to this celebration served to confirm for the author what many chaverim had told him verbally: that the kibbutz is still struggling with the problem of the "religious" holidays. Should they be celebrated at all, or should they be ignored? And if they are to be celebrated, what form should this observance take? This is an area in which Kiryat Yedidim, after more than thirty years, is still unsure of itself.

[9] For a description and history of this, and the other holidays of traditional Judaism, see Schauss, *The Jewish Festivals*.

The day of Rosh Hashana is a day of rest, and though the children in the grade school receive a holiday, those in the high school have classes as usual. The unimportance of Rosh Hashana in Kiryat Yedidim is symbolized by the fact that during our study the students in the high school did not know of its pending arrival, nor did they realize that it had arrived until one of their teachers happened to mention it.

The holiest day in the Jewish religious calendar—The Day of Atonement—is not celebrated at all in the kibbutz. Since its traditional meaning is entirely religious, there is no way, the chaverim feel, in which it can be reinterpreted. Hence, it is officially ignored by them, and treated as just another day. The children are not given a holiday from classes, as are children in the rest of the country; for—as the school principal explained to one mother—if the children are granted a holiday, one must explain it to them. For children who are taught atheism, how is one to tell them that the holiday is a day on which people repent of their sins toward God, as well as toward their fellowman? Although officially ignored, this holiday has not been forgotten by the chaverim. The writer repeatedly heard them facetiously asking each other how they were taking the "fast"— the Day of Atonement is traditionally a fast day—an indication that some of them may perhaps retain some guilt feelings about eating on that day.[10]

Two weeks after the New Year occurs the Festival of *Sukkot*. In ancient Palestine this was the fall harvest festival, but later the custom of living in "booths" during this festival was taken to be symbolic of the booths in which the

[10] It should be noted that the Day of Atonement, like the other religious holidays, is observed by the aged parents of the chaverim. Religious services are held by them in their own kosher dining room, and they are attended, as well, by many children of the youth groups who come from religious homes.

Israelites lived as they wandered for forty years in the wilderness. Since the kibbutz harvest season does not coincide with the date of the festival, Sukkot has no agricultural meaning for Kiryat Yedidim, nor does it attach any value to the latter interpretation of the festival. Hence, there is no festive meal and work is not stopped. The school children, however, are given a one-day vacation from classes and small "booths" are erected for them in the school areas.

Chanuka, the Feast of Lights, commemorates the victory of the Maccabees over the "Greeks." Falling in December, this holiday has always been a children's festival, and so it is celebrated in the kibbutz, with a number of children's parties in the various children's dormitories.[11]

The festival of Purim, which is celebrated in March, is traditionally a joyous occasion, celebrating the victory of the Jews of Persia over the wicked Haman, thanks to the efforts of Mordecai and Queen Esther. Later it began to symbolize the eventual destruction of antisemitism. Traditionally, presents were exchanged among the children, folk-plays were presented in the streets, and the Book of Esther was read in the synagogue. Like Chanuka, it emphasized the participation of the children. It is in this spirit that Purim is celebrated in the kibbutz. The nursery children have a costume party. The children in the grade school present a program of skits, dances, and songs for the adults; the high school has a similar program which is attended by many adults; and the latter have their own program of skits, each on successive nights. All are marked by the wearing of costumes, good humor, and general merriment.

The traditional Jewish holiday of most importance for

[11] Since the author was not present at a Chanuka celebration, no detailed account can be given.

Kiryat Yedidim is Pesach, or Passover. Occurring in April, Passover was originally a festival of spring. Later it came to commemorate the Exodus of the Israelites from Egypt. It is not too difficult to reinterpret the Exodus by changing its meaning from that of supernatural redemption to that of freedom in general, and to its attainment by natural means. It is only natural that a holiday which can thus synthesize two important values of kibbutz culture—nature and freedom—should receive considerable attention in Kiryat Yedidim. Preparations for the holiday are begun months in advance, and the precious rations of sugar, meat, and other delicacies are accumulated for that occasion. As Passover eve approaches, the dining room is decorated with flowers and greens, and Biblical verses, describing the spring, are hung on the walls.

The great event of the Passover celebration is the *Seder*, which traditionally consists of a festive meal and a long religious service, the latter being sung from a prescribed ritual known as the *Haggada*. The Federation has composed its own Haggada which retains many selections from the traditional, insofar as they are compatible with its secularist philosophy. It has added passages from Biblical and traditional Jewish literature, modern Hebrew poetry, and readings written by members of the kibbutzim. All the readings stress the twin themes of spring and freedom. The Seder is held in the large and newly constructed dining room of the high school. It is at this time that kibbutz hospitality is expressed at its greatest; for in spite of crowded conditions and the acute food shortage, friends and relatives—frequently numbering more than one hundred—are invited to partake of the festive meal and to spend the night, precisely as a European Jewish family would invite a few friends to their home for the celebration. Aside from the Seder, this is a memorable evening because of the excellence and abundance of the food. As noted above, the kibbutz, like the rest of the country, suffers from severe rationing. By contrast, the Seder meal is a Roman banquet. Because of its abundance, not all the food can be eaten—it is too much for persons whose stomachs have shrunk under a severe system of rationing. But this banquet is as important psychologically as it is gastronomically to the chaverim: at least once a year it is important to be able to have so much food that some of it must be wasted. The Seder attended by the author included an introductory speech by one of the chaverim, stressing the importance of freedom in our own time; musical selections by the choir; modern dances by some of the children; and the reading of the Haggada, section by section, by members and children of the kibbutz. Their own Seder is excellent, some of the chaverim commented to the author, but still they missed the beauty of the traditional Seder of their childhood with its elaborate ceremony and ritual, and would give much to witness one again.

The last traditional festival of the year, succeeding Passover by seven weeks, is Shavuot, Pentecost. Traditionally, Shavuot, like Passover and Tabernacles, is both an agricultural and an historical festival. Agriculturally, it is the festival of the "first fruits," *chag habikkurim;* historically, it supposedly commemorates the Revelation on Sinai. Kiryat Yedidim, of course, celebrates it only in its former meaning. As is true of all holidays, the celebration begins on the eve of the festival, with a festive meal, in a dining room decorated with first fruits. The next day, work ends at noon, and the main celebration consists of the offering of the first fruits to the Jewish National Fund (in ancient Palestine, they were offered to the Temple). This offering takes the form of a parade in which the offerings are displayed on "floats" decorated by the members of each branch. The representatives of each agricultural branch march from the main gate of the kibbutz to a specially constructed platform on the wide lawn in front of the dining room, followed by a parade of the young children and toddlers. As the name of each branch is called, its representative brings its offering to the platform to be judged, and prizes are awarded for the three best offerings—a roasted lamb and two cakes in the competition observed by the author. After the judging, there follows a succession of dances on the lawn. Each age group dances in order—the nursery children, grade school children, high school students, and younger chaverim. Following these, there is one huge dance in which all the parents dance with their children as partners, amidst general merriment. The latter dance is the climax of the celebration and is eagerly performed by the participants. The celebration is followed by the usual folk-dancing and light refreshments.

Some chaverim, as has been noted, are not content with the way in which Kiryat Yedidim observes its Jewish festivals, and feel that more thought should be given to this area of their social life. During the writer's stay in the kibbutz, a special meeting was held to discuss this problem, at which time the chairman of the cultural committee criticized the chaverim for neglecting these holidays, and complained that the old had been abolished, but that nothing new had been added to take its place. Another chaver, one of the kibbutz intellectuals, complained about the indifference to the Sabbath in Kiryat Yedidim. He recalled the "marvelous spirit" that had permeated his parental home on the Sabbath eve, and wondered why the same spirit could not be recaptured in the kibbutz. Why was it necessary, he asked, for so many chaverim to work on the Sabbath? The religious kibbutzim,[12] he continued, are no wealthier than Kiryat Yedidim, and yet they can afford to free their members for the Sabbath. He could, moreover, see no objection to the lighting of candles on Friday evening. Some people say that the lighting of candles is *petit bourgeois;* but, he protested, many *petit bourgeois* characteristics have entered the kibbutz, so why single out the lighting of the candles for special condemnation?

In addition to these "major" holidays and festivals of the traditional Jewish calendar, Kiryat Yedidim has emphasized a traditional secular date, reinterpreted a "minor" religious holiday, and revived—in new guise—an ancient Palestinian ritual. *Tu Bishvat* (literally, the fifteenth day of the Hebrew month of Shvat) was traditionally recognized as Arbor Day, the "new year of the trees." Occurring in January, this day was marked, if at all, by the eating of fruit from Palestine. But in modern Palestine Tu Bishvat has become an important day, symbolic of the reforestation needs of the country. In the kibbutz this is the day for the planting of new trees. Each year a different area of the kibbutz is selected for planting, and the entire population—carrying red flags and flags of The Movement—marches to the area. The procession is headed by the children, wearing garlands in their hair and carrying young saplings; and it marches to the music of the high school band. Arriving at the area the children first perform dances, symbolizing the growth

---

[12] There are a small number of religious kibbutzim in Israel with their own federation. They adhere to all the rituals of Orthodox Judaism and pattern their lives after Talmudic law.

of the trees and the opening of flowers, and then the representatives of all the groups in the kibbutz—the various adult "layers" and children's groups—plant a sapling in a symbolic ceremony. Finally, everyone has an opportunity to plant, usually in couples; one person placing the sapling in the hole which his partner has dug.

In ancient Palestine the first sheaf of the first grain (barley) was offered to the priest at the Temple, on the day after Passover. This was the *omer*. With the destruction of the Temple this ceremony was no longer observed, although it was remembered ritually in the synagogue service. Today the festival of the Omer is a major event in the kibbutz calendar, but its only relationship to the ancient ritual is its connection with agriculture. Revealing many of the characteristics of an American county fair, the chaverim—enjoying a half-day vacation from work—assemble in the fields to witness and to participate in a number of events. First each agricultural branch has competitions for its own workers: grapefruit wrapping, plowing a straight furrow with an Arab plow, starting a tractor blindfolded, catching a chicken, etc. This is followed by a performance of interpretive dancing presented by the sabras. Finally representatives from the various groups within the kibbutz cut the omer, the first sheaves.

Lag B'omer was, traditionally, the one joyous day in the period of semi-mourning that characterized the seven week interval between Passover and Pentecost. On this day (whose joyous character derives from various legendary events which were presumed to have occurred on this date) marriages, which were otherwise prohibited during this interval, were performed, and the children would go for a hike into the fields. In the kibbutz the date is marked only by the Youth Movement, and not by the adults. As in the shtetl the major event of the day is an all-day hike which is preceded on the previous night by a meeting of the entire "nest"—all of the chapters of The Movement in Kiryat Yedidim. At this meeting the political and ideological competence of the various chapters is tested by the leaders of The Movement. The all-day hike is similar to a scout jamboree, during which various scouting skills are displayed; and at night new members are officially inducted into The Movement, and others receive awards, in a solemn ceremony.

In addition to these traditional Jewish holidays, Kiryat Yedidim celebrates four modern festivals, two in May and two in November. The two in May are May Day and Israel's Independence Day. Since the State was only three years old at the time of the writer's study, no pattern had yet emerged for the celebration of its independence, except for the hanging of the picture of Theodore Herzl—the founder of modern Zionism—in the dining room, the listening to the official celebration in the city on the radio, and the placing of flowers on the graves in the *kibbutz* cemetery.[13] May Day, however, is a holiday of long standing. The dining room is decorated with the pictures of Lenin and Stalin (this was prior to the death of Stalin, of course), as the leaders of the international workers' movement. The kibbutz works only a half-day, and in the afternoon and

[13] Kiryat Yedidim is not sufficiently old to have established any clear pattern for burial and death ceremonies. No one died in the course of our study, so that we had no opportunity to observe a funeral at first hand; and unfortunately we failed to make detailed inquiries about this aspect of kibbutz culture. We do know that the dead are buried in a cemetery on the edge of the village, and that a simple, secular-type ceremony is held. The author regrets to say, however, that he does not know the specific content of this ceremony.

evening it joins the other kibbutzim in the area for a district celebration, which generally includes a series of speeches on the significance of the international workers' and socialist movements, and a concert.

In November, Kiryat Yedidim celebrates both its own anniversary and that of the Russian Revolution. The program for the former celebration witnessed by the author included some readings—serious and humorous—by a chaver, and a series of speeches by some of the vattikim, emphasizing the importance of this event. The program was followed by refreshments.

The latter celebration is more elaborate. No food is served, but the dining room is decorated with the Red and the Zionist flags, pictures of Lenin and Stalin, and an exhibit of Soviet propaganda pictures. There are usually addresses on the significance of the Revolution and on Soviet culture.

The celebration of these holidays, perfunctory though it is in some instances, serves at least five important functions in Kiryat Yedidim. In the first place, all of them provide an important and welcome relief from the daily routine of work. The chaverim work a long week—eight or nine hours a day, six days a week—and dedicated though they are, this work schedule in the hot Israeli sun takes its toll. The holidays, with their concomitant vacation from work, enable them to receive a hard-earned rest. But the holidays not only provide relief from the work routine, they also provide relief from the daily routine of living as well. Life in a small rural village possesses an inherent potentiality for boredom, unless checked by counter forces. The holidays provide this check in a combination of ways. They are the occasion for more, better, and special foods, for the festive decoration of the dining room, for the wearing of fresh and, sometimes, new clothing, for the witnessing of artistic performances, and for the meeting of guests who spend the holiday in the kibbutz. The special spirit that seems to pervade the kibbutz on the Sabbath and on holidays is perceptible to even the casual observer.

The holidays serve to promote an equally apparent social solidarity. The workaday life in the kibbutz precipitates many tensions and, at times, ill-will among chaverim. Much of this tension is not only dissipated but is also replaced with genuine cameraderie on holidays. This effect seems to be the result of physical rest, of joint participation in skits, choir, and ritual drama, and of joint rededication to common ideals. This latter fact—the rededication to common ideals—serves yet another function. It provides renewed faith in the future and in the ultimate realization of kibbutz goals. There are times when one can sense a profound lethargy in the chaverim, a lethargy induced by discouragement over their economic problems, their inability to achieve their social ideals, their political impotence in national affairs. But this lethargy seems to be displaced by genuine enthusiasm after a Passover Seder, an inspiring political address by one of their political leaders at a May Day Celebration, or an oration of emotional appeal by the leader of The Federation at their anniversary celebration.

In addition to these functions, served by all the celebrations, the Jewish festivals serve an additional unique function. The chaverim, in one sense, are in an anomalous situation, psychologically speaking. They are Zionists whose Zionism was a solution to, among other things, their repudiation of their fathers and the Jewish way of life of their fathers. Hence, though they call themselves Jews, the quality of their Jewishness involves some basic negative overtones.

The celebration of Jewish holidays, despite the elimination of the religious elements, provides them with positive Jewish identifications, both with the Jewish people as well as with its historic past. And apparently they feel a deep need for such identifications—else why bother to celebrate holidays which require such radical revision and reinterpretation?

More than Farmers

Although the kibbutz is proud to be a workers' community and emphasizes especially the moral value of agricultural work, the chaverim are not farmers in the psychological and cultural sense of that term, and they deliberately attempt to avoid such a status. It is true that they live in the country; they till the soil for a livelihood; and they insist upon doing their own work, including the dirty and the difficult. But their work in the *meshek*, or in the economic aspects of the kibbutz, is only one part of their lives; there are other important values in life, and these must be enjoyed as well. Hence, though labor is an ultimate value, work is not allowed to monopolize either one's time or one's interests. Farm work is the ideal calling, but the "farmer" is not the ideal personality. It will be remembered that many of the chaverim, and particularly the vattikim, were intellectuals for whom intellectual values were highly important. And though they had forsaken the intellectual life for the life of a worker, they had not given up their intellectual interests. The intellectual life, detached from physical labor and from the land, the kibbutz has always claimed, is artificial and parasitic; but physical labor, detached from intellectual and artistic values, is boorish and stultifying. What was needed was a synthesis of the two, and thus arose the notion of the "synthetic personality," as it is termed by The Movement, the person who combines in a harmonious whole an attachment to the soil; a joy in work; and an appreciation for, if not creativity in, art, science, and literature. It is not a "landed gentry," but a "landed intelligentsia," that represents the kibbutz's self-image.

Thus it is that, although the formal education of the average chaver rarely included college training and many of them did not complete high school, the intellectual level of Kiryat Yedidim is probably higher than that of the average urban community, and is incomparably higher than that of the average rural community. The casual conversation overheard in the fields includes literature, politics, science, international problems, and other intellectual topics. "Small talk" is rare. The most remarkable intellectual attainment of the chaverim is their linguistic competence. With the exception of the sabras (many of whom know at least some English in addition to their Hebrew), it is the rare person who does not speak and read three languages, and many know as many as six and seven. It is true, of course, that this linguistic facility is to some extent a result of immigration from their countries of birth. Yiddish and Polish, for example, are the native tongues for most of them, and Hebrew was added upon arrival in Palestine. In addition, many of the chaverim have taught themselves other languages—German, English, Russian, for example—in order to be able to read technical and literary works in their original. It might be noted that the decision to use only Hebrew as the language of daily use required for the chaverim, as well as for other early immigrants, a great intellectual drive and dedication. Hebrew is a difficult language for the Westerner, and it would have been considerably easier to have conversed in their native tongue, particularly after a hard day's work in the fields.

In addition to the relatively high intellectual level of the average chaver, there are several chaverim of exceptional intellectual interests and attainment. One vattika, a worker in the vegetable garden, has pioneered in experimental horticulture, and has developed a new variety of melon that is famous throughout the country. But her attainments do not cease with her scientific interests. She has written poetry, has taught herself many languages, and is acquainted with the masterpieces of world literature in their original. In a typical afternoon's work in the garden, she would discuss, with knowledge and insight, such writers as Freud, Schiller, Goethe, Steinbeck, Twain, and Arthur Miller.

In addition, Kiryat Yedidim includes among its members a number of creative artists, among whom are a composer, a painter, and a dramatist. These artists, however, are workers like everyone else who manage to find some leisure from their regular work for their art.

Although the intellectualism of many of the chaverim is readily apparent, the auto-didactic nature of their learning is equally apparent. One is struck, in discussion with them, with the absence of the qualification, the reservation, the tentative attitude. This characteristic may stem, too, from yet another aspect of their intellectualism—its consumptive rather than productive nature. In all areas of "Culture," the chaverim are primarily consumers rather than producers. In like manner, they are training their children to appreciate, but not to create art, science, and scholarship. Indeed, the intellectual or artistic creator, to the extent that he permits his intellectual productivity to interfere with his economic productivity, is not highly regarded. Since they are not engaged in productive scholarship and, indeed, are not trained in the tools of scholarship, the kibbutz intellectuals lack that primary destroyer of the dogmatic attitude—research.

Despite its emphasis on cultural and artistic experience, the attitude of Kiryat Yedidim towards the intellectual, as has been hinted above, is not one of unqualified respect. Although the intellectual is admired *qua* intellectual, he does not enjoy great respect *qua chaver* unless he combines efficiency in physical labor with his intellectuality. The ideal personality type, the "synthetic personality," is both intellectual and worker, one who excells in both activities. Very few people, however, have either the interest or the talent to become "synthetic personalities," and Kiryat Yedidim recognizes this fact by dividing its membership, roughly, into *tarbutnikim*, those who are interested primarily in the intellectual and political aspects of the kibbutz, and the *mishkistim*, those who are most concerned with its economic aspects. Despite the ideal of the "synthetic personality," it is rare, as one of the chaverim (who happened to be a tarbutnik) complained at a public meeting, that a tarbutnik is ever assigned to an economic committee, or that a mishkist is assigned to a cultural committee.

Since it is impossible for most chaverim to attain the ideal of the "synthetic personality," some will be good workers with little intellectual ability and others will be intellectuals with little ability in work. It is to be expected, given the moral value of work in kibbutz culture, that the former, although non-intellectual, are respected, while the latter are often viewed with either suspicion or derision. One of the chaverim, for example, is a colorful cosmopolite; he is at home in a number of languages, and he speaks with knowledge and insight about music, painting, literature— and even Moslem culture. In the United States he would have a number of avenues for success and prestige. But when the author praised him to other chaverim for his erudition and wit, the immediate retort was always, "oh, yes, he knows something, but he's a *batlan*." If he had worked hard *and* was cultured and witty, as well, he would have commanded great respect. But since he is eager to return to his painting or sculpture, his reading or his garden, he doesn't work hard. Hence, he has no regular work assignment, and oscillates between sanitation, irrigation, and the vegetable garden.

This general attitude towards the intellectual was well expressed when a question arose concerning the advisability of sending a talented high school student to study in a private school in the city. There was considerable opposition to this plan, headed by a highly respected vattik. In a town meeting, he argued that the kibbutz was interested in educating farmers, not intellectuals; intellectuals could come from the outside. The town meeting decided to send the student to study, but this attitude expressed by the vattik is nevertheless becoming more prevalent. Should it prevail, it will succeed in modifying the kibbutz self-image from that of a society of "synthetic personalities" to one of farmers. If that occurs, Kiryat Yedidim will be a farm, not a kibbutz.

In short, the attitude towards knowledge and art is highly practical, and the artist and intellectual receive little encouragement from the kibbutz. This, in one sense, is highly paradoxical. With respect to art, for example, Kiryat Yedidim, like other kibbutzim, shows great appreciation for artistic performances. Kibbutz concerts and art exhibits are filled to capacity, and foreign artists are unanimous in their reports that there is no more enthusiastic audience than the kibbutz. But Kiryat Yedidim, like other kibbutzim, is willing (if necessary) to gets its art from others, rather than to produce it itself. Hence, although it calls upon its artists when it requires art work—decoration for the dining room, designs of sets and costumes for plays, direction of and acting in local plays, direction of choir, instrumental recital, composition of music—it does not grant the artist leisure time for his art, nor does it grant him prestige purely on the basis of his art. To achieve respect he must show skill and diligence in physical labor.[14]

Some of the chaverim are sensitive to what they believe are the shortcomings of this attitude, and feel that it must be changed. In a speech, one chaver pleaded with the chaverim to grant its artists the leisure to pursue their work. "The culture of the kibbutz will not be created in Tel Aviv," he said, "It will be created only in the kibbutz." Therefore, he concluded, if Kiryat Yedidim does not grant leisure time to its writers and artists, it will have no culture at all. As a matter of fact, two artists have resigned from the kibbutz because of this attitude.

It should be noted, however, that although Kiryat Yedidim does not free its artists from the daily work routine so as to enable them to work at their art, it does attempt to provide them with periodic opportunities for study and for growth. After its dramatist, for example, had demonstrated that he was a conscientious and skilled field hand, and his creative ability was proved by having one of his plays produced by an important Israeli repertory company, he was given a six-month leave of absence to study drama and the

[14] This attitude is responsible for an interesting anomaly in the educational system of Kiryat Yedidim. Music, for example, is an important part of the school curriculum, and the kibbutz is proud of its high school orchestra and band. Nevertheless, when one of the students graduated and wished to continue his musical training, the kibbutz refused to appropriate funds for an instrument, and was content to let its previous investment in his training go to waste.

theater in Europe—all expenses paid by the kibbutz. A similar leave was granted its composer, although the kibbutz did not have to assume his traveling expenses. Kiryat Yedidim arranged for him to be sent as a representative to the Zionist Youth Movement in the United States and, although much of his time is devoted to official responsibilities, he has the opportunity in the course of his two-year stay of studying at an American conservatory, as well as of listening to good music.

Teachers, by the very nature of their work in the kibbutz, must devote their full time to intellectual work. And the attitude described above extends to them as well. For, although it is frequently and officially denied, there seems little question but that teachers are less highly respected than are manual workers. This is one of the reasons, in addition to the intrinsic difficulties of the job, that most chaverim are reluctant to become teachers, and often have to be drafted. It also accounts for the refusal of the sabras to become teachers. This attitude is particularly surprising in a community which emphasizes the importance of education, and which views its educational system as the crux of its new culture. It is not improbable that this attitude is retained by the chaverim as part of their shtetl heritage. For despite its emphasis on learning, the shtetl had little respect for the teacher. The shtetl teacher, we are told, is "looked down upon by the whole community . . . It is generally assumed that a man who teaches little children has fallen into his profession because he failed elsewhere."[15]

The prevailing attitude toward the teacher has not escaped the attention of the children; and the chaverim are fond of repeating the following anecdotes whose authenticity the

[15] Zborowski and Herzog, p. 89.

author cannot vouch for. Even if apocryphal, however, they clearly symbolize the status of the teacher. A group of five year olds, including a boy whose bald-headed father was a teacher, were bragging about their fathers. One boy claimed that his father was the best tractorist in the kibbutz; another said that his father was the best milker; the third claimed that his father was the finest gardener; the teacher's son announced that his father was the baldest man in the kibbutz. In another anecdote the children were recounting their fathers' occupations. One said his father was a tractorist; another that his father was a shepherd; a third said his father was an electrician; and the teacher's son said his father was a floor-sweeper (which, in fact, was his secondary occupation).

The teachers are sensitive about their position of inferiority, and try to "prove," when they have the opportunity, that they can work as hard as any manual worker. During school vacations, teachers are often assigned for a short time to some work detail, and a teacher in the grade school who was assigned to work in the kitchen told the author repeatedly that she intended to stand in front of the kitchen window in order to show the people that she could wash pots all days long as well as anyone else.

Although Kiryat Yedidim does not grant high prestige to its pure intellectuals, intellectual qualities, in conjunction with other characteristics, are important for the attainment of prestige as well as leadership. Hard and devoted manual labor, for all the importance of work in kibbutz culture, is not a sufficient condition for prestige and leadership. Such a person is respected, and if he is a skilled as well as a devoted worker he may become the foreman of his branch or even an important economic official. Should his behavior, moreover, correspond to the norms of kibbutz culture, he is then viewed as an admirable chaver and as an asset to Kiryat Yedidim. Nevertheless his opinions on non-economic matters are not sought at town meetings, nor are his ideas received with more than average attention in public debate. And this is the crux of the matter: the measure of one's prestige and the means to leadership in the kibbutz are the degree to which one's counsels are taken seriously in town meetings. But only a person with intellectual qualities possesses the knowledge on which to base his opinions and the linguistic skill which enables him to communicate his ideas in an articulate fashion. It is the combination of skilled and devoted work, conformity to kibbutz values, *and* intellectual attainments (in short, the "synthetic personality") that leads to prestige and leadership.

Despite the low prestige of the pure intellectuals, the interest displayed by many chaverim in cultural matters is intense. And the kibbutz attempts to satisfy these interests through the work of its cultural committee which offers a diversified cultural program throughout the year. Formal classes are held, conducted by members of the kibbutz, in English, Russian, Bible, Hebrew literature, biology, and other subjects for which there is a demand. The cultural committee, moreover, is in charge of a good library that includes books—cultural and scientific—in many languages, and a reading room which has the daily papers, as well as important literary and political journals.

The cultural committee also sponsors lectures on a wide variety of topics by lecturers from outside the kibbutz, although occasionally a kibbutz member who is noted for his competence in a particular field will lecture. Some of the lectures held during the author's stay were on such diverse topics as existentialism, genetics, Chagall, the economic problem of Israel, the new government in Poland, culture in the United States, and the contemporary Russian novel. The cultural committee also arranges for musical programs, usually chamber music or violin concerts. These musical programs are the most popular form of entertainment in Kiryat Yedidim, and they invariably attract a capacity audience. The chaverim have well-developed musical tastes, and they have little compunction about displaying their disapproval of a poor performance by walking out in the middle of the concert.

Kiryat Yedidim is generally included in the annual tour of the famous Israeli repertory company, *Habima*. This is a big event, and the entire membership turns out to witness the performance. The year of the author's study, they produced (in Hebrew, of course) *Death of a Salesman*.

The cultural committee also sponsors a weekly movie, an institution to which the chaverim respond with mixed feelings. On the one hand they look forward to "movie night," and it is rare that any other event, no matter how important, is allowed to take its place. On the other hand most of the movies shown in the kibbutz are made in Hollywood, and their plots almost always elicit unfavorable comment. Frequently many chaverim leave in the middle of the movie: "a waste of time" (*chaval al hazman*), is the way they put it. Nevertheless, they return each week.

Aside from the events sponsored by Kiryat Yedidim, there are cultural programs sponsored by the various kibbutz federations or by various cultural groups, which members of Kiryat Yedidim attend as a group. During the course of this study, such programs included a dramatic performance of Howard Fast's *My Glorious Brothers*, produced by the dramatic group of kibbutz Sarid; the annual national dance festival at kibbutz Dahlia; an extensive exhibit of the paintings of Marc Chagall at the art museum of kibbutz Ein Harod; and a ballet performed at the latter. These events constitute a favorite topic for conversation for many days after they are witnessed.

In addition to these group experiences, the average chaver enjoys certain cultural and artistic experiences of his own. Almost every room includes a small library, and many members do as much reading as their meager leisure hours permit. The Israel Broadcasting Company has a number of daily radio concerts, which many chaverim listen to regularly, and a visit to the city is rarely complete without attendance at some dramatic or musical performance. The daily newspaper, read by all, usually includes articles of a general cultural and political nature, and the Friday edition (corresponding to the American Sunday edition) devotes half its columns to discussions and criticism of art, music, literature, and politics, as well as to translations of articles in current American, Russian, and European magazines.

In short, the chaver is more than a farmer. He is a farmer with intellectual interests, which is to say that he is not a farmer at all. In a very important sense, this refusal to be "merely a farmer" is profoundly symbolized in the kibbutz habits of dress and personal appearance. Here, the contrast between the chaverim and other farmers, including those who live in Israeli cooperative settlements, is telling. The ordinary farmer is often unshaven, and he rarely changes from work clothes to "dress" clothes at the end of the day's work. The man of Kiryat Yedidim is seldom unshaven. At the end of his work, his first stop is the shower room, where he shaves and showers, and changes from his work clothes

to his "dress" clothes, which he wears the rest of the afternoon and evening.

But this emphasis on personal appearance is not only symbolic of the self-image of the chaverim; it is also important
for their conception of their daily lives. During the day,
one is a worker, but in the evening, one is a citizen. This is
another part of one's life—the part that includes being with
one's children and participating in the cultural and intellectual, as well as the social, life of the community. This
is when one reads, visits with friends, and attends lectures
or concerts; and this is the time when the chaver neither
looks nor acts the part of the farmer.

This same self-image accounts for their pleasant rooms
and attractive gardens; and it accounts for the high school
curriculum, whose broad cultural program can be equalled
in the United States only in the good private schools. The
absence of technical courses, or of practical courses with a
"home economics" orientation, clearly differentiates the
kibbutz high school from the ordinary rural high school.
Whether this education "takes" is a separate problem; of
importance here is the kibbutz self-image which this curriculum symbolizes.

It should be stressed, however, lest a distorted picture
of the chaverim be derived from the above description, that
not every chaver has intellectual interests. Although most
of the vattikim were European students before they decided
to emigrate, they arrived in Palestine at a very early age,
and few had completed their formal education. The later
settlers, moreover, had not had the same education as the
vattikim, and many of them had received only a grade school
education. Nevertheless, what is important for an understanding of the kibbutz is not the intellectual attainment of

the chaverim, but rather their intellectual interests. The average chaver, regardless of his formal education, lives in a cultural milieu which stresses the importance of intellectual and artistic values; he is motivated, therefore, to read books, attend lectures and concerts, and discuss matters of intellectual and political concern in daily conversation.

Despite this cultural milieu, however, many chaverim possess some of the characteristics of any rural community: provincialism, naïvete, conservatism. The provincialism of the chaverim is expressed in a number of ethnocentric attitudes, one example of which may be described here—their attitude towards clothing. Any departure from the style of dress found in the kibbutz is viewed with critical disdain. The chaver typically wears khaki pants or shorts and shirts. Ties, suits, and hats (other than work hats) are viewed as "bourgeois," and are eschewed, even for dress wear. The typical apparel of the chavera includes a blouse and skirt, or shorts or slacks for work, and perhaps a print dress for evenings. Make-up is avoided as "bourgeois." Clothing, as is well known, is often important for the marking of status distinctions, and it frequently has important symbolic significance. That the chaverim, therefore, should disdain "bourgeois" dress is understandable. But they react with equal criticism to the wearing of work clothes which may be different from the kibbutz style of work clothes. The author's wife, for example, elicited much comment by wearing a plaid shirt, since plaids are unknown in the kibbutz, and are identified only with Americans. A chaver who had recently returned from America was criticized for appearing in American denims or jeans, and one member commented that he "only wanted to show how Americanized he had become." Strong criticism was evoked by the author's wife when she wore shorts. Shorts worn by kibbutz women have elastic in the hems, so they fit snugly about the thighs. While the American shorts worn by the author's wife were much longer than these, they lacked the elastic, and the comment was so great that it was necessary to have elastic sewn into her shorts.

Conservatism is particularly characteristic of the women. For example, the kibbutz was presented with a pressure cooker which, in a communal kitchen, might be regarded as a blessing. It saves valuable space and time, both of which would contribute much to lessening the present complexities of the kitchen. Nevertheless, the kitchen staff refused to use it; they had never used one before and did not intend to begin now. The same attitude accounts for the absence of canned fruits and vegetables in the kibbutz. In the winter months, it has all the fruits and vegetables it needs. But there is a period in the summer when none are to be had. When the author's wife suggested that this shortage could be alleviated by canning fruits and vegetables in season, she was told that the kibbutz had never canned, and that there were no plans to can in the future. As one chavera put it, somewhat bitterly, "no canning will be done simply because it has never been done."

A classic example of the conservatism of the women, however, involves the scrubbing of the floor in the kitchen in which children's food is prepared. The floor is scrubbed every day, and it is always scrubbed in exactly the same way—starting from a certain wall, and proceeding to the opposite wall. One day, one of the women decided to relieve the monotony by starting at the opposite wall, although this was less practical. The other women were shocked by this innovation. The floor had *always* been scrubbed starting at the other wall, and that was the *correct* way. Feelings ran so high that one of the women walked out in protest, refusing to work until the floor was scrubbed in the traditional way.[16]

Kibbutz naïvete is best expressed in some of the notions it has concerning the outside world. Some of this naïvete is a function of its Marxist ideology, but much of it may be attributed to its restricted information concerning the outside world. For example, in discussing antisemitism in the United States, a chavera—by no means the least perceptive —pointed to the quota system characteristic of some universities as an example of antisemitism. The author agreed that this was a problem needing correction, but pointed out that some universities have abolished this system, and that that very year the university in which he taught had removed such restrictions from all its colleges. To this she replied, "Oh, that's because Truman wants to obtain the support of the Jews for the Atlantic Pact."

Despite these manifestations of a rural culture pattern, the previous generalization holds true: this is a community whose worldly sophistication is much higher than that of the average rural community, and whose intellectual interests and attainments are much above those of the average Western community—rural or urban.

---

[16] This conservatism of the women is probably best explained in conjunction with their greater insecurity, which will be discussed in a later chapter. Routine and ritual, as is well known, are one type of defense against insecurity, and any abrupt change in routine represents a symbolic, if not an intrinsic, threat to such a defense. In general (and in the above two examples) such conservatism is found among those women whom the chaverim term, the "primitive" types—those whose education, both formal and informal, is low.

CHAPTER 6

A commune to exist harmoniously, must be composed of individuals who are of one mind upon some question which to them shall appear so important as to take the place of religion, if it is not essentially religious . . .
The Communistic Societies in the United States
Charles Nordhoff

THE KIBBUTZ AS A POLITICAL COMMUNITY

From Utopian Sect to Political Community

IT IS APPARENT from the early history and pre-history of Kiryat Yedidim that there was little in the non-Zionist values or goals of these early settlers to distinguish their settlement from that of the many utopian communes that were established in the United States during the nineteenth century.[1] In common with the members of these utopian communities, these young chalutzim were opposed to private property, to social inequality, to the exploitation of man by man, and to the luxury and "decadence" of urban

[1] Although these utopian experiments are of no small importance for the development of a sound theory of social behavior, the decisive scientific analysis of these societies is yet to be made. In lieu of such a study, the reader is referred to Nordhoff, *The Communistic Societies in the United States;* Gide, *Communist and Cooperative Colonies;* and Holloway, *Heavens on Earth.*

living. Like the Utopians, the chalutzim believed that man could best realize his potentialities (*hagshama atzmit*) in a society in which property was collectively owned; where social equality was guaranteed by preventing the rise of invidious distinctions based on wealth, kinship, or power; where exploitation was precluded by prohibiting the use of hired labor, so that all the work in the community was to be performed by the members themselves (*avodah atzmit*); where the members were to live and work on the land and, as far as possible, produce all that was necessary for the satisfaction of their economic needs. Finally, in common with these utopian communities, the early kibbutz was a sectarian community—a community, that is, based on opposition to the "world" and membership in which demanded a voluntaristic commitment to the all-important ideals of the group.[2]

It should be pointed out, however, that there are basic differences between the early kibbutz and these utopian communities. Many of the latter were comprised principally of individuals of working-class background, whose intellectual interests were narrow and whose cultural horizons were limited; whereas the former were comprised principally of intellectuals who had deliberately chosen to adopt a worker's life, but whose cultural horizons were those of the "emancipated" middle classes. Another major difference between Kiryat Yedidim and the utopian societies is to be found in their differential attitudes to religion. Most of the utopian societies were religious in character, and were moti-

[2] For an analysis of the nature of the "sect," see Troeltsch, *The Social Teachings of the Christian Churches*.

Much of the theoretical framework of this and succeeding chapters dealing with the changing values of the kibbutz is based on Troeltsch's incisive analysis of the "sect type" and the "church type."

vated by the desire to return to primitive Christianity. Kiryat Yedidim, on the contrary, has always been actively opposed to religion, at least to those elements which are included in any conventional definition of that term. The kibbutz was to be a secular society, in which the emotional component of religion would be provided by nature, and the intellectual-explanatory component, by science.

Another difference between Kiryat Yedidim and the utopian societies (with the exception of the Oneida community) is to be found in their attitude towards sex, and to the general problem of the relationship between men and women. Some of the Utopians shared the conventional attitudes concerning the relationship between males and females, and were content to perpetuate this relationship in their new societies. This meant, as a rule, that such matters as sexual behavior, family structure, the sexual division of labor, and socialization of children were the same in the utopian communities as they were in the outside world. On the other hand, some of the utopians (the Shakers, for example) viewed both sex and marriage as evil, and based their lives on celibacy and on a minimum amount of interaction between the sexes. The Oneida community, however, revolutionized the traditional sexual relations. But the substitution of group marriage for monogamous marriage in this community, and the consequent communal rearing of children—a feature which it shared with the kibbutz—was based on the quasi-religious notions of John Humphrey Noyes concerning sex, procreation, and eugenics.[3] This is what distinguishes Oneida from Kiryat Yedidim.

---

[3] A detailed study of the Oneida experiment has never been made, though there have been some general descriptive accounts. See Parker, *A Yankee Saint*, and Noyes, *My Father's House*.

The latter also departed from the conventional practices, but it did so for political, cultural, and psychological reasons (all secular) which have already been examined.

The kibbutz, in brief, began as a utopian sect in which one's personal salvation was to be achieved through collective living in a community based on fellowship. In his following characterization of the "sect-type," Troeltsch may well have been describing the kibbutz in its early, formative years. The sects, he writes,

. . . are comparatively small groups; they aspire after personal inward perfection, and they aim at a direct personal fellowship between the members of each group. From the very beginning, therefore, they are forced to organize themselves in small groups, and to renounce the idea of dominating the world. Their attitude towards the world, the State, and Society may be indifferent, tolerant, or hostile, since they have no desire to control and incorporate these forms of social life; on the contrary they tend to avoid them.[4]

In attempting to find meaning in their own personal and social experience, the young men and women who founded the kibbutz felt it necessary to reject the world. Unlike others who, finding the world evil, are motivated to change it, these young people were interested primarily in withdrawing from it, and in establishing their own small world based on brotherhood and love, and within which they could find their own salvation.

In a gradual process, however, the main aim of Kiryat Yedidim has been changed from this early goal of providing personal salvation to that of expediting social revolution. To pursue our religious analogy it has changed from a "withdrawing" to a "militant" sect.[5] In short, though still

[4] Troeltsch, *Christian Churches*, p. 331
[5] These terms are suggested by Nottingham, p. 63.

opposed to the "world," Kiryat Yedidim now aspires to change the "world," to mold it in its own image, rather than to withdraw from it. Without pressing the analogy too far, its historical Jewish model is no longer the Essene[6] but the Prophet.

Put in secular terms it may be said that Kiryat Yedidim has become a political community, in which the outside society, rather than the individual chaver of the kibbutz, is its main object of change. This change in philosophy is found as early as the Second World Congress of The Federation. One of the resolutions adopted at this Congress stated:

In the center of our education stands the individual; in the center of our goal stands society—the kibbutz society. We believe in the individual, but not for his own sake. The individuality of the new man is only valuable to the degree that it helps to build a new society.

It is not easy to explain this change in orientation. But among the many factors responsible for the change at least three must be considered here. These are intra-kibbutz realities, extra-kibbutz realities, and the influence of the European Youth Movement. After the first early years of kibbutz existence, it was discovered that, once the early thrills derived from camping, from creating a new society, from being emancipated from urban conventions, and from dancing and singing all night, began to wear off, the problems of facing up to the reality situation could not be postponed. And it was discovered that "human nature" did not suddenly change because the social structure had changed.

[6] This obvious parallel to the Essenes was first observed in print, insofar as this writer knows, in Edmund Wilson, "The Scrolls from the Dead Sea."

Most of the difficulties inherent in the society from which the vattikim had escaped were to be found in the society they had established; and those that were absent found adequate substitutes in the unique problems that the new society engendered.[7] This realization came as a great shock to the youthful and idealistic settlers, whose kibbutz image was derived from their highly romantic and emotionally charged experiences in the Youth Movement and in Nevei Gila. Instead of succumbing, however, to either disillusionment or despair, the chaverim, together with the members of other kibbutzim, began to develop the notion that it was not the kibbutz social system, nor even human nature, that was at fault, but rather the larger society of which they were a part. It was not enough to create a perfect community for oneself, if the outside world, which was far from perfect, continued to exercise great influence on it. A small utopia in the midst of the larger wicked world could not succeed and, therefore, the entire world must be made into a utopia.

But there were many external difficulties, as well, that served to turn the concern of the chaverim from their own personal salvation to that of social salvation. There were the problems connected with the British rule in Palestine, and the desire to be rid of that rule; there was the problem of the relationship between Jews and Arabs, and how best to cope with it; and there was, finally, the whole problem of the relationship between the various groups of Jews within Palestine. From the day they had arrived in the country, the chaverim were faced with the fact that not all

[7] For a sensitive literary treatment of this problem by an individual who experienced it, the novel by Maletz, *Young Hearts*, is recommended. Certain aspects of this problem are also treated in the novel by Mosensohn, *Derech Gever*.

Jews were interested in Zionism, and that not all Zionists were sympathetic to the aims of these chalutzim. When they applied for jobs on the plantations owned by Jews, they were often refused employment, for the latter preferred to use cheap Arab labor, which they could exploit with impunity. This led to clashes with the plantation owners, which in turn often ended in physical combat with the police. These economic struggles taught the vattikim, as it taught other groups of workers in Palestine, that their rights could be promoted and protected only through a strong organization. Hence, the Histadrut, the General Federation of Labor, was founded in 1920.[8] It further became apparent

[8] The Histadrut (as of 1950) is a federation of nine countrywide trade unions and labor organizations. These are: (1) Agricultural Worker's Federation (to which the kibbutz members belong); (2) Union of Clerks and Office Employees; (3) Union of Engineers, Architects, and Surveyors; (4) Federation of Building Workers; (5) Union of Railway, Post, and Telegraph Workers; (6) Union of Electrical Workers; (7) Working Youth Federation; (8) Central Working Women's Council; (9) Palestine Labor League. These nine organizations elect the General Convention of the Histadrut, which in turn elects the General Council, whose executive body is the Central Executive Committee. But the Histadrut is not only a trade union organization. It is one of the largest entrepreneurs in the country, owning some of the country's most important business enterprises. A special body, uniting all these enterprises, is known as the *Chevrat Ovdim* and is co-terminous with the Histadrut— membership in the one automatically confers membership in the other.

Kiryat Yedidim, as a member of the Histadrut, is subject to its regulations concerning general working conditions, and to its discipline concerning national, as well as labor, problems which the Histadrut General Council considers within its jurisdiction. At the same time the kibbutz enjoys the many privileges of Histadrut membership. It buys supplies from the Histadrut's consumer's cooperative; it markets its products through its distributing cooperative, and participates in its trucking cooperative. Furthermore, the kibbutz participates in the excellent system of socialized medicine that is sponsored by the Histadrut—a system that provides Kiryat Yedidim with a clinic and a resident physician, dentist, and nurse, as well as with complete medical coverage including hospitalization. The Histadrut also provides Old Age Benefits for its members. See Kurland, *Cooperative Palestine*, and Muenzner, *Labor Enterprise in Palestine*.

that in the general economic and political arena of Palestine, the future of their own kibbutz could best be promoted and defended, if there were to be an increase in the number of kibbutzim with whom they could unite. All these factors, then, led to an increased identification with the labor movement, in general, and to a desire to increase the strength of their own kibbutz movement, in particular.

At the same time, the idea was beginning to develop that the social problem must be solved before it was possible to solve the individual problem. And though psychoanalysis and "utopian socialism," some of them were beginning to think, were all right in attempting to solve the problems of the individual, they could not solve the social problem. For this they turned to "scientific socialism." As one vattik phrased it, "when we had to find a scientific explanation for the political reality in Palestine, we met Marxism."

The immediate source of this Marxist influence came from the second large immigration of their Youth Movement from Europe early in the 1920's, many members of which had been strongly influenced by the European Communist Movement. In the early twenties, when a meeting was held to create a political organization which would include all members of The Movement, the attempt failed because many chaverim, still under the early anti-political emphasis of the early Youth Movement, were opposed to any political activity. A few years later, an attempt was made to unite the existing kibbutzim founded by members of The Movement into a federation based on social, educational, and political ties. This failed because of some opposition to the inclusion of a political program within the organization. In 1927, such an organization—The Federation—was eventually formed. This organization formulated the ideology

that served to transform Kiryat Yedidim from a "withdrawing" into a "militant" sect, from a utopian into a
political community.[9]

The Nature and Functions of Ideology

Life in Kiryat Yedidim is hard. The work day, which is
long and strenuous, is made even more difficult by a frequently oppressive climate. The work week lasts six days,
and there are no long weekends or extended holiday vacations. Hence, when Friday night arrives the people are
physically tired. Moreover, the kibbutz has attempted to
raise its standard of living by increasing its acreage but it
has not been able to increase its manpower proportionately;
and, as has been pointed out, it will not hire labor for ideological reasons. The barely sufficient labor supply represents, therefore, an omnipresent problem which is not infrequently solved by the entire kibbutz's giving up its one
day of rest in order to harvest a crop that would otherwise
rot in the ground.

The physical fatigue, which is an inevitable result of this
kind of work schedule, is exacerbated by some of the inconvenient living conditions. The dining room is crowded and
noisy, as are toilet and shower facilities. The latter, moreover, are often distant from the living quarters, and one

[9] Aside from its permanent importance for the ideological aspects of
kibbutz life, The Federation has many other functions as well. Acting
through its selected committees, it exercises jurisdiction over general
working conditions, educational policy and curriculum, expansion of
physical plant, the regulation of minimum standards in clothes, vacations, annual "vacation allowance," and many other details of kibbutz life.
It also performs a host of services for the individual kibbutzim, including
technical advice on all manner of agricultural and economic problems,
financial assistance, teacher training facilities, publication of books and
journals, provision for lectures and concerts, and guidance of young
kibbutzim in all aspects of social and economic life.

must sometimes tramp through mud and rain in order to get to them.

Nevertheless, few people, including those who have the opportunity of obtaining well-paying professional or governmental jobs, have left the kibbutz. But, while this is generally true of all the kibbutzim within The Federation, it is not the case in all other kibbutz federations, where many members are leaving. This has had a serious demoralizing effect on those who remain.

Why are the members of other kibbutz federations leaving now? Although kibbutz life is difficult, it is much easier today in the established kibbutzim than it was formerly, and then there were fewer resignations. When the members of one kibbutz first arrived in the country, the Jewish Agency wanted them to settle in the south, where the land was fertile and the area populated. They refused, insisting upon settling in a sub-tropical valley, where they would be forced to meet the combined challenge of poor soil, stifling heat, and possible Arab attacks. After all, they were chalutzim! Today, the Arabs are gone, the soil is fertile, and the effects of the heat are considerably mitigated by shade trees, cement houses, running water, and showers. Nevertheless, the year before this study was undertaken, 25 per cent of its population had resigned.

It would be false to convey the impression that there is only one answer to this question. There is a crisis today in the entire kibbutz movement, and Kiryat Yedidim does not constitute an exception to this generalization.[10] But one observation is immediately relevant. Because of the frustrations which almost every person experiences in any kibbutz, no one whose primary motivation for living in one is per-

[10] See Chapter 7.

sonal gratification would continue to live there. One remains, despite the personal frustrations entailed, because of a motive more powerful. This motive may be one or both of the following: the willingness to defer present for future happiness; or the conviction that personal frustration has meaning in the light of some higher value or ultimate end. In other words, one is willing to live in a kibbutz because of a belief in some value greater than one's own happiness, or because of a *faith* in a future much better than the present, or both. The members of The Federation have both. Their faith and belief, alike, are provided by their all important *hashkafat olam*, their *weltanschauung*. Hashkafat olam is an immensely important concept in Kiryat Yedidim and one which occupies a paramount place in their vocabulary of motives. The examples which follow are typical.

A chavera said that kibbutz life was very difficult, but that it was well worth it. "In two hundred and fifty years, they'll write about us."

Another chavera, stretched out on her bed at the end of an exhausting day, said that her work was becoming too hard for her. When the author commented jokingly that her work was for a good cause, she retorted quite seriously —"Yes, if we did not always have that cause uppermost in our minds, we could not continue our work here. That is what makes it possible for us to go on."

In discussing the problem of backward students in the high school, one of the teachers suggested that it might be necessary to send them to a trade school, but that they would still be taught the same amount of ideology. "This is vital. Without ideology, we would not be able to survive."

A field worker was pointing out the advantages of kibbutz life to the author, when his wife interrupted him to say that the disadvantages were much greater, and that it would be deceptive to deny this. The husband conceded that kibbutz life was "difficult," and that no one would remain if he thought only in terms of his "physical pleasures." It is not on this basis, he said, that the kibbutz can be made to appeal to outsiders or even to the children of the kibbutz. Ultimately, "living in a kibbutz is based on ideological conviction, and its appeal rests only on its superior ideology."

One of the "intellectuals" of the kibbutz expressed dissatisfaction with some Marxist interpretations in a newspaper article. "Nevertheless," he said at the end, "I value Marxism very highly. In times like ours when there is no faith and there is no God, Marxism does provide you with a *weltanschauung;* it does fit every theory and every science into a scheme and, thus, it brings order out of chaos."

These quotations introduce the main thesis of this chapter—that Kiryat Yedidim, in spite of its formal opposition to traditional religion, its avowed secularism, and its insistence on the "scientific" basis of its social analysis and predictions, is actually a "religious" community, in the technical meaning of that word, and that its faith provides the *élan* which some kibbutzim in other federations seem to lack.[11]

Analogies between religion and certain political movements are often proposed, but they are frequently con-

[11] But it is not an isolated community. Rather, it is part of a larger brotherhood of kibbutzim, all of which are members of a national federation—The Federation. Hence, the "religious" faith of Kiryat Yedidim was not evolved by its chaverim alone, nor is it unique to them. It was evolved, rather, by the leadership of The Federation and is shared by all affiliated kibbutzim. Since the faith which is here described is not the faith of Kiryat Yedidim alone, but the faith of its Federation, this faith will be referred to as the "faith of the kibbutz."

vincing only on a formal level. The "religious" character of Kiryat Yedidim, however, is probably its essential characteristic,[12] so that those principles of socio- and psycho-dynamics which serve to explain traditional religious faith provide the most effective tools for the analysis of kibbutz ideology.[13]

As has already been observed, Kiryat Yedidim (and all the other kibbutzim in The Federation) may be viewed as a "sect" rather than as a "church." Its sect-like nature is clearly revealed in its insistence upon separation from the "world" and its evils, in its insistence that it alone has a monopoly on the truth, and in its restriction of membership to those who, as adults, willingly join it on the basis of conviction. Its strength lies in its belief that it comprises one of the small groups of the "elect," who enjoy "grace" in this world and who are predestined for salvation in the next (after-the-revolution) world. Although it has renounced the "world," the contemporary kibbutz, unlike the kibbutz of the past and other contemporary sects, is not content to go its own way, seeking merely its own salvation (the "withdrawing" sect). Rather, the kibbutz is a militant sect, attempting to convert the "world" and to re-create it in its own image.

The faith of Kiryat Yedidim can be simply expressed.

---

[12] After living seven years in Kiryat Yedidim, its veterinarian (not a member) decided to move to a cooperative agricultural village (*moshav*). "I am simply tired of living with sectarians," he said, "and just want to live with farmers."

[13] The writer does not mean to imply that the kibbutz *weltanschauung* constitutes the only secular religion in the modern world, but it may well be the most highly systematic, perhaps the best example of a secular sect-type religion. Nor, in analyzing the kibbutz in religious terms, does the author mean to demean the importance of its ideology; on the contrary, only in these terms can its importance really be grasped.

The historic process inevitably and irrevocably leads to the ultimate triumph of socialism. In the socialist stage of man's history, all social evils will disappear, hence all evil in man will disappear. Unfortunately, however, the process of achieving this end will be one of both triumph and anguish. As a leader of The Federation has phrased it:

[We are living in a revolutionary era, in which] . . . the fate of the individual and of the community is interdependent. Every individual here faces a vital personal alternative: either to be swept into the stream that leads to the doomed yesterday, or to join the stream that is advancing to the new life that is being built.

Socialism will triumph even if victory comes only after the horrible suffering of war's hell. A third world war means the annihilation of whole countries and perhaps of whole continents. Nations and civilizations will be razed to the ground. The road to socialism will be drenched with blood and pain such as none of us here can even conjure up in our minds. The Second World War will seem like child's play in comparison. That is why all lovers of freedom are waging such a stubborn struggle for peace. If, however, the horror does come—it will be the last war of the 'ancien régime'. All its exploitation of scientific advancement for the destruction of humanity notwithstanding, it will not succeed. Gasping, bleeding, but victorious and emancipated, humanity will begin the great task of rebuilding that will lead to the world of social justice.

The kibbutz represents the future society of humanity and, as such, its members constitute the avant-garde of the class-conscious Jewish workers in Israel in their struggle for national and social liberation. In the words of the same leader:

We have the privilege of being one of the most decisive generations in the history of Israel. This is a glorious privilege, but it is laden with tremendous responsibilities. Only if we bear up under them will we not prove traitors to the great national and social mission placed upon us.

. . . [In this struggle there are various degrees of self-realization, but] . . .there is no higher degree than chalutz self-realization. Self-realization does not confer any extra privileges on the chaver. On the contrary. It places greater responsibility on you. The great privilege which chalutziut confers upon its adherents is the privilege of giving and not receiving, of paving roads and not traveling along those which have been paved by others long ago . . . And the highest degree of chalutz self-realization is kibbutz . . . It is the outpost on the front lines of the whole national and class battlefield. It is the forward position from which the first sally in each new attack is initiated, and it is the first to receive the blows of every enemy to the nation and the working class.

The new society, like the kibbutz, will be organized on the basis of collective living. When that day arrives, all the difficulties of contemporary kibbutz living will disappear— for these difficulties are primarily a result of the anomaly of being a "socialist island in the midst of a capitalist sea," of living in a "hostile environment." In the interim period, the chaver can find contentment not only in the realization that he is leading Israel and all of mankind to its ultimate goal, but also in the many satisfactions he is enjoying in the society of the future, despite its admitted difficulties.

. . . [It is true that the] kibbutz must be a home for those who live in it. However, a kibbutz which is only a home and nothing else is fated to degeneration and disruption. Life on an island of collectivism in the midst of the capitalist system's grim realities must of necessity be as grim as on the battlefields . . . Only the kibbutz, which exists as a vanguard weapon in the hands of the working class, only such a kibbutz has the power to withstand the murky stream of the way of life around it. Only the kibbutz which exists as a militant ideological collective . . . has the power to be a secure home for its members . . . [The day to day living in the kibbutz is often difficult and frustrating, but this can be overcome by a] clear *weltanschauung*, a crystallized political approach . . . consciousness of the mission that the kibbutz movement bears—unwavering faith that the kibbutz movement was and still is today the most important vanguard tool of the Jewish working class in its struggle for the realization of maximal Zionism, the dissolution of the existing system, and the construction of the socialist society.

With this statement of the essential doctrines of the faith of Kiryat Yedidim, we may now proceed to an examination of its more detailed beliefs and of their psychodynamic bases.

THE SOURCE OF TRUTH: THE PROPHET AND THE SACRED WRITINGS. The prophet of this faith is Karl Marx. Like other prophets before him, Marx had been able to predict future historic events; like them, he left his sacred writings which enable others to understand the course of these events. But like other prophets, Marx is not always clear, and his intentions are not always manifest. Hence, an interpreter is required and this function is served by Lenin. But even Lenin's works are not always self-evident; they too require exegesis. And the official exegete of the works of Lenin, as well as of Marx, is the Soviet Union. When a rival political leader, for example, took issue with a leader of The Federation by quoting from Lenin, the latter replied that quotations from Lenin without the "proper" interpretation of the text are worse than useless. There is only one kind of Marxism-Leninism, he reminded his opponent, and that is the kind that issues from the Soviet Union; any other kind is false.

The similarity between the attitude of the chaverim to a sacred text and the attitude of their fathers in the shtetl to their (the latter's) sacred text, is remarkable. The Bible was sacred, but it clearly required interpretation. This function was served by the Talmud. However, even the Talmud required clarification, and among the many and conflicting interpretations, that of Joseph Karo became the authoritative one. Functionally, also, Marxist writings serve the identical purposes in the kibbutz that the religious texts of Judaism served in the shtetl. Traditional Jewish literature had three functions: it was intellectual fare, enabling man to understand his universe; it was inspiration for combatting the daily struggles with a hostile world, providing a faith in the Messianic coming; and it was sacred literature, containing the wisdom of sages and prophets whose teachings were inspired and, hence, definitive.[14] Marxist literature serves the identical functions. It is intellectual fare, providing the only correct analysis of the world; it is inspiration for present political and economic struggles, providing faith in the ultimate victory of the proletarian revolution; and it is sacred and, therefore, infallible literature. The chaverim in Kiryat Yedidim and their fathers in the shtetl are not far apart, despite the theism of the latter, and the atheism of the former. Despite their rebellion against religion and their insistence on the "scientific" nature of their social analysis, the fact remains that the chaverim seem merely to have substituted Marxism for Judaism. The content of the belief is different, the psychodynamics of the belief are the same— a need for a faith which will justify current suffering and promise ultimate salvation. The truth of this faith is confirmed by the sacred texts, which can never be wrong. The Talmudic *pilpulist* (casuist) in the shtetl and the Marxist exegete in the kibbutz are the same, psychologically speaking.

[14] For an excellent description of these and other characteristics of Jewish sacred learning, see Zborowski and Herzog, ch. 3.

THE ABSOLUTE. The importance of the Soviet Union in the belief system of the kibbutz cannot be exaggerated. It is a combination of the Vatican and of heaven: from it, come authoritative pronouncements on important social, political, and intellectual matters;[15] toward it are directed the aspirations of all the downtrodden of the earth. Not only is the Soviet Union the center of peace, justice, and freedom, but everything in the Soviet Union is superior— its art, literature, science, technology are all superior to their counterparts in the rest of the world.[16] In a sense, it is a secular heaven, for it has already achieved what the kibbutz is still trying to achieve. Almost everyone, therefore, wants to visit the Soviet Union, in order to see this paradise for himself. Soviet propaganda journals, filled with glorious and romantic pictures of Soviet accomplishments, are accepted as unqualified truth. Comparisons with Israel and with the kibbutz are inevitable and, necessarily, invidious. This picture of the Soviet Union, in which near-perfect people live in a state of near-perfection, serves an important psycho-

[15] The intellectual domination of the Soviet Union is apparent in the choice of books which are read, the scientific theories that are accepted, the art which is appreciated. Lysenko, for example, was accepted immediately, and Mendelianism was branded as "bourgeois genetics." Psychoanalysis, out of favor in the Soviet Union, is under serious attack, and there is now much discussion of Pavlov and "reflexes." Lectures are frequently delivered in Kiryat Yedidim on literary and artistic topics "in the light of Marxism"—that is, in the light of the current Soviet "line" on these matters.

[16] This attitude, which is shared by the average and the intellectual chaver, alike, often results in abject and invidious comparisons between the Soviet Union and Israel, or between the Soviet Union and the kibbutz. A distinguished American educator waas escorted through the high school of Kiryat Yedidim by some of the educational officials of The Federation and by a local committee of teachers. To most of his questions the responses were, "we haven't got to that point yet, but in the Soviet Union . . ." or, "we don't have the proper textbooks, but in the Soviet Union . . ." or, "our teacher's training has not been fully explored, but in the Soviet Union . . ."

logical function in the lives of the chaverim. It proves that
Socialism, when not obstructed by Western Imperialism and
by a hostile government—as is the case with the kibbutz—
can create the perfect world and the perfect human nature
which their socialist faith promises, but which are so far
from realization in their own community. This vindication
of their faith gives the chaverim the courage to carry on.
Were their faith in the Soviet Union to be destroyed, it is
not at all improbable that their faith in their own experiment would be seriously shaken. How else can one account
for the tenacity with which the chaverim cling to this faith
which, normally, would have been shattered by the considerations raised below?

This faith, it should be stressed, is not merely a wistful
hope or a belief in an event that might occur in the distant
future. The kibbutz, in one sense, may be viewed as an
apocalyptic sect, which looks to the imminent end of the
capitalist world, and of the triumph of socialism. This triumph is not a matter of millenia, centuries, or even decades.
The goal of history, the chaverim believe, will be attained
in their own lifetime. Within the next five years, perhaps,
the Soviet Union will have won the cold and/or hot war,
the Red Army will have marched into Israel, and the Day
of Delivery for Israel and for all the other countries of the
world will have begun. These statements, it must be stressed,
are more than political propaganda or poetic fancy; they are
part of a pragmatic faith, and are expressed in daily activity.
In discussing the high school curriculum, for example, a
teacher said that the students do not want to study Arabic
but that this is of no grave concern, for when the Soviet
Union of the Near East is created—an event which will
occur shortly—they will become interested in Arabic.

The idealization of the Soviet Union, as a whole, is equalled only by the glorified picture of its leaders. The author heard chaverim discussing Stalin—his personality, his achievements, his brilliance, the miracles he had wrought in Russia—in the same glowing terms and with the same awe that a *chassid* would speak of his *rebbe*.[17] For many chaverim, Stalin was more than a charismatic leader—he was a semi-divine father, all-good and all-wise, whose every decision was to be accepted as true and good.

This idealization of the Soviet Union and its leadership stands in marked contradiction to the kibbutz ideals of liberty, and great intellectual effort is required to reconcile this obvious contradiction. As is true in any theological system, such an effort can succeed only if it is based on a profound faith or on an intense "will to believe." The chaverim, like Tertullian, must be willing to assert, ultimately, that they believe because "it is absurd." For it is absurd that a society which is so passionately devoted to the cause of freedom should believe in a dictatorship, and it is absurd for Zionists to place their faith in a country which has been consistently anti-Zionist. This will to believe seems to be based on their need for an absolute, and in another sense, on their need for a strong and good father to take the place of the one whom they had rejected.

That the Soviet Union, specifically, was chosen to satisfy this need may best be explained by reference to the kibbutz conception of "socialism." The chaverim are the spiritual heirs of three traditions: the Eighteenth Century Enlightenment, the French Revolution, and Nineteenth Century Liberalism. From these movements they acquired their values of secular humanism, social justice, and national liberation.

[17] A chassid is a follower of a wonder-working rabbi, or rebbe.

"Socialism," as they use that term, refers not merely to an economic system but to a total way of life which synthesizes these three values. When a chaver is asked, for example, which of the following values—justice, peace, socialism, brotherhood, freedom—he tries most strongly to inculcate into his children, he answers: "They all are equally important; they are all included in 'socialism.'"

But if socialism represents the synthesis of the values of the three traditions from which the chaverim are descended, the Russian Revolution (in their eyes) is their historic culmination. And since this Revolution attempted to establish socialism in the Soviet Union, the latter—like the kibbutz—must be dedicated to the principles of justice, peace, freedom, and brotherhood.

Given this argument—and its false (from our point of view) major premise—the rejection of the Soviet Union would be highly threatening to the chaverim: it would be tantamount to the rejection of socialism which, in turn, would constitute a rejection of the very values on which the kibbutz is based. Hence, instead of rejecting the major premise—the Soviet Union is a socialist society—they have clung to the anomalous belief in the benevolence of the Soviet Union, and their faith provides a ready answer for its own anomalies. The chaverim recognize that "true" communism has not yet been attained by the Soviet Union, that conditions there are far from democratic. Indeed, they admit that in some respects life in the Soviet Union is a "hell." Nevertheless, as one chaver put it, one must understand that the "United States is a paradise of fools; the Soviet Union is a hell of wise men." It is true that there is a dictatorship in the Soviet Union, but it is a dictatorship of the proletariat; and although the Russian masses may suffer severe hardship under the dictatorship, it is run for them and its procedures will be vindicated by its future results. Furthermore, it is superfluous to have more than one party in a Communist society, because all workers have but one opinion on political matters, and this opinion is always represented by the Communist Party. As one vattik expressed it, "no one in his right mind would want to oppose the Soviet Union, for there is nothing to oppose." The ultimate aim of the Soviet Union is the abolition of the dictatorship, an aim whose realization is prolonged primarily by the machinations of the Western countries, against whom it must defend itself. That it will eventually disappear, however, is inevitable.

The irrationality of their faith in the benevolence of the Soviet Union is equally apparent when it is remembered that the Soviet Union has always been hostile to Zionism. It has banned Hebrew culture, imprisoned Zionist leaders, and refused permission to Jews to migrate to Israel or to have any contact with world Jewry. But, say the chaverim, this *apparent* anti-Zionist behavior is not *really* anti-Zionist; it only appears that way to those who do not understand its true motivations. The Soviet Union has seemed to be anti-Zionist because Zionist activities in the past had taken place within the context of Turkish and British imperialism, and have often been dominated by American Jewish capitalists. That these are the grounds for its anti-Zionist attitude, is evident from the fact that when the British were about to abandon Palestine in 1947, Andrei Gromyko, the delegate from Russia, delivered a speech in the United Nations, referring to the "rights" of the "Jewish People" to a homeland in Palestine. Furthermore, in the Israel War of Liberation, it was Czechoslovakia which supplied the Jews with arms.[18]

---

[18] That Gromyko's speech might have been motivated by a desire to weaken the position of the British, rather than by sympathy with the

It is true that the Soviet Union has since continued to attack Zionism, but this is due to the anti-Soviet attitude of the present Israeli government. Were the political party with which the kibbutz is affiliated to gain power, the Soviet attitude would change. The Soviet refusal to allow Russian Jews to emigrate to Israel is also explicable. Since the present Israeli government is anti-Soviet, and since it is rapidly reducing Israel to the status of an American colony, the release of Russian Jews at this time would only mean that these Jews would be fighting against the Soviet Union in the future war which is being planned by the United States.

Not even the recent (1952) antisemitic events in the Soviet Union and its satellites have served to change the attitude of the kibbutz. The virulent antisemitism and anti-Zionism in the Slansky trials; the imprisonment by the Czech government of a leader of their (the kibbutz's) own political party, charged with being an anti-Soviet agent; and the antisemitic overtones of the arrest of the Moscow doctors—none of these served to shake their faith in the "justice" and in the "socialism" of the Communists. In a public statement, the Party with which the kibbutz is affiliated averred that it would remain faithful to its Zionist aspirations despite the "mistaken" actions of the Soviet Union, but that it would also remain faithful to the Soviet Union, which continues to be the center of world peace and international brotherhood. When the Soviet physicians were freed after the death of Stalin, The Party proclaimed to the world (via

---

Zionist cause; and that Czechoslovakia, as a Soviet satellite, was motivated by a desire to create unrest in the Near East, as well as by a need for American dollars (the arms were not given as a gift, and only dollars were accepted as payment) are considerations which the kibbutz refuses to entertain as possible motives. That the Soviet Union had not changed its policy is best indicated by the fact that the Communist Party in Israel which, presumably, was closer to the Soviet Union than is The Federation, continued its policy of virulent anti-Zionism.

its newspaper) that once again, "Socialist justice is vindicated."[19]

This attitude to the Soviet Union seems to be the typical attitude of the religious devotee to his God. God is always just, and if His justice is not always apparent, it may be attributed to the fact that the ways of the Lord are mysterious, and man cannot always understand them. Just as the religious person searches for a hint of God's favor in every obscure event, so the chaverim examine every statement of the Soviet leaders for the slightest hint of a pro-Zionist attitude. One might characterize this as genuine religious masochism, in which the faithful continue to love God, no matter how cruelly He has dealt with them; for even His cruelty can be interpreted as a sign of love, much as a father chastizes his children because he really loves them.

EVIL. The United States and her allies represent the Forces of Evil in the world. The United States, in particular, is responsible for most of the evil in Israel. This, despite the fact that it is the United States which permits Israeli representatives—including those of The Federation—to raise money for, and to promote immigration to Israel; which has granted considerable loans to the state of Israel; and

[19] Despite the above—and adding another anomaly to a situation already pregnant with anomalies—The Federation has been consistently and irrevocably opposed to the tiny Communist Party in Israel, and it has refused to cooperate with the Comintern or its successor, the Cominform. The one immediate avenue of expulsion from The Federation and any of its affiliated kibbutzim is membership in, or even flirtation with, the Communist Party. The manifest reason for this reaction is obvious: The Federation is based on both socialism *and* Zionism, both principles being coordinate, rather than one being subordinate to the other. The Communist Party, on the other hand, is—and always has been—anti-Zionist in both word and deed. The hostility between The Federation and the Communist Party is mutual. The latter views the entire kibbutz movement as a product of bourgeois romanticism, which serves as a retreat from the political arena of class struggle. *Kol Ha-Am*, the organ of the Communist Party, is most vitriolic when it attacks The Party and The Federation.

which permits Americans to send contributions of millions of dollars every year to Israel—all of which are illegal in the Soviet Union. America, nevertheless, is execrated and the Soviet Union is praised.

This paradox, like the ones examined earlier, can be understood only in terms of the belief system of Kiryat Yedidim. For the kibbutz and its Federation there exist only two categories of people: capitalists and proletariat. The capitalists, because they are capitalists, are morally evil, so that it becomes a moral duty to defeat them. The workers, on the other hand, because they are workers, are noble; they embody all value. Hence it is a moral duty to fight for, and to uphold them. Not only is their cause just, but *they* are just.

Now the Soviet Union is a "Workers' State." It is a dictatorship, to be sure, and this is unfortunate. But it is a dictatorship run by workers and for workers; it is a proletarian dictatorship. And in the future, when the dictatorship will have disappeared, the Soviet Union will be a democracy of workers, based on the principles of justice, equality, and freedom.

The United States, on the other hand, is a Capitalist society. Democratic in appearance, it is, in fact, a "dictatorship" run by capitalists and for capitalists. And should the power of the capitalists be threatened by a militant workers' movement, the democratic façade would crumble, and the true nature of the "dictatorship" would become apparent.

Hence the present "cold war" is perceived by The Federation as a moral war, as a struggle between the proletariat —"the forces of peace and of progress"—and the capitalist—"the forces of war and of subjugation." Since the United States is perceived as the spearhead of the latter forces, it is the symbol of all that the chaverim hate.

Analyzed in terms of the psychodynamics of religious

belief, the chaverim, it seems, have a need to polarize their world into good and evil, into God and Satan. They have, in short, an intense need to love and an intense need to hate; and what is more, they abhor uncertainty and cannot tolerate ambivalence. Hence, all their hatred is channeled in one direction, and all their love in another. In psychoanalytic terms, there has been a split of the synthetic father figure into a "good" father *imago*, who can do no wrong and who can be loved unqualifiedly, and a bad father *imago*, who can never do right and who can be hated unqualifiedly. The distorted perception of both the Soviet Union and the United States may stem, then, from this need to polarize their emotions.

This distorted perception is responsible, furthermore, for the extreme suspicion with which the chaverim perceive the non-Soviet world. The world, it is believed, is hostile, and wishes to destroy the kibbutz movement. A constant refrain in the newspapers and journals, a refrain which is repeated in conversation, is that they live in a *seviva oyenet*, a hostile environment. It is true, of course, that many people both in and out of Israel are opposed to kibbutz living. It is also true that as members of an opposition political party, The Federation has incurred the hostility of the government. In discussing this problem, many chaverim interpret this hostility in the following manner. The Israeli government wants to receive loans from the United States government. The latter is opposed to the kibbutz movement, and has agreed to grant Israel its requested loans only if the kibbutzim are weakened, if not destroyed. The government of Israel, therefore, has become hostile to the kibbutzim in order to obtain its loans.

It is believed, moreover, that the American government, working through its State Department, employs agents to spy on the kibbutzim. Shortly after we arrived in Kiryat Yedidim, it was thought that we were spies, and for some time it was difficult to obtain cooperation for our study. Eventually, it was decided that we really were what we had claimed to be—scientists—and most of those who had been openly hostile to us became friendly. But even at the end of the study, some of the people retained their suspicions of us, and two chaverim told us quite candidly that they still thought we were spies.

Political matters, then, are not merely political; they are matters of ideology.[20] And in the absence of traditional religion, ideology becomes religion. This accounts for the emotional energy which the chaverim invest in politics. Political meetings are of the nature of religious Councils, and political pronouncements assume the overtones of religious Confessions; for political decisions are more than temporary, pragmatic actions designed to win elections, control patronage, or promote personal careers or political fortunes. They are moral events, whose consequences involve the ultimate salvation of mankind. Political differences are not merely differences of opinion; they are matters of Truth and Error, of right and wrong. Differences in opinion can be tolerated, respected, compromised; but one cannot tolerate that which is wrong, and one cannot compromise with the Truth. Hence, political discussions with those with whom the chaverim are in disagreement are always emo-

20 It is the author's impression that this relationship between politics and ideology is generally true for Israelis as a group. Without suggesting here a "national character" trait, it may be noted that the visitor to Israel is immediately struck by the intensity of emotions aroused by politics or political discussions. Americans, after all, become aroused only once every four years, but for at least those Israelis who settled in the country prior to 1948 (that is, before the waves of "oriental" migrations) politics seems to be not a mere hobby, but a vital, day-to-day activity.

tional, and personal friendship with individuals of different political views is difficult, if not impossible. A chaver with whom the author had been very friendly refused to talk to him when he learned that the author was in favor of the Marshall Plan. A chavera, who had many friends in another kibbutz, and who had formerly spent much time with them, said that she could no longer spend more than two days in that kibbutz, because their political opinions made her "sick." One of the gentlest of chaverim became unrecognizable when he discussed the United States, so great was the hostility aroused by the topic. Political matters, in short, evoke the affect and emotional involvement that we generally associate with ultimate life commitments.

We are now in a position to examine the paramount role which the belief system of Kiryat Yedidim plays in its total adjustment. Any kibbutz, in its aspect of a farmers' village, comes to an end if its constituent members leave the community. But every kibbutz, at least in its inception and conception, is more than an agricultural village; it is a community of visionaries, dedicated to the achievement of a new society based on brotherhood, as symbolized by communism in property, social equality, and self-labor. Hence, a kibbutz *qua* kibbutz can come to an end, although its entire membership remains intact, by the abandonment of its original vision. Now the daily routine of any community is frequently dull, and in a pioneering community—such as a kibbutz—it is also strenuous and enervating. It is not too difficult, as the few books written by kibbutz members testify,[21] to lose one's original vision and to perceive the

[21] See the novels by Maletz and Mosensohn already referred to. Since the completion of this monograph, a book written by a member of an "American" kibbutz brings out this same point. Weingarten, *Life in a Kibbutz.*

kibbutz primarily as an agricultural village. When this happens the dominant motives of the kibbutz are little different from those of any Western community: a higher standard of living and greater personal and present gratifications. If these needs cannot be satisfied by the traditional social structure of the kibbutz, one may (other things being equal) seek to satisfy them outside the kibbutz, or change its social structure in such a way that it will satisfy these needs.

This, very briefly, constitutes the contemporary "crisis" in the entire kibbutz movement.[22] On the one hand, the resignation rate in some kibbutzim, on the part of those whose "normal" personal needs are not being satisfied, is alarmingly high. On the other hand many kibbutzim, in order to check the spread of these resignations and to arrest the growing discontent, have introduced innovations which threaten the continuity of the kibbutz *qua* kibbutz. By permitting, even encouraging, the introduction of industry, hired labor, and private property, these kibbutzim are beginning to develop a system of social classes based on property, power, and prestige—a system which may well mean the end of the kibbutz viewed as a brotherhood of those who till the soil and live from the labor of their own hands.

Although all kibbutzim are confronted by this "crisis," those in two federations are least threatened by it—as measured by a much smaller percentage of resignations and by a greater devotion to their original ideals of self-labor and communal property. These are the small federation of religious kibbutzim and The Federation, of which Kiryat Yedidim is a member.[23] Despite their profound theological

[22] See Chapter 7.
[23] It is no accident that the members of Kiryat Yedidim speak of these religious kibbutzim with great admiration, despite their unqualified disagreement with their religious values.

differences both federations share one important characteristic: their belief in a system of transcendent values which gives meaning to their struggles—the boredom and difficulty of the daily routine—and which imbues them with a conviction that their original vision, though far from attainment in the present, may yet be attained in a Messianic future. Hence their principled opposition to innovation in the traditional social structure of the kibbutz. The system of transcendent values for the one is Judaism (with its transcendental God); for the other it is Marxism, with its apocalyptic vision of History.

Before the establishment of the State, all kibbutzim shared at least one transcendent value—Zionism. And while they still viewed themselves as instruments for the attainment of this goal, the "crisis" through which they are now passing was only partly nascent. It was only after one of the main goals of Zionism—a Jewish State—was achieved that the "crisis" reached its present acute state in those kibbutzim which share neither the transcendental values of Judaism nor the transcendent values of Marxism. It is the author's hypothesis that, without some system of transcendent values to give it meaning, the utopian vision of brotherly love must give way to the realistic vision of "normalcy" based on the mundane values of the "world." This, at least, is a plausible explanation for the differences that are found among the various kibbutzim with respect to their adherence to their historic institutions. And if this hypothesis is valid, then the faith of Kiryat Yedidim is a crucial element in maintaining the integrity of its social structure—an element which informs, rather than reflects, its humanistic culture.

Kiryat Yedidim, then, is not merely an agricultural village; it is a religious community, membership in which is contingent upon acceptance of its political ideology. This means that the kibbutz is a selective rather than an open society. But if the kibbutz is to remain a selective, sect-like society, it must not only recruit its membership selectively, so as to ensure homogeneity in ideology; it must also have some technique to provide for the continuance of this homogeneity, and for the preclusion of schism based on ideological differences. This is a problem that the ordinary village does not face, for in the latter, any person—no matter what his political or religious beliefs—can, and does, establish residence. The kibbutzim in The Federation achieve ideological homogeneity by what is called *kollectiviut ra'ayonit*, "ideological collectivism." This means that the members of Kiryat Yedidim are pledged to accept any majority decision of the kibbutz, The Federation, and The Party. Before a decision is made, any member has the right to fight for his own opinion on the matter under discussion. Once a vote has been taken, however, he is obliged to accept the decision and, if it has certain practical consequences, to work for their achievement or implementation. This means that the kibbutz and The Federation can always present a united front on any political or ideological issue. This homogeneity, of course, gives The Federation much greater strength than its numerical size might warrant. Moreover, although this is not a totalitarian technique,[24]

---

[24] The Federation has often been charged by its political enemies with being totalitarian and dictatorial because of its "ideological collectivism." This charge would be valid if the kibbutz were truly a village. But if the kibbutz be viewed as a religious community, the concept of kollectiviut ra'ayonit is intelligible. No religious community allows differences of opinion concerning its faith; if it did, its faith would be destroyed. No one may remain within Methodism, Judaism, Catholicism, for example, if he refuses to abide by the basic tenets of these respective religions. The same is true of Kiryat Yedidim. Kibbutz decisions, furthermore, are arrived at democratically, and may be revoked in the same manner.

kollectiviut ra'ayonit enables the kibbutz to take extreme
stands on any issue, because it need not compromise in order
to appease a minority faction. This is precisely what The
Federation has always done; it has always been extreme and
has never compromised.[25] Since it is convinced of the truth

---

[25] For the Israeli specialist another factor contributing to the extreme
intransigence of The Federation should be noted—the continuous conflict
between the Second and Third Aliya. The Second Aliya, it will be
remembered, refers to those immigrants, primarily Russian, who migrated
to Palestine between 1904 and the outbreak of the First World War,
while the Third Aliya refers to the predominantly Polish immigration of
the years immediately following the First World War. The former, in
the main, were political revolutionaries upon arrival, while the latter were
often *petit bourgeois* romantics. The realism of the former allowed them
to perceive the true nature of the Soviet Union, against whose policies
they have always been implacable foes. The romanticism of the Third
Aliya was more receptive to the influence of the Soviet propaganda
machine. The members of the Second Aliya, because of their seniority,
assumed leadership positions in the influential Histadrut and in the Palestine section of the Jewish Agency for Palestine. The Third Aliya
has always resented the power and prestige of the Second Aliya; and the
more politically extreme individuals who came during the Third Aliya
and who now belong to The Party have refused to join the political party
organized primarily by members of the Second Aliya. They have further
refused to enter into a coalition government with the latter party. They
reserve most of their hostility for Ben Gurion, its leader, and the strong
affect which he arouses in them leads one to speculate about their perceptions of him. Is he perceived only as a political opponent, or is he
perhaps perceived as symbolic of the father whom they had rejected? In
either event, it is not unlikely that the strong pro-Sovietism of The Federation developed in typical "schismogenic" fashion against the equally
strong anti-Sovietism of its opponents. (Since going to press the author
has read in the *New York Times* that The Party has consented to join
the new government to be headed by Mr. Ben Gurion. This fact would
serve to qualify the author's characterization of The Party's leadership
found on page 217. The author still feels that this characterization is valid,
however, and he will stand by it unless The Party remains in the government throughout its entire tenure. It is his prediction that, short of renewed warfare between Israel and the Arab states, The Party will resign
from the government before its tenure expires.)

and righteousness of its cause and since it has not had to compromise with its convictions, it has consistently taken its stand with the "truth" as it sees it, no matter how extreme that stand might be. As a vattik has put it:

We have always been extreme. We were extreme in demanding *hagshama* (immigration), rather than remaining Zionists in the Diaspora. In Palestine we were extreme in demanding return to the land and to agriculture. In agriculture, we were extreme in demanding kibbutz. In kibbutz, we were extreme in demanding (geographical) border kibbutzim. Hence, there are deep psychological roots for our political extremism. We are always on the border.

CHAPTER 7

Between the conception
And the creation
Between the emotion
And the response
Falls the Shadow
　　　　T. S. Eliot, *The Hollow Men*

THE CRISIS IN THE KIBBUTZ

Indications and Interpretations of Crisis

LIKE THE kibbutz movement as a whole, Kiryat Yedidim is passing through a critical period in its history. This might represent a transitional phase in its development or it might be of more serious import. Whatever its meaning, however, no one questions the fact that the movement is facing a serious crisis. The crisis in Kiryat Yedidim is not so acute as that confronting other kibbutzim,[1] but its proportions, nevertheless, are of serious magnitude. The indices of this "crisis" may be classified into those conditions that would represent some degree of malfunction in any society, and those that are so indicative only within this unique cultural configuration.

The first indication of crisis within the former category is intra-kibbutz tension. It should be remarked in this connection that Kiryat Yedidim, like Israel in general, is char-

---

[1] The reasons for this discrepancy are suggested above, 176–178.

acterized by what may be termed a "crisis psychology";
but this is not the source of the "tension" referred to here.
Each day seems to bring a new "crisis" to the kibbutz, and it
no sooner overcomes one before it is necessary to face
another. The grapefruit must be harvested immediately,
lest they rot, but there are not enough workers; the grapes
have to be picked immediately, before the bottom drops out
of the market. The high school students are drafted from
their classes for a special task "for the last time," only to
be recalled a month later, again "for the last time." In the
fields, the chaverim always manage to find a "vital" topic
for discussion, as if Kiryat Yedidim were only a year old,
and as if they did not have two town meetings a week for
the discussion of "vital" problems. The threatened resignation of a foreman, the newest move of the United States
concerning Israel, the latest action of the government which
"discriminates" against the workers, and a score of other
topics of conversation produce a feeling of daily crisis.

However important this "crisis psychology" is for an
understanding of the kibbutz, it does not produce those tensions that are regarded here as an indication of social dys-
phoria. This "crisis psychology" is not unique to the kibbutz; moreover, its net effect is probably a heightening,
rather than a lowering, of social vitality.

The tension that is important for this discussion is that
which is aroused within the context of the kibbutz social
structure and its unique values, and that lowers the sense of
social well-being of the chaverim. For the chaverim are
fully aware of the adverse consequences of such tension.
Commenting on the appearance of an American visitor, for
example, a chavera remarked that she had a face "like a
Madonna; it is such a quiet face. We cannot have such a

face in the kibbutz." When asked why, she explained that when people live and work together there is inevitably much tension, and everyone quarrels and shouts. Again, when a number of chaverim, during the course of this study, traveled together on a vacation to the South, they were impressed by the spirit of fellowship which permeated the group. "Somehow," said one chaver, "it required a trip one hundred miles from home to remind us that those around us are our chaverim, and that the person you had barely said hello to in the past, was really a wonderful companion." The reason for this sudden camaraderie, said a chavera, was the "absence of tension. Suddenly, you are not working with the others under the usual strain, and there are no arguments, and there is no tension. For once, I felt real peace and friendship."

The felt sources of tension in Kiryat Yedidim are usually "objectively" unimportant, and in the past they would have been glossed over by the chaverim. Today, with the kibbutz undergoing a crisis which challenges its existence, these sources become psychologically important. One such tension involves the shortage of clothing. As a chavera explained:

You want a new dress, and it's your turn to get one, but the *machsanait* (the woman in charge of the clothing store) tells you that there are no more points (clothing was rationed in Israel), or that the youth group has used all the material, or that there is a large backlog of orders. But I want my dress now, and all I care for is the fact that by rights I should have it now, and I don't want to wait another two months.

Someone else stresses the tensions of the dining room. The struggle for food, due to the shortage, and the noise and turmoil, due to the overcrowded conditions, are at times unbearable. The kitchen staff is overworked and, as a result, irritable. Consequently, they become angry with the chaverim who make some unusual request, and these, in turn, become angry with the staff. Then there is the constant consideration that not everyone likes the menu served on a particular day. "You come into the dining room," says one member,

. . . and see that they have eggs and onions. But you don't want onions; only eggs. So you ask the waiter to bring you eggs without onions. But they're busy, and they don't get around to you, and you walk out without eating. This may happen once or twice, and then you get mad. After all, this is your home, you work here, and you have to eat. It's a small thing, but it's very irritating.

Others point to the constant necessity for interaction, even when one is not in the mood, as a source of tension:

In the city, if you have a fight with a business colleague, it's not so bad; you only see him during business hours anyway. But here you have a fight with a chaver, and he is more than a business colleague. He's a chaver of the kibbutz; he's your friend, and you must live with him and see him every day. It's not pleasant.

Others stress the lack of social and psychological privacy which results from this kind of interaction. "It's no fun," remarked a sensitive chavera, "to be naked before everyone." Another chavera, emerging from the shower room which, miraculously, she had had to herself, remarked: "a shower in peace and quiet—how pleasant it is."

Although the "regimentation" that certain critics of socialism regard as intrinsic to a planned society is not characteristic of Kiryat Yedidim, there can be no doubt but that one's choices are restricted in a social system of this type. Whether or not these restrictions are greater than those found in other societies is difficult to decide, short of an intensive study of this specific problem. If they are not greater, they are different. If a woman wants a new dress, for example, she may not choose its style, but is limited to the two or three to be found in the sewing room. If a couple wishes to move into different housing, they may do so only with the permission of the "social committee" which determines whether their request is reasonable. Should a chaver desire a temporary leave from the kibbutz, he must acquire the approval of the town meeting. In short, the maintenance of equality has meant that certain types of personal decisions have been subordinated to the approval of the group or to one of its delegated committees. And some chaverim complain that this hegemony of the group over, what they consider to be, their private lives is a source of no small irritation.

In discussing these and other problems with some of the chaverim, the author pointed out that many of these problems arise in city living as well, and that they are not unique to Kiryat Yedidim. They agreed; but, observed a chavera, there is one difference. Since they are living in the kibbutz, the chaverim can always say that if only they lived in the city, in a private house, they would have none of these problems. Since this alternative always exists, they can blame these irritations on the kibbutz.

A second indication of crisis may be found in the increasing frequency of resignations from the kibbutz, though the percentage is much smaller in Kiryat Yedidim than in other kibbutzim. In the first twenty years of its existence, when physical conditions were primitive and difficult, approximately ten people resigned from Kiryat Yedidim. In the next ten years, when the standard of living had risen and economic conditions in the kibbutz were at least as good as in the cities, the same number of people left. The year of this study, two couples left Kiryat Yedidim for the cities. Resignations are both a sign and a cause of the crisis. Every resignation is a source of demoralization in the kibbutz, as every resignation constitutes an explicit threat to its claim of superiority for its way of life.

Not only are more people leaving Kiryat Yedidim now than in the past, but—and this is a third index—many more chaverim have taken jobs which keep them outside the kibbutz most of the day or the week. Kiryat Yedidim, it will be recalled, is a constituent member of three larger national organizations—the General Federation of Labor (Histadrut), a kibbutz federation, and a political party. These organizations require skilled personnel for executive posts, and all kibbutzim contribute some of its members to work in these bodies. Kiryat Yedidim, however, has contributed more than its quota, and there is considerable resentment toward the chaverim who work in these jobs, when it is apparent that there is a great labor shortage in the kibbutz itself. Granting the element of sincere devotion to a cause which motivates these outside workers, the fact remains that, for some, this work enables them to live in the city and to escape many of the rigors of kibbutz life, while sharing its benefits. When it is remembered that most of these workers are vattikim and leaders in the kibbutz, this exodus represents a serious crisis.

These three conditions constitute universal indices of poor morale; that is, any society which shows evidence of considerable in-group tension, and in which dissatisfaction is great enough to lead to a desire to live elsewhere, is in a critical state.

But the degree of social crisis must be measured not only by those conditions that constitute a threat to the healthy survival of a society, but also by those conditions that constitute a threat to its unique cultural heritage. Kiryat Yedidim came into existence in order to realize certain moral values. Any internal threat to these values also constitutes a threat to its survival—not only its survival as a society, but its survival as a kibbutz. And there are some serious indications of such threats in Kiryat Yedidim.

The first and most important—one that Kiryat Yedidim views with considerable alarm—is the gradual introduction of private property and the seeming inability of the kibbutz to cope with this problem. In the past there was no private property in Kiryat Yedidim. Gradually, however, it began to permit its members to own such personal effects as books and fountain pens. Recently there has been a sharp increase in the acquisition of private property, again, however, to a much lesser extent than in other kibbutzim. Nevertheless, many chaverim have no compunctions about keeping such presents as radios, clothes, or furniture which in the past would have been turned over (and the kibbutz would have expected them to be turned over) to the kibbutz.

At present, the flagrant examples of private property in Kiryat Yedidim are the private ownership of a refrigerator and of an automobile. A couple received a small refrigerator from relatives outside the country, which they have kept for themselves. This not only enables them to have ice water— a real luxury—but also, since the man works in the city, they can have ice cream or cold beer. Such a violation of the kibbutz values of public ownership, sharing, and equality would have been unthinkable in the past, however much the couple may have justified it by saying—as the present violators say—that they are merely the custodians of the refrigerator until its owners arrive in Israel. The automobile was inherited by a chaver from European relatives. He has kept the car, he claims, because his wife lives in the city, and he can visit her in the evenings without losing a day's work. This reason, however justified, is irrelevant; what matters is that this act constitutes a violation of crucial values of kibbutz culture.

More important, however, is, not that a few individuals have violated its most important values, but that Kiryat Yedidim has been unable to deal with them. In the past, a chaver would have been publicly denounced for a much smaller violation, whereas today no sanctions are brought to bear against these violators of major values. Some justify this by saying that since the kibbutz cannot at this time provide for the material comforts of its members to the degree that it would like, it overlooks those occasions in which a chaver has an opportunity to do something for himself. This justification is not convincing. The reason for its lack of action seems, rather, to be that Kiryat Yedidim is afraid to take any action lest it touch a flame to a powder keg. Almost everyone in the kibbutz has accumulated some private property, and any action taken against the two flagrant violators might lead to action against the minor violators, as well. Since no one dares to predict what this might lead to, nothing is done at all. The fact remains that, should this trend towards the increase in private property continue, it might well mean the end of Kiryat Yedidim as a kibbutz. This increased desire for private property, then, constitutes an important index for "crisis."[2]

[2] An important check on this increase is to be found in the attitude of the sabras. The desire for private property is not characteristic of the sabras, who often criticize this "backsliding" on the part of their elders.

A second major value whose future existence is threatened is that of the paramount importance of group experiences. There seems to be little doubt but that Kiryat Yedidim is in the midst of a general trend from a completely community-centered society to one in which there is a much greater degree of privacy. This is manifest in a number of ways. In the first place there is a significant centrifugal movement from the dining room, as the center for the activities of the chaverim, to private living rooms. Nostalgic vattikim point to the good old days when the chaverim spent their evenings in the dining room, singing, dancing, and conversing. Today, the dining room is empty in the evenings, the chaverim preferring to remain in their own rooms with their children or a few friends. Some chaverim, in an attempt to find greater privacy, obtain their food in the dining room and retire with it to their own rooms, where they eat their meals alone or with their spouses. Still others are beginning to object to the use of communal showers, and managed to obtain lumber and pipes with which they constructed private showers outside their own rooms. When this trend threatened to become a universal practice, the town meeting prohibited all private showers on the ground that they were eyesores.

Kiryat Yedidim has taken cognizance of this greater demand for privacy on the part of its members. In the past, for example, when the chaverim spent their evenings in the dining room, light refreshments were left out on the tables. Now that they remain in their rooms with a few friends, they like to have tea or coffee and, perhaps, a cookie or piece of cake there and the kibbutz has officially recognized this to the extent of providing the chaverim with private rations of tea or coffee and sugar each month. An even more significant indication of the official recognition of the need for greater privacy may be seen in its new housing development. The units include private showers and toilets for each couple, and the rooms are constructed in an L-shape, which assures greater privacy to each spouse.

Despite such concessions, however, the leaders of Kiryat Yedidim and of The Federation view this trend from group to private experience with considerable alarm, as constituting a departure from a primary kibbutz value. Within Kiryat Yedidim, for example, an entire meeting was devoted to it during our study; people constantly talk about it; and articles in various kibbutz publications are written about it. The rallying cry of the opponents of this "centrifugal" movement is the "kumkum!" or tea kettle. The desire to drink tea with one's friends in the privacy of one's own room has become the symbol of this seeming dissolution of the camaraderie and family spirit that characterized the kibbutz in the past.

The Federation, too, is disturbed by this trend toward greater privacy. In a recent annual convention, the discussions centered about two main problems: the increase in both private property and in privacy. The convention was particularly disturbed by the increasing trend toward private showers and toilets and the trend away from the dining room as a communal center. It attributed these trends to the fact that the kibbutzim were becoming crowded with youth groups and new immigrants and that, as a consequence, the chaverim no longer possessed the feeling of "home" towards their own kibbutz. This interpretation, while possessing some merit, is hardly a satisfactory explanation, as will be indicated below.

Another index of crisis is the reluctance of many chaverim to accept official responsibilities in the kibbutz. It was noted that the chaverim view this reluctance with a certain pride. In other societies, they point out, people fight for power and prestige, whereas in the kibbutz, they avoid it. But this phenomenon, particularly when it is accompanied by a progressive decrease in the number of people who attend town meetings, is amenable to another—and less flattering—interpretation. In the past, town meetings were regularly attended by almost the entire kibbutz membership; today, the average attendance is less than 50 per cent. And, of those who do attend, only a small percentage participate actively in the meetings, while others complain that the meetings are boring. Taking all these facts into account, the reluctance to assume public office may be interpreted as a sign of indifference and of social irresponsibility. The fact is that no complex community can survive unless responsibilities are delegated; and, if people are reluctant to accept these responsibilities, they reveal—consciously or unconsciously—a certain indifference to the welfare and future of their group. It is true that other societies show a much higher incidence of such indifference than does the kibbutz. But the *raison d'être* of the kibbutz is its difference from other societies. It is based on mutual aid and on the value of the group. Should its indifference approximate the degree of indifference shown in other societies, this would not only indicate that these values have been abandoned, but it would be necessary to appoint professional managers to operate the kibbutz. This would mean the end of its values of equality and of freedom, as they are understood by the chaverim today. Again, Kiryat Yedidim, as a kibbutz, would cease to exist.

There seems to be little question, then, that the social and cultural survival of Kiryat Yedidim are seriously threatened.

There is considerable disagreement, however, as to how this crisis is to be explained. An analysis of it suggests that conditions both within the kibbutz and external to it have contributed to the present situation.

The chaverim tend to attribute all problems within the kibbutz to external conditions and, particularly, to governmental opposition. The government, they point out, is headed by a "reformist" party, and is actively opposed to the kibbutz movement. There is some justification for this claim. The present coalition government, like any government, wants to remain in power, and it views the kibbutzim, a large percentage of whose membership are in an opposition party, as a political threat. Furthermore, the government is anti-Soviet and is, on principle, opposed to the pro-Soviet attitude of many of the kibbutzim. Nevertheless, if asked to point to specific measures taken by the government to weaken the kibbutzim, the chaverim can point to few specific acts. The one act which is constantly mentioned is the dissolution of the Palmach, the shock troops which played such an important role in the War of National Liberation. It is true that most of the Palmach members were members of kibbutzim, but whether its dissolution was motivated by anti-kibbutz sentiment or not is a moot point. Granting, however, the validity of this charge, it is difficult to see how this act, or any other governmental act, has seriously contributed to the kibbutz crisis, as a whole, or to any of the indices of this crisis described above.

Aside from the government, whose role, to say the least, is controversial, there is another external condition which has had some influence on the kibbutz: the changed climate of opinion in the country as a whole concerning the kibbutz movement. In the past, when the country was still in a primitive, pioneering state, the kibbutzim were viewed with great respect by the rest of the country; and to be a chaver kibbutz was to be a national hero. For the chaver was the very symbol of the *chalutz*, the pioneer, the prototype of the new Jew. It was he who colonized the most dangerous parts of the country, who protected the borders from Arab marauders, who drained the swamps, and who made the deserts fertile. Hence, wherever he went he was honored. But this picture has changed since Independence. On the one hand, the earliest immigrants are tired of pioneering, of fighting, and of sacrifice. Their only desire is to return to a normal existence, and pioneering heroes are no longer important symbols. For the recent great wave of oriental immigration, on the other hand, the kibbutzim are of no significance, for these immigrants possess no cultural values that would assign importance to kibbutz life or to kibbutz ideals. At best, therefore, the kibbutzim are viewed with indifference.

This changed climate of opinion has deeply affected Kiryat Yedidim. Chaverim frequently exclaim, in hurt tones, that they are no longer respected when they enter the cities, and that their khaki dress, formerly a mark of prestige, has now become a symbol of inferiority. Moreover, they claim, it is they who continue to live in the hot deserts and on the dangerous borders, and it is they who disrupt their normal lives by taking in immigrants for rehabilitation, while the inhabitants of the cities compete for economic luxuries and professional careers.

This latter claim—and it is a just claim—is a potent factor in the ease with which some chaverim have abandoned important kibbutz values. Since their arrival in the country, the chaverim, together with its other Jewish inhabitants, have had to face an almost endless series of objective crises. From the very beginning, they have had to conquer the harsh physical environment, to defend their lives and property against Arab attacks, to fight the British, to bring in and rehabilitate refugees, to strive for economic and social improvement. There was seldom a moment's surcease from these tasks. And all this time they were motivated by high ideals and profound convictions. The War of Liberation and the establishment of the state marked a turning point in the history of Jewish Palestine. For the achievement of Independence marked the end of a long period of struggle and, it was hoped, a long period of sacrifice as well. As one Israeli put it, expressing what is probably a typical attitude:

Until the State was declared, we went through one crisis after another. We lived in a state of high emotional pitch. Now that the State is here, we are tired, simply tired, and we want to sit back and relax. We have made all the sacrifices we are capable of, and now, enough.

This attitude, which represents an emotional and moral letdown on the part of the older immigration, constitutes the normal attitude of the new immigration. And this attitude is expressed in a desire for material goods, for comforts, for personal careers, for worldly success. It is within this larger social context that the crisis in the kibbutz must be viewed. Many chaverim resent the fact that the kibbutz continues to exact sacrifices from them and continues to demand that they live in accordance with its high ideals, while the other segments of the population have abandoned their pioneering convictions. Hence, they argue, if the kibbutz will not grant them a greater degree of material comfort, why not obtain it for themselves?

Although this external situation has contributed to the

crisis in Kiryat Yedidim, it is the author's impression that the basic causes for the crisis are to be found *within* Kiryat Yedidim, and may be attributed to the social structure, the values of the kibbutz, and the changing psychology of its members.

The psychological changes that are important in this discussion are those changes that have been brought about by the process of aging. The kibbutz had its origin in a youth movement and, like the youth movement, it provided an outlet and a way of life for a rebellious youth which was searching for a better world and which believed that such a world could be achieved within its own lifetime, if only the structure of society could be changed. The way of life it chose—with its stress on hardship, sacrifice, sharing, and group living—was eminently suited for idealistic adolescents. But the vattikim are no longer adolescents, much as many of their leaders would like them to be. They are now middle-aged, the *sturm und drang* period of their lives is over, and they are content to settle down to a comfortable middle-age. They still believe in the just society, collective living, group experience, and their other original ideals. But they no longer have the psychological compulsions that motivated their lives in the past. The values remain, but the fanaticism is gone. In fact, the kibbutz in this respect has become like many churches, in which all the religious virtues are extolled, but in which their inner meaning has become lost. The socialist phrases which, in the beginning, were living realities have become clichés to be recited at official occasions. The words are repeated, but the original fire is missing. The reason is, of course, that no one can live in a permanent revolution.

But the aging process has not only affected the socialist

ardor of the chaverim, it has affected their communal ardor
as well. The group experiences that characterized the early
history of the kibbutz—the evening meetings, dances and
song, group conversation, and the sharing of experiences—
these are phenomena of youth. The retirement to their own
rooms and the substitution of private for group experiences
is not a result of the influx of strangers, as the convention
of The Federation suggested. It represents, rather, an inevitable retreat on the part of middle-aged people from the
group-centered activities of an adolescent youth movement
to interests which are more congenial to their own age—
children, friends, and personal concerns.

In short, the psychological needs that characterized the
chaverim as adolescents have long disappeared, so that
some of the communal institutions which were designed to
satisfy those needs are no longer functional, and others have
become dysfunctional. If the kibbutz leadership could distinguish between the temporary, adolescent values of kibbutz culture and its permanent, moral values, it could probably solve this problem. For it is apparent that kibbutz living entails two features which are not always consistent and
which are not necessarily connected. These are the values
of sharing and cooperation, on the one hand, and the values
of communal living and of group experience, on the other.
There is no reason to believe that the abandonment of the
latter two values would necessarily endanger the survival of
the former. Indeed, there is some reason to believe that it
might have the reverse effect. Until now, however, kibbutz
leadership sees both these features of kibbutz living as crucial
to its moral survival. Hence, communal living remains an
integral feature of kibbutz life. But this intimacy and frequency of interaction, no longer congenial to the needs of

the older chaverim, have generated much of the tension in Kiryat Yedidim today.

Social Structure and Psychological Tensions

Although the process of aging has led to a shift in some basic attitudes of the chaverim, advancing age has contributed to the crisis in Kiryat Yedidim for yet another, and probably more important, reason—one which is intrinsic to its social structure.

The kibbutz social structure places a strong accent on youth. Despite the retreat from adolescent attitudes and behavior discussed above, many characteristics of youth remain indelibly stamped on the culture of Kiryat Yedidim as well as on the personalities of its members. The name of the youth movement of their adolescence is now the name of their political faction. Mates are termed *bachur* and *bachura*—young man and young woman—although they may be more than fifty years of age. The Yiddish form of the diminutive—"ke"—which is added to the proper name of the young child, is retained by a chaver, although he may now be a grey-haired man. Kibbutz dress—open shirt and khaki pants for males, and white blouse and dirndl skirt or shorts for the female—is the mark of the Youth Movement. And, finally, the personality characteristics of the leadership of the kibbutz federation—characteristics which impel it to remain as a perpetual opposition, to refuse to assume governmental responsibility, to remain the permanent rebel and critic—are the characteristics of the rebellious adolescent, not of the mature political leader.*

The high evaluation of youth which characterizes the kibbutz, an evaluation which probably has its psychologi-

* See footnote 25, page 199.

cal roots in the rebellion of the vattikim against their elders, has had a considerable influence on the patterns of interaction between the young and the old. Both prestige and power in Kiryat Yedidim are functions of ability rather than of age, so that the foreman of an agricultural branch may be a young man, although the other workers in the branch are old. Young people enjoy social equality with their elders, and there is little, if any, differential prestige based on age, *qua* age, in either the formal or the informal structure of the kibbutz. All are called by first names, regardless of age or position, and the social distance that usually separates different ages by the Euro-American asymetrical system of appellation—the young calling their elders by their surnames, preceded by a "Mr." or "Mrs.," and the elders calling the young by their first names—is absent. The opinions of younger people, whether in formal meetings or in informal discussions, are received with the same respect as are those of older people.

But this emphasis on youth and on the equality that exists between the young and the old create a potentiality for a condition of inequality—an inequality in which the young assume the superior, and the old the inferior, status. In Kiryat Yedidim, this potentiality has given rise to the "problem of the aged." For if all men are equals, and if an important criterion for prestige is ability and, more particularly, ability in work, it would soon become evident that all men are not equals, for as one grows older he cannot work so hard as those who are younger.

This, then, is a social system whose extreme emphasis on equality has, paradoxically, led to inequality. The absence of a formal age-grading prestige system within the adult group (age-grading is sharp throughout childhood) has created a prestige vacuum which has been filled by an informal age-grading in terms of which the youth become more important than their elders because of their superior economic abilities. As a result, older chaverim find themselves being gradually displaced from their economic positions and, as a result, their most important prestige-achieving device—skill in work—is lost. This is an important source of psychological insecurity.

Kibbutz family structure further contributes to this problem. Since the nuclear family does not exist as a structural unit in Kiryat Yedidim, children are not subservient to their parents, for they do not belong to a social group that includes themselves and their parents—that is, to a family group. Instead, their identifications are with two groups— their age peers, on the one hand, and the entire kibbutz, on the other. This psychological identification with two "membership groups" has important social consequences when these adolescents become official members of the kibbutz and become full-time workers in its economy. As members of their peer groups, these young people remain distinct from the older people. But, as members of the kibbutz, they are in free competition with the older people—a competition in which the best man is allowed to win; and frequently the best man is the younger man, because of his physical superiority.

That this situation is a source of considerable insecurity for the older people may be illustrated by two examples. A respected vattika, who continues to work in the fields despite her age, complained one especially hot day that it was becoming increasingly difficult to work in the terrible heat. When the vattikim were younger, she said, the heat had proven no great difficulty, but now that they were getting older, it was almost impossible to continue working in the summers. She suggested that a small settlement on the mountain be built for the older people, to which they could retire. There, they could escape the heat, and at the same time they would not be a burden to the younger people. Despite her complaints, however, she refused to take longer rest periods or to retire to her room in the heat of the afternoon. Later that day, one of the men told her that he had found an ideal place for her to work—a shady spot, which was relatively cool. "That's wonderful!" exclaimed one of the younger women. The vattika turned to her and said with bitterness, "What's so wonderful about that? Why do you wish to sadden me?"

A vattik approached the problem of aging with greater insight and less passion. He had recently retired from a non-agricultural job, as he wanted to return to the fields and, since he is an expert in one of the important agricultural branches, he wanted to reënter that branch. He knew, however, that he would have to struggle for such a job since the members of that branch did not want any "old" men (he was fifty-two). They wanted young men who possessed physical strength; and his experience of thirty-two years in this branch meant little to them, as they already had one expert. There was little he could do about it, because:

. . . a man has his pride, you know . . . Of course, the kibbutz can always find room for me and others my age, in some branch, doing something dull and unimportant. That would be the economic solution to the problem, but it wouldn't be the human solution. The only men who do not face this problem are those who have taken jobs outside the kibbutz, in one capacity or another. But I don't want to pay the price (separation from his family during the week).

Here, then, can be found a major reason for the increasing number of people who prefer to work outside, as well as for much of the tension found within the kibbutz. The older people who work outside the kibbutz are not confronted with the "problem of the aged." Since they work in political, intellectual, governmental, or trade union activities, they are not at a disadvantage in competition with younger men. On the contrary, their greater experience and knowledge gives them an advantage. Hence, work outside the kibbutz is not a threat to their self-respect; it enhances it. Those who remain in the kibbutz, however, and continue to measure their worth by its criterion of efficient labor are constantly threatened by diminished self-respect, and this threat is a potent factor in the increased tension found in the kibbutz.

The social structure of the kibbutz is responsible for a problem of even more serious proportions—"the problem of the woman." In discussing the crisis in Kiryat Yedidim, no attempt was made to analyze the relative contributions of the sexes to this crisis. The fact is, however, that it is the women who are primarily responsible for the crisis. Almost all resignations are instigated by the women; the increased demand for private property and for greater privacy is found most strongly in the women; most of the tension in the kibbutz is caused by the women. It should come as no surprise, therefore, that many women in Kiryat Yedidim are unhappy in their role. Hence, it is no accident that, with the exception of politics, nothing occupies so much attention in the kibbutz as "the problem of the woman," *ba-ayat ha-chavera*. This phrase, constantly on the lips of the chaverim, was the subject of a number of town meetings during the writer's stay in Kiryat Yedidim. It is no exaggeration to say that if Kiryat Yedidim should ever disintegrate, the "problem of the woman" will be one of the main contributing factors.

In a society in which the equality of the sexes is a fundamental premise, and in which the emancipation of women is a major goal, the fact that there exists a "problem of the woman" requires analysis. It will be recalled from previous discussion that the Youth Movement, from which many kibbutz values are derived, was strongly feminist in orientation. The woman in bourgeois society, it believed, was subjugated to the male and tied to her home and family. This "biological tragedy of woman" forced her into menial roles, such as house cleaning, cooking, and other domestic duties, and prevented her from taking her place beside the man in the fields, the workshop, the laboratory, and the lecture hall. In the new society all this was to be changed. The woman would be relieved of her domestic burdens by means of the various institutions of collective living, and she could then take her place as man's equal in all the activities of life. The communal dining room would free her from the burden of cooking; the communal nurseries, from the responsibilities of raising children; the small rooms, from the job of cleaning. Hence, woman would be "emancipated from the yoke of domestic service" (*shichrur ha-isha mehaol shel sherut*).

In a formal sense, the kibbutz has been successful in this task. In an official statement, The Federation has proudly proclaimed:

We have given her equal rights, we have emancipated her from the economic yoke, we have emancipated her from the burden of the raising of children, we have emancipated her from the feeling of "belonging" to her husband, the provider and the one who commands, we have given her a new society, we broke the shackles that chained her hands.[3]

Despite these many accomplishments, the statement goes on to imply that, somehow, the woman has not found her salvation. For it concludes with this sentence: "And we forgot that the hands had been chained for hundreds of years, that an organ which does not function for such a long time, becomes paralyzed." It is this paralysis—perhaps it is something else?—to which we must turn.

In spite of the "emancipation" which they have experienced in the kibbutz, there is considerable sentiment among the women—much of it barely conscious or articulate—that they would prefer not to have been "emancipated." Almost every couple who has left the kibbutz has done so because of the unhappiness of the woman; and there seem to be a number of women who would like to leave, but remain because of their husbands. One vattika admitted that she has often thought of leaving Kiryat Yedidim, but has not done so because her husband could be happy nowhere else. Another vattika frequently expressed a desire to be a housewife, and to have a house and kitchen of her own. A female ideologue admitted that after a hard day's work even she has sometimes thought how much more pleasant life would be if she had her own home, took care of her own children, and did her own cooking. Finally, at a town meeting devoted to the "problem of the woman," one of the most respected women in Kiryat Yedidim—the wife of a leader of the kibbutz movement—publicly proclaimed that the kibbutz women had not achieved what they had originally hoped for; as for herself, after thirty years in Kiryat Yedidim she could pronounce her life a disappointment.

[3] Quoted by the Veteran Settler, *op. cit.*

These are strong words. What can account for such low morale? In the first place, many women report that they find kibbutz life physically too strenuous. The difficult physical environment, the absence of many simple comforts, the meager food, the long hours of work frequently under poor conditions, the poor sanitation, the crowding and the noise in public places—all have made life increasingly difficult. As a result, many women are physically tired. But this, however correct, is hardly the entire answer. Physical conditions are much better today than they were in the past when there was little complaint; and it is not sufficient to point out that the women are older and therefore find these conditions increasingly difficult, for the morale of the younger women is not always higher than that of the older women. It is worthwhile to note in this connection, however, that the female sabras do not find the physical conditions especially difficult.

A second source of the women's poor morale is that many women are dissatisfied with their economic roles. The Federation claims, with some justification, that the solution of the woman's economic problem would mean the end of her dissatisfaction. The woman must be "rooted in the life of the kibbutz economy," a recent convention of The Federation proclaimed. "Only this can restore her feeling of complete partnership and citizenship in the kibbutz."[4]

In view of its emphasis on the economic equality of the sexes, how is it that the women have not become "rooted" in the economic life of the kibbutz? It has already been noted that when the vattikim first settled on the land, there was no sexual division of labor. Women, like men, worked in the fields and drove tractors; men, like women, worked

4 *Ibid.*

in the kitchen and in the laundry. Men and women, it was assumed, were equal and could perform their jobs equally well. It was soon discovered, however, that men and women were not equal. For obvious biological reasons, women could not undertake many of the physical tasks of which the men were capable; tractor driving, harvesting, and other heavy labor proved too difficult for them. Moreover, women were compelled at times to take temporary leave from that physical labor of which they were capable. A pregnant woman, for example, could not work too long, even in the vegetable garden, and a nursing mother had to work near the Infants House in order to be able to feed her child. Hence, as the kibbutz grew older and the birth rate increased, more and more women were forced to leave the "productive" branches of the economy and enter its "service" branches. But as they left the "productive" branches, it was necessary that their places be filled, and they were filled by men. The result was that the women found themselves in the same jobs from which they were supposed to have been emancipated—cooking, cleaning, laundering, teaching, caring for children, etc. In short, they have not been freed from the "yoke" of domestic responsibilities, as the table on page 226 indicates.

An examination of these figures reveals the significant fact that of 113 physically able women, only 14—12 per cent—work permanently in any agricultural branch, while the overwhelming majority—88 per cent—work in service branches. These figures, properly interpreted, explain much of the discontent of the women. In the first place, although most of the women probably have no desire to return to heavy field work and are for the most part content to engage in the traditional "women's work," (with certain qualifica-

tions to be noted below) the early values of the youth movement are still operative to a considerable extent, so that
women develop a certain feeling of inferiority as a result
of working in these "menial" tasks. This feeling is exacerbated by the fact that the kibbutz values most highly those
branches which bring in the greatest economic returns. The
"service" branches in which the women are concentrated

Economic Distribution of Women in Kiryat Yedidim, 1951

Branch of Work	Number Permanently Assigned
Education	35
Youth leadership	2
Clinic	2
Office	2
Laundry and clothing storehouse	11
High school kitchen	1
Poultry	5
Vegetable garden	4
Landscaping	2
Orchards	2
Dairy	1
Total, regularly assigned	67
Not regularly assigned	46
TOTAL	113

bring in no returns; in fact, they are responsible for most
of the kibbutz expenditures. These two factors conspire to
reduce the women, in their own eyes, to second-class
citizens.

Secondly, many of the "service" jobs are boring, and the
working conditions are poor, so that workers in these

branches receive little job-satisfaction and, in some cases, hate their work. This is particularly true of work in the kitchen, which is so difficult that no woman will accept kitchen duty as a regular assignment, and it must be filled by a rotation system. Women view their kitchen assignments, usually of one or two years duration, as a period of slavery. They become nervous, irritable, and all but impossible to get along with. One woman said that if the conditions in the kitchen are not improved, there will be an explosion among the women, "which is the only thing that will wake up the men." She was referring to a major explosion, for there are plenty of minor ones. One afternoon, for example, as the tension in the kitchen mounted, one of the women ran from the kitchen in a burst of hysterical crying, and two hours later she was still crying in the shower rooms.

But it is not only in the kitchen that working conditions are poor. In one of the nurseries there was no running water and therefore no toilet facilities until quite recently, so that the nurses had to bring water from downstairs, and carry chamber pots up and down the steps each time they were needed. In another nursery, recently erected, no provision was made for a play yard—an oversight which made the work of the nurse very difficult as she could never leave the children alone. She was promised a play yard, but had to wait many months for its construction. The Infants House, to give still another example, did not have hot water facilities until three years prior to the author's study. Hence, the nurses had to carry hot water for the infants' baths from the kitchen, a distance of at least one city block.

These technical deficiencies could be remedied, of course, and this would improve the lot of the women considerably.

But there are at least two reasons why Kiryat Yedidim is slow in this regard. In the first place, as has been pointed out, the service branches do not bring an income to the kibbutz, and the men feel that if it is a question of a new tractor or a new dishwasher, of a new milking machine or plumbing in the nursery, the "economic" needs must take precedence over the "service" needs. The psychological adjustment of the women, the men agree, is very important, but there can be no adjustment of any kind unless the kibbutz remains solvent. Hence, the needs of the agricultural branches must be satisfied first. The women, moreover, find themselves in a vicious circle in this respect. The decisions regarding purchases and capital investments are usually made by the Economic Committee (*vaadat meshek*). But since few are employed in the agricultural branches, women are seldom represented on the Economic Committee. Hence, the technical requirements of their branches have no one to argue their case. They could, of course, bring their problems before a town meeting, but they seldom do so. In a society which emphasizes the importance of "productive" work, such problems as hot water, toilet facilities, or a new refrigerator seem "trivial," and they are consequently reluctant to speak out.

A second source of job dissatisfaction among the women is also revealed in the Table. According to this table, forty-six—41 per cent—of the women have no regular work assignments. This means that almost half the women do not choose their own work in accordance with their talents or interests, but are assigned to a job by the work-assignment chairmen. These jobs include working in the kitchens, cleaning latrines and shower rooms, assisting nurses and nursery teachers, ironing and sorting in the laundry room.

As unassigned workers, they may be constantly shifted from one job to another, depending upon the needs of a particular branch for additional labor. It is this group of women with no permanent work assignment, whose work is both difficult and boring, which provides one of the greatest threats to the future of the kibbutz. The woman co-chairman of the work-assignment committee, in commenting on this large percentage of women without regular work assignments, wrote that many women consequently receive "no satisfaction at all from their work, which has undesirable results, socially."[5]

Even if all the women were to receive regular work assignments, however, and even if the physical conditions of their work were to be improved, their work dissatisfaction would remain, for the "emancipation of women from the yoke of domestic service," has lead to a paradoxical result. It is true that the kibbutz social structure enables the woman to be free from the manifold activities of the ordinary housewife. But what has been substituted for the traditional routine of housekeeping, as the Table indicates, is more housekeeping—and a restricted and narrow kind of housekeeping at that. Instead of cooking and sewing and baking and cleaning and laundering and caring for children, the woman in Kiryat Yedidim cooks *or* sews *or* launders *or* takes care of children for eight hours a day. She has become a specialist in one aspect of housekeeping. But this new housekeeping is more boring and less rewarding than the traditional type. For, in the latter, the activities of the woman are diverse— her day at least has variety. Moreover, there is a certain degree of initiative and creativity involved in the traditional

[5] Taken from an article in the weekly newspaper of Kiryat Yedidim of August 24, 1951.

type of housekeeping. But in the kibbutz system, where domestic service has become specialized, a woman performs the same activity all day long in a job which often, because of its specialized nature, calls for little skill or initiative. It is small wonder, then, given this combination of low prestige, difficult working conditions, and monotony, that the chavera has found little happiness in her economic activities.

Even those women who enjoy their work show signs of insecurity in it. The women who work in the agricultural branches of the kibbutz, for example, seem to feel a constant need to "prove" that they are as capable and as efficient as the men. Working in the fields with both men and women for almost a year, the author observed that women often work longer than the men, remaining in the fields beyond quitting time; that women take fewer and shorter recesses than do the men; that they take off less time for breakfast or lunch; and that, in general, they work at a harder pace than do the men, who work more leisurely. Hence, even those women who have achieved economic "emancipation" are still not "emancipated" psychologically.

Those women who enjoy their "service" jobs, which include almost all the women in the educational system, also betray signs of insecurity in their work. This insecurity stems from three sources. In the first place, some nurses are not really convinced that the system of collective education is "right," and they therefore doubt the desirability and usefulness of their own work. In the majority of instances, the nurses for the various children's groups studied would indicate their own doubts and questions by asking us for our impressions. Is the system really good? Are the children normal? Are they too aggressive? Is the incidence of enuresis too high? Do the children feel secure?—and a host of other questions that are of deep concern to them. Secondly, they feel insecure about the children's love. Being relieved from the care of their own children, they seem somehow to have a great need to be loved by the children in their charge. The children's love, moreover, is proof that they are doing a good job. But they are never quite sure that they really are loved. Hence, many of them emphasize how much more they have accomplished with the children in their charge than other nurses could have accomplished; or how much the children love them, even more than they love their own parents; or how much the children miss them when they are separated. Finally, the nurses are insecure in their relations with the parents. They are sensitive to the opinions of the parents concerning their work—so much so that a nurse may even reject an educational technique that she considers to be psychologically sound, if parents disapprove. One nurse, for example, after an extended study of nursery school techniques, decided to apply some of her newly acquired theories to her own group of children. When the children did not want to eat, she did not pressure them to do so, and their remaining food was returned to the kitchen. Soon the rumor began to spread that the children did not like her, "for they did not eat." She became extremely anxious about this criticism and returned to the previous technique of trying to compel the children to eat.[6]

The nurses are conscious of the serious responsibility involved in rearing eight or sixteen children, and frequently wonder if they are carrying out this responsibility well. If a

[6] This example illustrates, equally well, the conservatism of the kibbutz—its resistance to change—as well as the great pressure which the group can unwittingly exert on the individual. It should be noted that this incident occurred several years prior to the author's study, and that children are no longer pressured to eat all their food.

nurse feels that she is "slipping" or that the parents disapprove of her work, she has no alternative but to resign, however much she may love her work. In the course of this
study, three nurses resigned from their jobs for these reasons.

There are two other roles, in addition to the economic
one, in which the woman feels frustrated and insecure—her
maternal and sexual roles. It is safe to state—what the kibbutz educational leaders are aware of—that many mothers
have not reconciled themselves to the system of collective
education and the resultant separation from their children.
This separation is a profoundly frustrating experience for
many of the mothers, for it is viewed by them as another
deprivation of their feminine prerogatives. Particularly difficult is the separation from their children at night, and the
impossibility of seeing them first thing in the morning. One
mother, although an activist and a feminist, complained bitterly about the fact that the kibbutz is officially opposed to
the parents' putting their children to bed.

Life in the kibbutz is difficult. The showers and toilets we are
forced to use are enough to warrant such a statement. But to
that must be added the noisy and hurried dining room, the
hard work day, the lack of real recreation. We really don't
have much, and even for books we must wait in line. All we
have left is our children, and we don't even have them, for they
are in the children's house. And now they even took *hashkava*
(putting the children to bed) away from us. Why? The "experts" say that the parents spoil them when they put them to
bed. This may be true, but you have to think of the parents
sometimes, too, and not always of the children.

Equally frustrating for many mothers is the fact that they
cannot see their children when the latter first awaken in the
morning, and many resent the fact that the nurses, and not
they, have this privilege. One mother said that she would

"put up with anything," if she could have that privilege. This woman, a kibbutz intellectual, offered a solution to this problem. If a system were to be devised whereby each mother would have her children with her for a few days each year—in which she could be with them the entire day, put them to bed at night, and greet them first thing in the morning then, she feels, this frustration would be considerably attenuated, if not eliminated. The intensity of this frustration is best illustrated by a vattika who was in charge of her grandchild while his parents were on vacation. It happened that all the children in her grandson's group were ill at this time, so that he had to sleep in her room. When asked how she enjoyed this unique experience, she replied that she had not slept the entire night, for she lay awake thinking how thrilled she would be the next morning to awaken and find her grandchild there with her. The frustration of deepseated maternal feelings, it may be concluded, is another source of the "problem of the woman."[7]

Finally, mention must be made of the insecurity that women, and particularly middle-aged women, have concerning their sexual role. Climate and hard labor contribute to a more rapid aging of kibbutz women than is the case, let us say, in middle-class urban American women. The women feel keenly this aging process; for the realization that they are losing their sexual attractiveness is highly threatening, as it is in any Western society. But it is particularly threatening in the kibbutz, where the marriage bond is based only on love, so that a union does not have to be continued because of the many extraneous factors

[7] At least for those mothers who were not born and/or raised in Kiryat Yedidim—that is, those mothers who themselves are not a product of a system of collective education; for there is evidence that the majority of sabra mothers do not share this feeling of frustration.

that conspire to perpetuate a marriage in our society after love has passed. Charming and still physically attractive middle-aged women may be heard to refer, in many different ways and on different occasions, to their age and to their loss of beauty. One evening, for example, when the author was sitting in the dining room with a very attractive and young looking middle-aged woman, with whose husband the author's wife was sitting, another woman came by and jocularly remarked that we had all made a good exchange. The author agreed, but his companion remarked that it was a good exchange for everyone but the author. Her husband, she said, had received a young woman; the author's wife, an older man; and she, a young man. But the author, she said, was "stuck with an old woman."

It is this insecurity that has probably led the older women to a renewed interest in clothes. In the past, women were content to wear shorts, slacks, or skirts and blouses. Indeed, they insisted on it. Today, however, they insist on wearing dresses; and one of the major tension spots in the kibbutz, as has been observed, is the women's clothing store and sewing room, where women complain that they have not received an equitable share—either quantitatively or qualitatively—of the dress allowance. Moreover, since women receive only one good dress every other year, they resent those women who wear elaborate or stylish dresses, or who display a wide and varied wardrobe. An American visitor, for example, was sharply criticized for wearing a different dress every evening since, it was pointed out, the average chavera had only two or three changes. The desire to remain young in appearance has led some women to use a dye to conceal their grey hairs; some have even advocated the use of cosmetics—a suggestion unheard of thirty years ago.

It should be finally noted, as a backdrop to the foregoing discussion, that the women do not have, on the whole, either the political consciousness or the intellectual interests of the men. There are intellectuals among the women, to be sure, and some women are intensely political. But these are few and they are found, for the most part, only among the vattikot—the first settlers of the kibbutz. The majority cannot justify their frustrations in terms of some larger intellectual or political meaning, nor can they obtain satisfactions from intellectual or political activities. For them there remain only gossip and children for their leisure activities, both of which accentuate their frustrations: children, because the women feel that they see too little of them, and gossip, because it only reinforces already critical attitudes.

All these factors have produced the "problem of the woman." And the "problem of the woman," in turn, is most responsible for much of the crisis in the kibbutz, at least those aspects which involve reluctance of members to assume positions of responsibility, withdrawal from group to private experiences, the increase in private property, and the heightening of group tension. Because they are unhappy in their roles, the women have no desire to assume social responsibility; because, consequently, they wish to find their happiness in their private lives, they often resent the time which their spouses devote to these activities. Since they are insecure in their sexual roles, they feel a need for more and nicer clothes; and since the kibbutz cannot satisfy this demand, they have fewer and fewer compunctions about acquiring them on their own initiative. Finally, since they feel frustrated in so many roles—maternal, sexual, and economic—they are responsible for much of the tension in the kibbutz.

Social Myth and Disillusionment

There is a third internal reason for the crisis in Kiryat Yedidim: a spirit of disillusionment which seems to have entered kibbutz life. One senses from conversations, and even hears explicitly, that the chaverim feel that they have not achieved what they had hoped. Some seem to feel that all their struggles have not been worthwhile, that their sacrifices have been in vain. This disillusionment is expressed with respect to the three focal concepts in their *weltanschauung:* Zionism, socialism, and Man; and it may be traced to the mythos of that *weltanschauung.*

First, there is disillusionment about the Zionist ideal— the Jewish State and the Jewish People. Somehow the achievement of this ideal has not proved to be the great event which they had anticipated. And if the Zionist goal is seen to lack greatness, how can one remain enthusiastic about one of its means, the kibbutz? This disillusionment is expressed by many vattikim, although it is frequently disguised. The following sentiments expressed by a vattika while reminiscing about her life in Palestine are fairly typical:

In the past, the country was different. The spirit of *chalutziut* (pioneership) was felt every place. We did not think that the country would become what it is now. It is not the fulfillment of our dreams. Somehow we had hoped for something different . . . When we came here we made great sacrifices, because we had great ideals, and now it may all be destroyed. The new immigration wants to live in the cities, they want to continue to lead the same ugly lives they lived in the Diaspora. Oh, the Jews are a difficult people, a very difficult people . . . The other day we received new furniture for our new room, and I told my friends that I would rather not take it. I would rather go back to the days of tents and straw beds, because then life had a purpose. Now, the spirit of those days is gone.

More important, however, is the disillusionment which many feel about their new society—the kibbutz. This disillusionment may be inferred, in the first place, from the insecurity which many chaverim manifest concerning the achievements of the kibbutz. One is constantly asked, for example, how it is possible to return to America after having lived in Israel and, more particularly, in the kibbutz. Every return seems to be interpreted by the chaverim as a rejection which constitutes a threat to their own security and weakens their confidence in their creation. Chaverim constantly ask what one thinks about this or that aspect of kibbutz living, and it soon becomes evident that what they want is not candid opinion, but praise. This may be recognized as a typical insecurity pattern, in which one's own lack of confidence in the worth of what he has is bolstered by the reassurance of others. This feeling of insecurity is most noticeable, however, in the refrain, "I don't think we have anything to be ashamed about," that frequently follows a chaver's own evaluation of the kibbutz school system, its children, its cultural program, and other aspects of its society and culture.

Finally, there is the disillusionment concerning the type of human being that the kibbutz has produced—or rather, not produced. The kibbutz, it will be remembered, was originally conceived as a means to an end—the creation of the new man. Instead of the selfish, aggressive personality created by urban capitalism, there would emerge, as a result of the new social order, a kindly, altruistic personality. This end has not been achieved. The chaverim, as a group, represent the range of personality types found in any society. But, in terms of kibbutz aspirations, this is not sufficient. As one chaver, a kibbutz leader, put it:

When we first came here, we all came from cities, and we left the cities with the idea of founding a simple society, where we could create real human beings. Somehow we have fallen from that ideal. At first we did have that type of society, but not any longer. And above all, we have not succeeded in discovering Man (*limtzo et ha-adam*). What we were really looking for was Man.

But if the new society has not succeeded in creating the new Man, if people in the kibbutz are little different from people in other types of society, why continue to lead the morally rigorous life demanded by the kibbutz? If the means do not achieve the desired end, why perpetuate the means?

The kind of disillusionment described here is of a special nature. Few people and fewer societies ever achieve their ultimate goals, and yet they do not succumb to disillusionment. Moreover few societies have attained the high quality of ethical living achieved by the kibbutz. Disillusionment is probably induced by a great discrepancy between achievement and aspiration levels, a state of affairs which often results from the belief in near-utopian ideals and in the belief that a certain technique constitutes a sufficient means for the attainment of the ideals. This seems to apply to the disillusionment of the chaverim, for their disillusionment results from the discrepancy between the real and the ideal kibbutz. The ideal kibbutz is compounded of three images: the romantic vision of the Youth Movement with its promise of an ideal society if man could only free himself from the bonds of urban artificiality; the "scientific" predictions of

Marxism, according to which human brotherhood could be attained if capitalist exploitation were abolished; and the brief, but ecstatic experience in Nevei Gila[8] in which an ideal society and an ideal humanity were, in fact, momentarily attained. The ideal kibbutz, in short, is an "organic community" in which the attainment of social justice, economic equality, and individual freedom has produced a group without tensions. It is a brotherhood of men who love rather than hate, who are cooperative rather than competitive, who are altruistic rather than selfish. The ideal kibbutz is a New Society, which has created a New Man.

That such a goal is ever capable of achievement is, at best, dubious. To believe that it is capable of achievement within one generation is an obviously utopian belief, provided by a mythos which had succeeded in capturing the emotional and moral zeal of idealistic adolescents. But this utopian vision of society and of man has refused to die. It has, on the contrary, remained an integral part of kibbutz aspirations, constituting its most important self-image. Compared with this myth, any reality would be found wanting.

[8] See above, pp. 53–55.

CHAPTER 8

The representatives of a given order will label as utopian all conceptions of existence which *from their point of view* can in principle never be realized ... This reluctance to transcend the *status quo* tends towards the view of regarding something that is unrealizable merely in the given order as completely unrealizable in any order, so that by obscuring these distinctions one can suppress the validity of the claims of the relative utopia. By calling everything utopian that goes beyond the present existing order, one sets at rest the anxiety that might arise from the relative utopias that are realizable in another order.

Karl Mannheim, *Ideology and Utopia*

EPILOGUE

THE ROLE played by conflict and competition in both the personality and social dynamics of the West has been of such paramount importance that thinkers as diverse as Augustine and Freud have postulated aggression as an innate, universal human drive. Although it is extraordinarily difficult to put this hypothesis to the acid test of scientific investigation, anthropologists have long been suspicious of propositions—such as this aggression hypothesis—which seek to find the wellsprings of social motives in the organism, or which assign a causative role to biology in the ordering of man's social structures. The notorious diversity of human behavior and of social forms, which has been so richly documented in the rapidly growing literature of ethnography, is sufficient evidence, anthropologists believe, for the validity of their suspicions. For, if all human beings are members of the same biological species, then presumably differences in behavior discovered by cross-cultural research are to be ascribed to differential learning contexts, rather than to different biological structures; and since societies have been recorded which emphasize cooperation and mutual aid rather than competition and conflict, it follows that aggression is a learned rather than an innate drive. Hence, statements which assert the universality of aggression are, accordingly, false, for they are derived from a culture-bound assumption concerning the innateness of aggression.

Other anthropologists are not so confident about the meaning of the ethnographic evidence. It is true that many societies, such as the Ifaluk or the Pueblo Indians, exhibit little if any aggressive behavior within their social structures. But, it is proper to ask, does this mean that there are no manifestations of aggression in other aspects of their cultural behavior—in religion, for example—or that there are no expressions of aggression in their non-institutionalized interpersonal relations? And even if the latter question be answered in the negative, still another problem must be confronted: does the absence of overt aggressive behavior mean an absence of covert aggressive drive, a drive which may be repressed but which finds expression in some disguised form or in fantasy-aggression? The record reveals that many themes in the folklore, and many aspects of the interpersonal relations, of the peace-loving Zuni, for example, are characterized by aggression; while the highly cooperative Ifaluk believe in, and exorcise, malevolent ghosts.

If we may generalize from these two examples, we may say that it is possible for societies to evolve social structures which either preclude or minimize the expression of aggression, but that it is impossible for societies to evolve personality structures from which the aggression drive is absent; so that some expression of aggression will be found in any society.

This statement need occasion no surprise. It is probably impossible for any society to assure its members a completely non-frustrating existence. In the process of growing up, to take but one example, it is inevitable that children's needs be frustrated, regardless of the socialization techniques employed to ensure impulse control. If only from this one source of frustration, everyone will develop some degree of aggression. But the systematic frustrations imposed by society because of the necessity for some degree of social control, are not the only sources of social frustration. Disappointments, privations, failures, rejections—these characterize the human situation everywhere; and these and other such experiences constitute frustrating situations for members of any society, however differentially they may be conceived, and regardless of their differences in magnitude from society to society.

Nor is social life—either through its social structure, the vagaries of one's life fate, or the character of interpersonal relations—the only source of frustration. Nature, expressing herself in illness, drought, flood, and death, is a frustrating agency par excellence. Hence it seems a safe guess that the aggression drive is universal, however much its expression may be muted within the social structures of certain societies; and one need not assume its innateness in order to account for its universality.

But only an unredeemed romantic would have assumed in the first place that aggression could be absent from social life. And only a person with a rigid defense against his own imperious and guilt arousing drives could have believed it possible for the members of any community to love each other unqualifiedly. What is possible—and what in fact we do find—is that a society's culture be so structured as to elicit a minimum of aggression drive from its members, that its social organization be so ordered as to demand little aggression in the motivational system of its members to ensure its successful functioning, and that its cultural heritage channel the existing aggression into socially sanctioned activities that neither disrupt the affiliative character of interpersonal relations in the society nor threaten the psychological integration of its component members.

Kiryat Yedidim has attempted to achieve both the possible and, if the author is correct in his previous statements, the impossible. The "primitivistic" and romantic notions of the early Youth Movement, and the interlude of brotherly love that characterized its experiences in Nevei Gila, imbued the vattikim with the conviction that it was possible to create a new Man if only certain impediments of the old order were removed. And their new culture—the kibbutz —was to order social life in such a way as to guarantee the implementation of that early vision and perpetuate the character of those early experiences. One of the reasons for the present crisis in Kiryat Yedidim, as we have tried to show, is that it has not been entirely successful in achieving this aim, so that the chaverim have developed a vague feeling of disillusionment with their accomplishment—the kibbutz.

Instead of locating the failure to attain their aim in its essentially utopian, and therefore unattainable, character, however, they have attributed the failure to external factors, and have been led thereby to dissipate much of their energies in politics.[1]

Although it may have fallen short of its utopian vision of Man, Kiryat Yedidim need not be disillusioned with the social edifice which it has erected. On the contrary, if a valid measure of the successful functioning of a group is the degree to which its behavior corresponds to its values, Kiryat Yedidim can be justly proud of its accomplishment. For the kibbutz *is* characterized by a high degree of equality, freedom, self-labor, communal ownership, and so on. The ideal of brotherly love, to be sure, has been the most difficult to achieve, and it is marked by the least success. Rivalry, envy, jealousy, gossip, and backbiting are probably as prevalent in Kiryat Yedidim as in other communities. But though it is impossible, in the author's opinion, to remove these characteristics from any society, Kiryat Yedidim does not constitute a crucial test for measuring the degree to which a cooperative culture can succeed in reducing their expression. There have been important obstacles, essentially irrelevant to the cooperative culture of the kibbutz, which have

[1] It is this latter characteristic, as has already been noted, which distinguishes Kiryat Yedidim and The Federation from many other kibbutzim. None of the other federations shares either the Marxist orientation of The Federation or its principle of political discipline. This orientation, paradoxically enough, stems from its opposition to the "materialistic" values of Western culture, and from its dedication to the principles of freedom and brotherhood. But in its relative isolation from the Western liberal tradition, The Federation succumbed to the humanitarian rhetoric of Marxist propaganda and has since persisted in its distorted perception of the Soviet Union. Regardless of the reasons, however, The Federation has remained pro-Soviet and, therefore, in serious conflict with other kibbutz federations.

prevented the attainment of a greater degree of brotherhood in Kiryat Yedidim; and, although these obstacles already have been noted, it may be useful to emphasize some of them within the present context.

It should be observed in the first place that the kibbutz experiment has taken place under highly adverse external conditions, physical as well as social. The malarial swampland on which the vattikim chose to settle was not a propitious location either for village life or for agriculture, however important it may have been for the strategy of Zionist settlement. The hardships involved in making this land both habitable and economically profitable have taken their toll on both the stamina and health of the chaverim. Malaria, arthritis, and physical fatigue do not contribute to the forming of amiable, kindly personalities. And, though they have succeeded in creating fertile fields and a pleasant village, the chaverim still suffer material hardships. Even today, they have only inadequate facilities to cope with either of their climatic extremes, and moods and tempers fluctuate perceptibly with environmental changes.

But it is not only the physical environment that causes material hardships. The absence of an abundant and diversified diet, the overcrowded and noisy dining room, the din and dinginess of the shower rooms, the long distance to the overused and frequently inefficient toilets—malodorous in summer and muddy in winter—all take heavy psychological tolls. Add to these the almost constant pressure of an acute labor shortage, and the inevitable strains induced by the consequent long work week and not infrequent labor drafts, and it may not be remiss to suggest that though material progress may not be a necessary condition for greater brotherhood in the kibbutz, it would surely serve to alleviate many of the tensions which currently stand in its way. It will be of some importance to observe in this regard whether the new housing project for the vattikim, with its indoor plumbing, greater space, and more comforts, will contribute to the lessening of tension.

Social, no less than physical, conditions have contributed to the hardships encountered by the kibbutz and, hence, to the difficulty of attaining greater brotherhood. Kiryat Yedidim, like other kibbutzim (and indeed the entire country), has labored under almost incessant social pressures and tensions from its very inception. A mere enumeration of some of these pressures will suffice to indicate their order of magnitude: Arab marauders, the Arab riots of 1929 and 1937, the struggle against the British for a more liberal immigration and land settlement policy, World War II (with Rommel at their back door), the War for Independence, the many border "incidents" since the War, the internal struggles among competing political factions, the taxing of their strained facilities by the acceptance of European (and recently, Oriental) youth groups for both training and rehabilitation—these and more have kept the chaverim in a constant state of tension. Never have they known the luxury of a prolonged period of relative rest and quiet, a necessary condition for both biological and psychological homeostasis.

All the tensions enumerated above, tensions which stem from the necessities of their Zionist commitments or from the exigencies of pioneer life—both irrelevant to the cooperative social structure of the kibbutz—have been accentuated by a dominant aspect of the culture of Kiryat Yedidim —its emphasis on "group dynamics." This emphasis is an effective obstacle to the deep-seated need of many chaverim for privacy. It is all but impossible for the average chaver to enjoy more than a few moments of solitude; even the privacy which most people enjoy at meals or in the shower is impossible. As some chaverim observed, it is entirely possible to cooperate with other people even when one does not love them; but unless one loves them, it is all but impossible to be in constant interaction with them. And it is this impossibility which the kibbutz in effect imposes on its members by its value of group dynamics and its consequent institutions of communal living.

In a year at Kiryat Yedidim, the author never heard a member complain that he was unhappy because the group owned his house, his tools, or his land. Nor did anyone express resentment over the fact that his contribution to the economic welfare of the kibbutz was greater than his returns, since he was a more efficient worker or had fewer children than another. But he frequently heard complaints about the noise and crowdedness of kibbutz communal institutions, the absence of privacy, and the constant exposure to the public eye. The chaverim are willing to share property and skills, but many of them resent the sharing of experiences; and this resentment has been a major source of tension in the kibbutz and an obstacle to brotherhood.

A third obstacle which Kiryat Yedidim has had to meet is the influence of the "world" and its values, an obstacle which has become even more formidable since the establishment of the State. The reference group for the chaverim, to be sure, is the socialist world, including the other kibbutzim; relative to the latter groups their own deprivations have been entirely normal. Nevertheless, the chaverim are not isolated from the "world," nor impervious to its influence. Their contact with, or knowledge of, others who enjoy a higher standard of living, have a greater measure of privacy, whose lives are not bound by decisions of a group, has introduced an element of dissatisfaction into their lives, hence an element of strain into their social system. The chaverim have discovered that they, too, would like to have refrigerators, easy chairs, attractive clothes, and the like; and, if the kibbutz is unwilling to sanction these "luxuries," some of them are willing to act contrary to its injunctions. But violations of the group's norms induce guilt feelings in the violators, conflict between them and the non-violators, and envy of the former by the latter. Such a state of affairs is hardly conducive to brotherly-love.[2]

This disruptive influence of the "world" is not too significant, however, unless it be related to yet another obstacle with which Kiryat Yedidim has been confronted: the early background of its adult members. Kiryat Yedidim has been in existence for but a brief generation; its founders are removed by only a few years from the non-kibbutz culture in which they had spent their formative periods. Private property, the traditional Western family, parental rearing of children, white-collar labor and entrepreneurship—these were the accepted and "natural" values of their early milieu. Only by rebelling against these acquired values were they able to sever their physical roots, migrate to Palestine, and create a culture whose values in many—but not in all— respects were contrary to their "natural" values.

If some of the hypotheses of both psychoanalytic and learning theory—the tenacious influence of early experiences stressed in the former theory, and the importance of

[2] The Federation is aware of the obstacle imposed by the outside world when it asserts that it is difficult, if not impossible, to build an "island of socialism within a sea of capitalism." But its ideology attributes this difficulty to the "hostility" of the environment, rather than to its lure which the author considers to be the more formidable obstacle.

reinforcement in the latter—are even partially correct, it would be naïve to assume that the chaverim would have discarded these early values easily. They have not. For some it is "collective education" which has been most difficult to accept; for others the absence of "comforts"; for still others it is the absence of private property; for a smaller number, all three. In any event the influence of the "world," whose values correspond with those values which the chaverim had acquired early in life, serves as a constant stimulus to "regress" to those early values.

If it be true that the present "crisis" in the kibbutz represents a conflict between values acquired earlier and those acquired later in the lives of the chaverim, it would be unwarranted to judge the success of the kibbutz, in either its cooperative or communal dimensions, by the behavior of the adult generation. The measure of its success is rather to be found in the behavior of those who were born and reared in it, those for whom its values presumably are as "natural" as were the contrary values for the parents. These individuals constituted the primary subjects of our study, and they will be described in a second volume to be published on Kiryat Yedidim. Since the data on the sabras is only now in process of analysis, however, little of an empirical nature can be offered at this time. Certain theoretical considerations, as well as some impressions of the author, may be worth considering, however.

On the positive side, it has been noted in various sections of this monograph that the sabras seem to accept as "natural," hence as desirable, certain aspects of kibbutz culture which some of their elders have never entirely accepted. With one doubtful exception, the sabras, for example, view "collective education" as the only sensible way to rear children; and the females betray few of the gnawing doubts that continue, even after thirty years, to plague some of their mothers. The sabras, moreover, seem to accept the public ownership of property as a social "given," much as they accept the climate about them as a physical "given." Nor have they displayed a strong tendency to accumulate private property. On the contrary, it is from this group that the opposition to the introduction of private property has been most articulate.

The survival of a culture depends, ultimately, upon the motivational system of the members of its society; it is not sufficient that they cognitively accept its values. Unless they possess those psychological characteristics which, at the very least, are consistent with that society's cultural characteristics, the perpetuation of the culture—within a democratic framework at any rate—is doubtful. Although an analysis of sabra personality structure has not yet been undertaken, it may be observed at this time that certain aspects of sabra character are entirely consistent with kibbutz culture so that, presumably, they would be motivated to perpetuate it.

Among the many psychological characteristics which are probably necessary for the survival of kibbutz culture the following are surely among the most important: identification with the group, a sense of security within the group, an absence of intense acquisitive drives, the absence of intense success strivings, a willingness to assume social responsibilities. There is some evidence to indicate that the sabras possess these characteristics to a high degree.[3]

[3] The evidence, which consists of responses to the Bavelas Moral Ideology Test and the Stewart Emotional Response Test, is summarized in Spiro, "Education in a Collective Settlement in Israel."

On the negative side, two questions might be raised without at this time attempting to answer them. First, is it possible to maintain a kibbutz, and not simply a collective farm, without the emotional-ethical dynamic that motivated the original founders? What happens to the original vision of the kibbutz when, to put it in Weber's terms, the "routinization of charisma" sets in? a process which seems to be inevitable in the natural history of any social group. The sabras do not have the same problems with which their parents struggled, and it is unlikely that they are the idealistic rebels that their parents were. The sabras, unlike their parents, did not forge the ideals of a revolution, ideals which were acquired only through long and painful struggles with parents and self, with nature and society. They have acquired them, instead, by the ordinary and relatively passive ways in which the values of any community are acquired by its children. We are, in short, raising a simple but fundamental question: Will Kiryat Yedidim remain a kibbutz with all the motivational overtones which this term implies, when, to use the terms of Karl Mannheim, the "utopia" of the fathers has become the "ideology" of the sons?

The second question which has to be raised is to what extent, having received an academic rather than a vocational education, and having been inculcated with a respect and an appreciation for science and art, the sabras will remain content to live their lives in a small Israeli village? Is it possible for the lure of the "world" with its laboratories and lecture halls, opera houses and art museums, to constitute a potent force in the disintegration of the kibbutz, even though the sabras have no doubts concerning the desirability of public ownership, social equality, and "collective education"?

Until the year in which our field work was conducted,

the "lure" of the outside world had not been sufficiently strong to threaten the survival of the kibbutz. In its entire history not one person who had been born and raised in Kiryat Yedidim had left it. Nor is this a function of sabra ignorance concerning the outside world. The sabras have had many opportunities to learn of non-kibbutz life in books and movies, and in their many visits to the cities. Some have lived in a city for a year or two after graduating from high school; still others have had the experience of traveling abroad. Nevertheless, every child of Kiryat Yedidim has chosen to remain within it upon becoming an adult.

On the other hand, should the artistic and intellectual values which Kiryat Yedidim has attempted to inculcate in its children, with such great expenditures of energy and money, not "take"; if books and concerts and art exhibits did not capture the imagination of the sabras, Kiryat Yedidim could remain a village of cooperative farmers, although it would cease to be a kibbutz.

In short, if the sabras are to demonstrate the staying power of the kibbutz, they must accept the ethical values of Kiryat Yedidim, be motivated to implement these values within its traditional institutional structure, and be attracted to the scientific and artistic values of the "world" without, thereby, becoming discontent with their village life.

This, too, is the dream of their fathers, who have, as it were, wagered their past on their children's future. The ethnographer will do well to study this dream in detail. For though ethnography deals with fact rather than fantasy, the type of fantasy found in a given society may be its most important fact. Kiryat Yedidim came into being on the basis of one dream; its future may depend upon the realization of another.

CHAPTER 9

POSTSCRIPT:
THE KIBBUTZ IN 1970

LESLIE Y. RABKIN
AND MELFORD E. SPIRO

T HE STUDY OF Kiryat Yedidim, on which this book is based, was conducted in 1950–51 by Melford and Audrey Spiro. Since that time, many changes have occurred in the kibbutz, some of which were recorded in the new preface to the 1963 edition. This, however, is not only a cursory treatment, but it is based on a brief visit to Kiryat Yedidim in 1962. In the meantime, Leslie and Karen Rabkin have spent one-and-a-half years in the kibbutz (January 1967-July 1968) and have been in frequent contact with the kibbutz since that time. It was deemed desirable that the present volume be brought up to date on the basis of their findings. The data found in this chapter were supplied by Leslie Rabkin, in response to a set of questions proposed by Melford Spiro. The text represents their joint effort.

Introduction

The Six Day War (1967) marked a turning point in kibbutz history, just as it did in Israeli society at large. As a galvanizer and crystallizer of the changes long pressing for expression in the kibbutz, this dramatic event surpasses even the ideological split of the 1940's. This was the war fought by the second generation, and they emerged from the six days of blood and sand to find the verities and mythologies of the past dissolved into dust. Unformulated and vague as their desires remain, the concerns and experiences of this younger generation are seeking outlets in every realm of kibbutz life. Their groping toward new beliefs, new encounters with self and others, has a tense ambivalence about it. Their feelings echo Voltaire's epigram: "One owes respect to the living; but to the dead one owes nothing but the truth."

The "living," in the kibbutz context, refers, of course, to the parental generation, the promulgators of the ideology which has so long circumscribed their life and learning. The "dead" are the comrades who fell in battle, nearly 200 of whom (more than a quarter of the total) were members of kibbutzim. Kiryat Yedidim lost five of its young men in the war and several since. It is little wonder that since the war sabras evince not so much a concern with ideology, or long-range schemes, or any clear critique of kibbutz education, or the kibbutz way of life, but an introspectiveness emerging out of the shock of war. As one twenty-one year old put it: "We went through a lot of years in a few days. We grew up fast. We still can carry on, but not so much as children anymore." There was, in his musing, as in that of the others, a pervasive feeling of having lost childhood in an apocalyptic moment.

So long fed on the exploits of the parental generation— as chalutzim, as the freedom fighters of 1948, and as the heroes of Sinai—suddenly they found themselves fighting in *their* war and achieving glories to match those so long held up to them as exemplars. They were the heroes of this battle, their blood was soaked into the stones of Jerusalem, they had proved themselves as fighters. The trauma liberated the youth from the tensions generated by the older generation's sense of disappointment in them. (Cf. pp. 247-52.)

The kibbutz, as observed in January 1967, had an air of listlessness and drift. This reflected the more pervasive sense of doubt which marked the larger Israeli society, suffering under a severe economic recession after a period of over-expansion and overspending. More than ten years of relative peace since the 1956 Sinai Campaign appeared to have sapped the reserves of pioneering spirit, and the country seemed uncertain about its goals. Much of the discontent was focused on the younger generation, characterized by some as the "discotheque generation," interested primarily in pleasure-seeking and self-interest.

The kibbutz situation was similar, if less dramatic. A noticeable feeling of anomie was apparent among the founding generation which, gathering force over time, seemed to be compounded of a number of factors. These included the natural processes of aging, with the concomitant weakening of physical power; the loss (with the economically-determined severe cutback in work in the factory) of a sense of productivity; an emotional vacuum brought on by their own waning interest in ideological concerns; and the frustrations wrought by a continuing and seemingly endless sense of being outsiders to the real seats of (governmental) power. These frustrations were often projected onto the younger generation who were felt to be ungrateful recipients of a glorious tradition, who lived in the kibbutz "because they were born there," not out of ideological conviction.

Much of this was changed by the Six Day War. But the war did not change everything, nor are all kibbutz changes responsive to the war alone. In addition, other historical events, such as the Sinai Campaign, have also left their impact on the kibbutz. Moreover, events internal to the kibbutz have also had their effect. Thus, the normalization of living, rise in living standards, new responsibilities, the shock waves of technological innovation, the "sudden" appearance of a generation of old people, the growth in kibbutz size and complexity, the downgrading of the mythical kibbutznik, the opening outward of kibbutz society, the enhanced educational level, the institutionalization of privacy—these and others have all had their impact.

Having pointed to some of the stimuli for change that have occurred in Kiryat Yedidim in the past twenty years, we can now turn to an examination of the changes themselves—without, however, losing sight of the equally important continuities.

Change and Continuity in Ideology

JUDAISM. There is no sign, in Kiryat Yedidim, of a changing attitude to traditional Jewish culture. Even among the old, where one might have expected a return to a concern with their original world, one hears little—positive or negative—about Judaism. Among the sabras, too, there is no sign of a turn to religion. On the contrary, the attitudes of twenty years ago are still extant. Thus, one can still hear the usual derisive remarks when a bearded, kaftan-wearing, orthodox Jew appears on a movie screen.

Typical is the remark of a sabra to the prayer service at the wailing wall. "Feh! What are they doing here! It's so primitive, idol worship. Why do they keep the women on one side? Why do you want to put that stuff [*phylacteries*] on?" In general, the attitude toward such symbols of orthodox Judaism ranges from outright antipathy to indifference. As in the past, however, there remains a grudging admiration for religious kibbutzniks. They are seen as good, even dedicated, workers who happen to have an irrational involvement with religion. In addition the sabras feel a bit awed by their dedication to learning (even if it is religious learning): they even get up an hour early to study Bible!

There is, of course, a great searching going on among all Israeli youth, no less so among kibbutz youth, about the direction in which they are headed, but thus far at least it has not taken a religious form. On the other hand, there is a desire on the part of some young people for the introduction of traditional symbols. Some, for example, would like to more meaningfully separate the Sabbath eve from the rest of the week, even by the lighting of candles. After all, one of them said, "It *is* a special time—not religious only—and it should be something special."

ZIONISM. Although the sabras feel an intense identification with their country, their identification has little to do with Zionist ideology. It is rooted, rather, in a feel for place, their army experience, and an ambivalent defense of their world against the perceived machinations and ruthlessness of the rest of the world. Ambivalent because the outside world still has its powerful allure. And what better way is there to reduce dissonance than to inflate the value

of one's own culture? Nationalism is very much alive, of
course, but it is related more to security than to ideology.

Sabras see diaspora Jews as strangers—as indeed they are.
To be sure, they see the tie between Israeli and non-Israeli
Jews which is implicit in the shared ethnic label, but this
has little power in the face of the differences between them
which they see in almost every aspect of life. Nor do
sabras talk very much about Zionist notions, other than in
a general, semi-mocking way. Even those who go abroad
as Zionist emissaries don't seem to be fired with abstract
ideology. Rather, they enjoy training young people for a
life of agriculture and bringing a work ethic to (what they
initially perceive to be) spoiled children, and providing
them with an aura of Israeli (not Jewish) culture. They
want the young people whom they train to go and work
in Israel and to become Israelis. They know the country
needs new hands, and although they place no particular
value on immigration, they prefer that the immigrants
consist of their own trainees rather than—or at least in
addition to—the "unselected" immigrants who clog the
cities. For some, bringing someone to Israel also provides
personal satisfaction as well as a vindication of their way
of life.

As in so many other things the sabra attitude toward
Zionism is the consequence of "normalization." The idea
of Zionism implies an alternative to it. For the normalized
sabra, the goals of Zionism are the realities of his life.
Therefore, for him, Zionism is a dead issue.

MARXISM AND THE SOVIET ORIENTATION. The issue of
Communism, of the Soviet Union as the mentor of the new
society, of world revolution—these also are dead issues,

but for different reasons. As late as June 1967, however, there were still some vattikim who maintained a lingering attachment to the Soviet Union. This attachment was compounded of three things: their continuing fascination with Marxist philosophy, their memory of the role that Russia had played in helping to create the State of Israel, and sentimental visions based on the original promise of the Russian Revolution.

The reaction of these vattikim to the "revelation" of the true nature of Soviet policy in regard to the Middle East and the Jews of Russia had a faintly tragi-comic aspect. At one impassioned postwar kibbutz meeting, for example, a vattika vigorously protested that she would never again sing the Internationale, and that the red flag (representing worker solidarity) should never again be unfurled at kibbutz celebrations. (The Internationale was played at the 1968 Independence Day celebration, although most of the participants seemed embarrassed by it, and the number who joined in was relatively small.) In another gesture, the library cancelled all its subscriptions to Soviet periodicals. These were subsequently reinstated, with the explanation that they were inexpensive and, besides, it was important to know what was going on in the Soviet Union.

For the younger generation, no intellectualization about the matter was necessary. They had returned from six days of peering into the barrels of Kalatchnikov rifles, of desert struggles against M-15 tanks, and of dogfights with MIG 21's. If there had been any earlier residues of ideological illusions, they were now totally dissipated.

It can be noted here that the prediction (*supra*, p. 186) that the kibbutz faith in itself would be shaken if the Soviet Union proved to be a false Messiah has not been borne out.

More important, for the ideologically oriented sabras, the severance of ties with the Soviet model had a liberating effect. As with much else, they no longer felt they lived in the shadow of something larger and greater than themselves: the Soviets had *not* created a true socialism after which all other attempts, the kibbutz included, were only pale imitations. The uniqueness of the kibbutz became even more dramatically spotlighted by its seeming importance in other parts of the world. The kibbutz movement has been called upon by a wide variety of countries to help in the setting up of agricultural communes, and the kibbutz society has often been cited by African leaders as the model they aspire to for their own people. The intellectual stamp of approval came from none other than Sartre who, after a visit, cited the kibbutz (not the Soviet Union!) as the true exemplar of socialist doctrine.

The following anecdote illustrates the new feeling of the superiority of kibbutz socialism to Soviet Communism. In a visit to the kibbutz, several Soviet officials asked to see a "typical" kibbutz flat, and were taken to one of the newer two-room apartments. They were incredulous that these were the rooms of an "average" kibbutznik, and implied that they must really belong to some "official." Nor could they believe that there did not exist an elite group of bureaucratic officialdom in the kibbutz. Finally, taken to the dairy, they could not believe that the cows produced some 7000 liters of milk a year, double the figure that the visitors could cite for their own herds.

Change and Continuity in the
Economic and Political Domains

SOCIALISM AND COMMUNAL OWNERSHIP. Kibbutz socialism is very much alive in Kiryat Yedidim, but the changes
already noted in the preface to the 1963 edition have been
accelerated. As with every other aspect of life, the Six Day
War acted as the supreme catalyst for these changes. Thus,
there has been a marked—not to say (when compared to
1956) revolutionary—increase in the amount of, and toler-
ance for, private ownership as well. There are still grum-
blers and diehards in this area, but they are few and mainly
confined to vattikim. If there is any tension among the
younger members about this fact, it is more a reflection of
discomfort with the inequalities this has created and,
simply, of jealousy of the more fortunate. Nevertheless, all
things considered, Meir's new tape recorder and camera,
Yigal's fur-collared coat, Sara's new rug, Yaacov's bicycle,
etc., etc., elicit little comment. Some aroused high school
students may see these private acquisitions as "deviations,"
but most are happy to use father's new Pentax.

There are at least four reasons why this increase in
private property has created little friction. (1) Those who
have acquired personal effects do not flaunt them—there
is no conspicuous consumption. Moreover, they are quite
willing to share them when asked. (2) "Things" still have
no effect on one's standing in the community, the contribution one makes to the group being far more important, so
that a member's possessions have no impact on his work
patterns. (3) The increase in private property is now almost incorporated into the ideology. Not only are some

things seen as a legitimate extension of "to each according to his needs"—a musician's tape recorder, for example—but it is now accepted that the private and public sectors of life can grow and expand together. Few would deny the dangers involved in this philosophy, but the idea that self-development must counterpoint group-development has taken root in (what seems to be) an irreversible manner. (4) It is a source of kibbutz pride that they have been able to maintain—at least as much as anyone in Israel "maintains"—a standard of living which allows for these goods.[1] To be sure, this "pride" is also partly defensive, nurtured by the fear of falling behind the standard of living available in the city, since too great a discrepancy is seen as a lure to leaving.

Despite this increase in private property, the basic socialist orientation of the kibbutz, with its emphasis on the public ownership of the means of production (and other capital goods) has persisted with undiminished strength. For the young people, no less than their parents, communal ownership continues to be an accepted way of life, a viable one, and an honored one. Conversations on the future of the kibbutz rarely reflect any disbelief in communal ownership. Even when private *consumption* is viewed as desirable, no accompanying attitudes are expressed in regard to *production*. An occasional dreamer or malcontent may envision the ownership of his own truck, for example, but

---

[1] Twenty years ago, it will be recalled, an isolated case of the acquisition of a refrigerator was the occasion for a minor crisis (*supra,* p. 207). Today *everyone* over thirty has been provided with a small refrigerator. This is symbolic of the basic ideological change which has occurred in this domain.

on both realistic and dissonance-reduction grounds such a person would also indicate that this would mean harder work and less recompense than obtain in the kibbutz.

In sum, there has been almost total persistence in the value of socialism as a way of life. It is accepted as a right and just way of life, with the proviso that within the socialist structure the individual be allowed to develop himself. The primary change has been in attitude, not in behavior. As is true of attitudes toward all kibbutz values, so too in the case of socialism, there has been a marked decrease in the passion with which it is defended—it simply *is*, and for most chaverim, young and old, that is enough.

ASCETIC ORIENTATION. The increase in private ownership reflects a change not only in attitudes to possessions, but in attitudes to material things as well. Most of the private property that has entered the kibbutz falls into the category of "luxuries." For the most part, the kibbutz has abandoned its early asceticism, though, to be sure, certain residues of this earlier value remain. Indeed, some of the roots of the ascetic tradition may be inferred from those residues. It is interesting, for example, though hardly unpredictable, that there is some criticism of the new consumption patterns of the kibbutz on the part of a group of ideologues in the high school. These adolescents often criticize the "softness" of life in the kibbutz, and the turning away from former ideological attitudes. They see the chaverim as overly concerned with the good things of life at the expense of hard work, ideological commitment, and the original communal spirit of kibbutz life. It is important to note, however, that in most cases this asceticism is diminished soon after high school graduation and, especially, following the first sexual liaison. (Asceticism as a defense against sensuality would seem to be indicated.)

It should be made clear that the end of the ascetic tradition has not signified the development of a different mystique; it simply means the development of new wants and expectations, as well as an acceptance of a strain of color and élan in everyday life. This can be seen, for example, in the attitude of the women toward clothing, jewelry, and make-up, most dramatically demonstrated on Friday night, when the entrance of each woman into the dining room is watched and commented on in respect to her clothing and appearance. New dresses, coats, rings, necklaces, and even earrings, all make their appearance at the Sabbath dinner, and this is now an accepted thing, even a source of communal pride: "See, we can dress as nicely as the women in the city!" [2] In addition, there is now a hairdresser in the kibbutz, there have been women's exercise groups, and there is a wide use of facial creams and the like.

Again, much of the force behind this change comes from the war. A significant reaction set in after the war, not only in dress, but in characteristic forms of interpersonal relations. This change might be characterized as responsive to a "live for today, for tomorrow we die" feeling, to a sense of the absurdity of trivial formalities and outmoded restrictions in the face of such a powerful event, and to a feeling of release engendered by the ending of the state of tension which had so long overlayed everyday life.

Some of the consequences of the attenuation of the as-

[2] There is a certain sensitivity which remains among kibbutz women about their appearance in the city. They often talk about going to town, all dressed up, and being asked in a shop, "What kibbutz are you from?"

cetic ideal have not been very happy from the kibbutz point of view. Some sabras, for example, have reacted by overstressing their desire for a good time, to the point of violating kibbutz values. Thus, several young men have found ways to earn money on the side in order to get things they wanted or to have a "big night" in Tel Aviv. (For those who work outside the kibbutz, full- or part-time, there is little trouble in accomplishing this.) One said: "Listen, we get an allowance of 150 pounds a year—why, I can spend that in one night in Tel Aviv!" Those who engage in such acts are rather discreet about it, although most people, no doubt, are aware of it. From the kibbutz point of view, another troubling aspect of this change is that many people spend a great deal of time and money fixing up their rooms, and this reinforces their growing desire to spend more time there.

As a final comment on this change, it is to be noted that there is an even greater emphasis than before on rendering the physical environment more attractive, nothing being spared to achieve this end. The beauty of the kibbutz is a source of pride to all, and four full-time landscapers and gardeners see to its maintenance—this in an economy that suffers from a perennial labor shortage.

EMPHASIS ON LABOR. There has been an important continuity and a noticeable change in the realities of and attitudes toward work. Work, like everything else in the traditional value hierarchy, has been demythologized by the second generation. No longer a "calling" or a sacred duty, work is something one does because, alternatively, there is no choice—the community depends on it; one has been reared as a worker and expects to do it; and the ethos insists upon it. The latter point deserves to be stressed; work may have lost its messianic aspect, but it still is a core value of kibbutz life.

There is a marked continuity in the dedication with which most chaverim carry out their work, but, at the same time, there is no longer an aura of transcendence about backbreaking physical labor, especially when it can be performed with the aid of a mechanical device. The young look with pity upon the old-timers who still insist upon doing things the hard way, the emphasis for the young being on output, efficiency, new methods, improvements. Related to the latter change is the development of a sense of professionalism about one's work.

The status of work, as well as attitudes to work, is also changing. Although there is still some prestige attached to a man on a big tractor (or, even better, a Caterpillar earth mover), this is no longer the ultimate image. The respect shown to workers of the brain is growing, though it is all connected with "visibility"; that is, the kibbutz wants to *see* you working, not just hear about it. To "make an impression" is still an important clue to kibbutz living.

"Visibility" not only refers to results but also, of course, to physical presence. Hence, there continue to be mixed feelings about those who work outside the kibbutz, although, to be sure, there are a number of reasons for this. There is the ever-present fear that someone outside will defect which is still felt as a severe blow to community unity (no matter that it has almost never happened). There is also some envy of the freedom of the outside worker, and there is a felt need for him to perform some local duty as a kind of sign of covenant, to show he really belongs. Whatever the feelings, however, the phenomenon is a growing one, not only in terms of full- or part-time work outside the kibbutz, but also in the amount of contact that outside jobs entail.

In work, far more than in the social sphere, the kibbutz has become far more open than it was in 1950. One chaver works for the Israeli aircraft industry, another for Israel Broadcasting, still another is in charge of a heavy-equipment cooperative which works from the upper Galilee to Eilat. A young chaver spends a few days in Jerusalem each week in scientific research, and another manages a fire-fighting equipment cooperative. The managers of the orchards have to deal with external processing and exporting services, nurses have periodic refresher courses at the inter-kibbutz educational extension center, two girls are studying physiotherapy at the Wingate Institute, several chaverim each year work for The Movement in Tel Aviv, in the United States, and elsewhere,

And then there is the factory, already alluded to in the 1963 preface. Industry has taken hold in the entire kibbutz movement. A recent exhibition of kibbutz manufacture in Tel Aviv had items from more than twenty kibbutzim. There are furniture producers and preserve processers, sprinkler pipe factories and toilet seat makers. And there are those who still worry about it, anxious lest kibbutz industry, which is the largest money-maker for many kibbutzim, lead to changes in the kibbutz structure.

Although, on the one hand, the factory in Kiryat Yedidim has not been a notably successful enterprise, it has not added—as it has in other kibbutzim—to the problem of hired labor. But the latter problem nevertheless remains, for hired labor is still found in other economic branches. Kibbutz labor continues to be in short supply, and the only solution for the pressing shortage, especially at the harvest seasons, is to hire outside labor. But this continues to raise the same moral problems which it raised in the past, and, as in the past, the answer seems to be *ain brerah*, there is no alternative—the crops must be picked, and on time. Besides, so it is argued, kibbutz hired labor is different from the normal meaning of "hired labor," since the hired workers labor side by side with the chaverim.

KIBBUTZ GOVERNANCE AND THE CLASSLESS SOCIETY. The basic structure of kibbutz governance, as described in Chapter 4, has changed very little. Rather than only one, two secretaries are now elected, one an older person and one a younger. This innovation reflects the demographic changes in the kibbutz population and the realization that the sabras require someone closer to their needs and problems as their representative. As in the past, it is still difficult to entice members into leadership roles, and for the same reason: the extra responsibility without commensurate rewards has little appeal to anyone. Still, every office does finally get filled.

The increase in population has resulted in an important change in secretariat and committee functioning. Increasingly, problems which had formerly been brought to the town meeting are handled by the secretariat, in camera. This new procedure not only saves time, but it allows greater privacy to the individual, while still maintaining the basic system of community decision-making. It also provides a more reasonable forum for airing problems. Indeed, there has been a growing disenchantment with large-scale community voting on all issues, especially those (primarily personal) which many cannot understand and to which they react only reflexively. Nevertheless, the town meeting remains an important, functioning unit in kibbutz social structure. It is seen as—and it is—the one forum where all members can receive at least basic information on the over-all functioning of different branches of the economy and on all those other problems about which they would otherwise, given the size and complexity of the present kibbutz, remain unaware.

The rotation in leadership positions and in committee memberships has continued to preclude the development of an entrenched bureaucracy and no other processes have given rise to the formation of social classes. The kibbutz remains in all essentials a classless society. To be sure, there are more or less clearly identified social categories—the intellectuals, the work horses, the idlers, the characters, etc. —but there are no invidious markers of social prestige, no inequalities in property or in power associated with them. No group is privileged vis-à-vis other groups, none exercises economic power or political control over another. Indeed, of all the Utopian dreams of the founders, the dream of the classless society is perhaps the closest to fulfillment.

Compared with the situation twenty years ago, kibbutz egalitarianism persists with almost no change, although it is not without its strains. Egalitarianism is maintained in all aspects of the formal social structure—an equal voice in kibbutz affairs, the rotation of "black work" assignments, equality in housing, in eating, in financial arrangements, and in all other domains. The relative prestige of their parents continues to have little effect on their children's status. Status continues to be achieved. To be sure, children are designated very early as being their "father's son" or "mother's daughter," and these generalized stereotypes do influence the kibbutz' perceptions of the child. But the latter easily outgrows these stereotypes and his status and prestige, alike, are achieved by his own efforts.

Change and Continuity in the Domestic Domain

MARRIAGE AND SEX. The marriage patterns observed among the small group of sabras twenty years ago have persisted, Marriage takes place fairly early, soon after the end of army service, but there are few pre- or mid-army marriages. The kibbutz encourages early marriage. It is seen (though this remains mainly subverbal) as the best means of cementing the ties of the young to the kibbutz—especially when marriage is quickly followed by children.

Those who remain unmarried past their middle twenties are viewed with much concern and (especially in the case of girls) no effort is spared in attempting to increase their opportunity to find a mate. It is indeed hard for an unmarried girl of twenty-six to find a mate—the local marriage pool has few, if any, candidates, and the chances of meeting strangers are very small. Hence, she may be sent or allowed to go to the city to work in the Federation offices, to study, or even to go abroad to live with relatives.

Much of the structuring of kibbutz life revolves around the family (the married couple and their children)—so that the bachelor is something of an outsider—and, emotionally, the marriage relationship is of unsurpassed importance. As was true twenty years ago, marriage is at least as important as the peer group, and, in addition, married couples share an intimacy—the intimacy which comes from sharing of inner feelings, longings, and desires —which is not found to a great extent among peers. Indeed, if there is any relationship in which intimacy is expressed in the kibbutz, it is in marriage.

In this connection it is important to observe the considerable change that has occurred in the freedom with which spouses express their affection in public. What was referred to earlier as the "public admission of relationship" (*supra*, p. 117) has moved to still another stage of "normalization." Previously, even when the idea of a married couple eating, traveling, socializing together had become a perfectly acceptable norm of kibbutz life, one still rarely witnessed any kind of public physical display between spouses. After the war, however, it became much more common to see couples walking arm-in-arm or hand-in-hand along the paths. The importance of the war in galvanizing these responses can be inferred from the additional observation that with the passage of time less of this behavior is evident. It was as if the emotions engendered by the war and its dangers were allowed a period of free expression, following which they were again inhibited as constituting too rich a brew for normal everyday life. In fact, critical comments were expressed about a couple, recently returned to the kibbutz from another where they had been living for a year, because of their frequent hand-holding and public display of affection.

Emphasis on the dimension of intimacy is not intended to minimize the importance of the sexual dimension of marriage—especially since in not a few cases his spouse is the only sexual partner an individual has had. In the sexual domain there has been little change in the past twenty years. The sexual code of The Movement is still the standard for behavior. Sexual intercourse is still taboo in the high school, and few, if any, *males* have had any sexual experience prior to graduation. Among the females, however, there is a substantial percentage of non-virgins in the graduating class. This difference is not surprising since the females tend to have older boy friends in the army or in the kibbutz.

As compared with twenty years ago there are many more couples among the high-school students and they begin at an earlier age—in 1968, for example, several eighth-grade girls had twelfth-grade boy friends. Moreover, these couples seem to engage in more sexual activity (including intercourse), and there have been several cases of teen-age pregnancies, with abortions arranged. Nevertheless, the ethos of the high school remains rather puritanical. Even in a recent graduating class, there was much concern about one girl who seemed to be rather promiscuous.[3]

In the kibbutz, too, sexual attitudes retain much of the puritanism found twenty years ago, but not as strong. Unlike then, chaverim *do* tell dirty jokes—though mild ones; they *do* look at *Playboy* center folds, and they *do* look over a pretty face or body. But it is still true that sabras tend to be rather staid about such matters, most of the sexual kidding and concern emanating from non-sabras or from those sabras who have a great deal of contact in the larger world.

---

[3] So far as other forms of adolescent sexual behavior are concerned, masturbation is engaged in, with a generally permissive air about it. Homosexuality does not exist—although there is the usual quota of early adolescent male wrestling, and of female friendships involving mutual examining and exploration. There has been only one (known) case of sexual "deviation," a young man who was finally expelled from high school because of sexual voyeurism.

With respect to sexual behavior it is still the case that both normatively and actually there is very limited sexual activity and experience before marriage, and that when it occurs it typically leads to marriage. Of course, Israeli norms in general prescribe that one has only one boy friend or girl friend at a time, and that within this relationship sex is taken for granted. To be "popular," in the American sense, and to "date" many boys or girls, marks one as promiscuous since it is assumed that one is sleeping with them all. Still, sexual experimentation in Kiryat Yedidim does not necessarily end in marriage, and affairs are not unknown, the typical affair involving an older male and a young—twenty to twenty-two year old—female.

It is important to observe that although children of Kiryat Yedidim marry and have sexual relations with other children of the kibbutz, there still has not been even one marriage (or affair) between children from the same kevutza. The self-designated "sibling" relationship among members of the kevutza still persists—as does the "how-can-you-marry-someone-you-sat-next-to-on-the-potty?" theme. We are still convinced that this is a function of deep-seated repression of libidinal drives (for reasons explained in Spiro, *Children of the Kibbutz*, pp. 347-349). The sabras themselves deny erotic feelings toward members of their own kevutza, but they themselves are not sure, as one put it, if it is "sociological" (referring to the amount of time they spend together, group pressures, and peer-group socialization) or "psychological" (involving repression, because of the problems it would raise).

As in many non-Western societies (but for different reasons), the sabras' choices and opportunities in mate selection are rather limited. Although when asked what they seek in marriage, they are likely to mention (as do

Americans) such things as understanding, respect, love, etc., they have less opportunity to build up these idealized images, so that they tend to create these attributes more after the fact, or else, knowingly or not, they settle for less. For this reason, they usually marry someone they have known over a period of time (usually someone they have met in high school) rather than taking a chance on someone more "daring" or unknown. Those whose exposure to the romantic notions of the outside world has been greater, or who (for whatever reason) have romantic fantasies of their own, are often frustrated in finding a mate who both matches the fantasies and allows for the security which comes from marrying "one of their own."

Typically, then, kibbutz children find their mates from within the kibbutz movement—from their own kibbutz or from other kibbutzim in The Federation. Indeed, The Federation has taken an active role in helping to arrange the latter marriages. Thus, it has established a marriage bureau which functions as a marriage broker, and it sponsors a vacation week (at a kibbutz-owned hotel) for unmarried persons under thirty, and another for those over thirty. At least two young men from Kiryat Yedidim have found brides in this manner. To be sure, marriages do occur with persons from kibbutzim in other federations, as well as with persons from outside the kibbutz movement, but these are much less frequent.[4]

Marriages continue to be stable, divorce being an extremely rare occurrence. Among the sabras, there have

---

[4] In inter-kibbutz marriages, the usual procedure is for the couple to spend one year at each mate's kibbutz, deciding thereafter in which to settle. Depending on the feeling toward the couple—based on personality factors and need for certain skills—each kibbutz makes a determined effort to woo the couple.

been only three cases of divorce (one woman, however, has been divorced twice), all three involving marriages with non-kibbutzniks. Divorce is perceived by the kibbutz as an undesirable solution to a problematic marriage, and every effort is made to patch things up between couples. The kibbutz keeps a watchful eye out for potential sources of marital disturbance, particularly of the "third party" type. In one such case, when a married man and a younger unmarried sabra were having an affair which threatened his marriage, the girl was sent to Tel Aviv to work in The Federation offices.

In addition to public pressure, there are other (psychological and realistic) pressures against divorce: the presence of children, the desire or need of one of the partners to leave the kibbutz, the fact that the unmarried state (made even more difficult with advancing age) is not a particularly happy one in the kibbutz. It is of interest to note the frequency with which couples who have weathered a stormy period will then, in a kind of covenant with themselves (and the kibbutz), produce a new child.

FAMILY. Sabras as parents have changed little from what was observed twenty years ago. They are fond of children, and they have them (relative to other non-Oriental Jews in Israel) with what seems like reckless abandon. In addition to their fondness for children, there is also group pressure on childless couples and on those with few children. In part this pressure reflects two general attitudes—that the country needs more children, and that the kibbutz movement can really grow only from within. For the mothers, however, still other factors are operative in the trend to larger families. Pregnancy provides the mother with some degree of narcissistic gratification in the form of community interest and attention; it provides her with an opportunity for creation denied to or unused by most women; it cements her ties to kibbutz and husband; for some it provides a welcome respite from work; and, most important, it allows for an approved one-to-one intimacy of an intensity not found in any other relationship, including marriage.

Unlike their own parents, sabra parents are relatively free of anxiety in relations with their children; at the same time they are not terribly intimate with them (at any age). In general their attitude seems to be: "they (the children) are there; they're mine; I play with them, and thus demonstrate my good parenting to myself and to the kibbutz; but that's it—and that's enough." Sabra parents simply do not possess—because there is no need for them to acquire— the range and variety of responses that a mother or father in a nuclear family structure must acquire. They do not know how to discipline a child and, when they (very rarely) do, they are embarrassed by the child's acting up and their own helplessness. Nor do they know how to spend an extended time with their children—longer, that is, than the usual two-hour afternoon play period. They see their role primarily as gratifiers, and they are quite content to delegate the socializing responsibilities to the nurses and teachers. An occasional mother, especially a primipara, may express a yearning for more interaction with her infant, but this desire usually disappears with the birth of the second baby. Moreover, sabra mothers (and fathers) almost never express a desire for more interaction with their older children.

In general, sabra fathers are more relaxed about parenting than mothers. They have no ambivalence (as do the mothers) about their sex role, and they are not perceived in an ambivalent way by their children. For the fathers (much more than the mothers) children are a diversion and break from the workaday life, and they genuinely appear to like and enjoy being with them. Many mothers, on the other hand, give the impression that they merely put up with them, or that they are something symbolic for them. It is no accident, then, that there seems to be more restlessness in the children's houses when mothers put the children to bed than when fathers do. Perhaps—though here we are speculating—the sabra mothers are in some ways more similar in feeling to their mothers than is supposed. Perhaps they, too, are ambivalent and somewhat confused—accepting the system, but not getting a great deal of emotional satisfaction from it.

COLLECTIVE EDUCATION. The sensitivity of kibbutz educators about collective education is no secret. At the same time, there is a basic acceptance of the system on the part of the sabras. Everyone perceives a sharp discontinuity between the pre- and post-high-school system. The former period—childhood—is seen as a "Garden of Eden." The child's life is idealized: after all, children are cared for, pampered, loved, needed, even spoiled. With entrance into the high school, however, there is a sudden break: innocence and freedom are lost, hard work becomes the norm, demands begin to be made, repressions are strengthened; and the spoiled child is now perceived by most kibbutzniks as a somewhat bewildered, somewhat depressed adolescent, distant from self and parents, who clings to the peer group for his psychic salvation.

On the whole, collective education has changed very

little in the past twenty years, the main change consisting of more personal care for the children by reducing the size of the peer groups. (In part this change has been responsive to criticism, in part it represents the natural desire of the kibbutz to improve the standards of child care.) Concretely, in the infant house each group of six infants now has two nurses, at least one of whom has had special training; and the same ratio of six to two persists until nursery-school age. Another change is found in the greater opportunity which parents (particularly mothers) now have for being with their infants. Mothers are officially given time off from work each day to visit their children until the latter reach the age of one-and-one-half, and often three. In general, there is a greater sense of openness concerning parental contacts in both the infant and the children's houses, than there was twenty years ago.

In sum, collective education has been maintained by the sabras. As in everything else, of course, they wish it to be as "normalized" as possible with its sharp edges rounded off as much as possible, but there is no question about their acceptance of it. They accept it not only because it is felt to be good, but because of the freedom it allows them as parents.

Sabra Personality

THE NEW MAN. The kibbutz, but more especially—it will be recalled—its system of collective education, was intended to bring about a "new man." It is interesting, then, that the latter concept has little place in kibbutz thinking these days. For vattikim and sabras, alike, there is a feeling of (what might be called) disillusionment with this notion. For the former, the feeling of disappointment with their children (already noted twenty years ago) continues to be widespread. Given the exorbitant dreams with which they began, this was inevitable.

At the same time, many aspects of their dream were realized only too well, and they don't like the results. They wanted their children to be independent, but they now complain that they are alienated from them; they wanted to be strong and brave—the counter to the ghetto image— but now that they reveal these attributes, they complain that they have lost a certain softness and sensitivity along the way; they wanted them to become objective, scientific, rational, and now that they exhibit these traits, they complain that somehow the subjective, humanistic, irrational aspects of personality are missing; they themselves wanted to—and did—give the young "everything," and now they call them "passive" because "of all we do for them."

For the sabras, the goal is not a "new man," but something much less dramatic—the "normalization" of life—for they do feel different from others, and they understand, to some extent, why the differences (in terms of radically variant life experiences and educational practices) exist. When they are in the army they are often met with a barrage of banter and ribbing, some light, some penetrating, about being from a kibbutz. They may argue, but most of them feel vulnerable. Without the support of the group, they feel exposed and uncertain, and it is at this time, if at all, that a real sense of doubt about kibbutz life sets in. If they are "new men," the feeling goes, then they are in the nature of deviants from a more general norm.

The doubting process is partly a result of the failure of their ideological education, and partly of their relative helplessness when cut off from group support. They come to feel that they don't want to be special. They want to be like the others they meet; the latter (in their eyes) have goals, something ahead of them to strive for on their own, while they can only move along a narrow, pre-determined track. It is not that they are totally without appreciation of the value their education may have had, especially in respect to the learning of concern for one's group, of team work, and of sharing. But they are more apt to be concerned with what has been "missing" in their lives, than with what self-consciously marks them off from their peers.

This self-doubting is attenuated as time goes on. By the time they have undergone the long process of finding their niche in the kibbutz, getting married, raising a family, and increasing their life experiences, most of them are able to evaluate more fairly and accurately the differences between themselves and others. But one never hears a sabra talk about his desire to create in *his* son a "new man." He may say that one of the advantages which keeps him in the kibbutz is that his children will have a good life, but in looking toward the child's future, he is apt to dwell on the deficiencies of the kibbutz educational system and to muse about his own inadequate education. The latter point is related to the changing kibbutz attitudes to higher education and careerism.

HIGHER EDUCATION AND CAREERISM. The changing attitudes toward higher education are the most dramatic index of change in the kibbutz world. There is an overwhelming desire on the part of the kibbutz sabras to continue their studies, expand their horizons, fulfill their intellectual needs; and the kibbutz has had to respond to these desires.

This does not mean that the earlier negative attitude to "careerism" has been entirely abandoned. Rather, although a balance between personal ambition and group responsibility is still insisted upon, the earlier attitude has been modified to allow a greater latitude in the extent of a chaver's career involvement.

Sabra educational strivings are the result of a confluence of factors. In the first place, learning is seen as a personal, autonomous act—a way to achieve a feeling of competence—in contrast to the "forced-feeding" which their earlier education appears to them to have been. In interviews, they speak movingly and passionately about their desire to learn—to do it by and for themselves, because they simply want to know about something. It is also seen as something of a "test" which they wish to put to themselves. This conception of learning has been a source of consternation in some kibbutz circles. In the past, it will be recalled, the desire to pursue a course of study which was not of immediate economic relevance—e.g., engineering, agronomy, mechanics, accounting—was brushed aside unless the individual wished to teach the subject in the high school. However, in 1968, a thirty-two-year-old son of the kibbutz won his long, hard struggle to obtain a leave of absence for one year in order to study sociology—with no commitment to become a teacher. Although the first sabra, he was not the first chaver who was granted permission to continue his studies. One veteran, a man in his sixties, had always wanted to study philosophy, and he was finally given a year off to go to town to study. There are now about fifteen young people studying outside on a full- or part-time basis.

A second reason for the sabra desire for higher education stems from the feeling of intellectual inadequacy which some of them have, and which, in great part, they attribute to their high-school education. As their perceptions of the complexities of the larger world (to which they are now exposed with far less ideological rigidity) expand, the greater is their desire to come to grips with and comprehend that world.

Finally, going away to study is seen by some as a way to temporarily escape the confines of kibbutz living. This is not a cynical attitude, but rather a wistful dream of temporary freedom, not too different from the desire (so well known to us) to have a vacation from all the responsibilities which comprise the normal routine of living. Since the usual outlets for achieving this freedom—travel, job shifts, change of residence—are typically lacking in the kibbutz, study becomes all the more important. It must be emphasized, however, that nobody is interested in higher education as a way to escape the kibbutz permanently.

There is, among the thoughtful chaverim, a growing recognition and acceptance of these educational needs, and one chaver has even been instrumental in an attempt to create a kibbutz university. Any forecast of future kibbutz needs, he points out, demonstrates the need for increased technological and general intellectual sophistication. If these needs are to be met, young men and women will have to enter upon advanced studies, and it would be to the kibbutz' advantage to have them provided in a kibbutz framework.

Careerism (as distinguished from study for intellectual growth) is a more difficult problem; the kibbutz has had to confront this issue on several occasions, but has never satisfactorily resolved it. Careerism is still a word with negative

connotations. To be a careerist is to be outside the framework of the collective, to be pursuing self-aggrandizing
goals rather than communal ones. Some believe that since
the kibbutz, after all, is a commune, career ambitions must
remain subservient to the basic tenets of kibbutz collectivism. Others feel that certain activities and professions
simply cannot be practiced within the confines of an agriculturally based economy.

GROUP DYNAMICS AND PRIVACY. Collective education, it
will be recalled, had as one of its aims the creation of a
personality that was group- rather than individual-oriented.
In one of its original meanings, the sabras *are* group-ori-
ented: they identify with and feel a sense of responsibility
for the group. In another of its meanings—a persistent desire to engage in group interaction—sabras are not group-
oriented. They seek for and cherish a sense of privacy. In
this they are little different from other members of the
kibbutz. Indeed there has been and continues to be a
greater acceptance in the kibbutz of the need—noted
twenty years ago—for greater privacy. (The new refrigerators are a good index of the acceptance of privacy and
of the focal importance of one's own room.) But the quest
for greater privacy has not been without a struggle or without criticism, nor has its achievement reached the point
where all discontent with the constant pressure of group
interaction and public opinion has abated. As one chaver
said, one still must have "the hide of an elephant" to put
up with the intrusion of public opinion into every realm of
life. "It's all right," as another one said, "if you're the sort
of person who's in the middle, accepting the idea and way
of life of the kibbutz and acting 'straight'. But be careful

if you want something special, or deviate from the norms!"

Still it cannot be doubted that the group-dynamics emphasis, so characteristic of the earlier period, has been increasingly attenuated over the years. Even the "official" ideology might be said to stress the *mutual* enhancement of the group and the individual within the group. To be sure, there is still no end to the pressure of group demands and expectations, but life, as lived from day to day, is based more and more on personal preferences and desires—including the freedom to be alone. (This is not inconsistent with the continuing importance of the group itself—and especially the peer group—as the prime source of identification and security.)

The Continuing Crisis

Of course, the crisis continues—kibbutz life is built on crises; one is resolved only for another to crop up. The crises (*supra*, Chapter 7), pointed to twenty years ago—work, women, ideology, old age, etc.—are chronic problems and their final resolution remains problematic; but attempts are always and ever being made to resolve them. Let us look at two of the critical problems which seemed rather salient twenty years ago: the problem of the woman and the problem of the aged.

SEXUAL EQUALITY AND THE PROBLEM OF THE WOMAN. A conversation with a bright young recent high-school graduate may be a good start here. The high school, he said, wants to raise boys and girls to be alike, and they are, outwardly at least. But a girl who takes on some important position and does well at it, is then snidely referred to as a "man." If she does badly, however, she is met with "Oh, she's just a girl!" On the other hand, if she is *too* feminine, or at least very concerned about her femininity—e.g., by wearing make-up—she is referred to as a prostitute.

In the kibbutz itself, however, the situation is less drastic. Women do take on the full range of leadership roles, and one never hears any comments about their "masculinity." Nor is there any sneering of the "just a girl" type, although there is some ambivalence (similar to our own) about a driving, over-assertive female. And there is no doubt that the burgeoning interest in "femininity" is an acceptable part of adult kibbutz life—and to an ever-increasing degree.

On the level of social structure, the kibbutz has succeeded in providing a framework for women to participate in decision-making processes and the maintenance of community life. It is equally clear however (as Yonina Talmon-Garber has pointed out) that there has been "a fairly clear-cut though fairly flexible sex-role differentiation (which) has emerged in internal family activities as well as in work assignments and in nomination to committees and central offices." [5] Thus, in the area of work assignments, the trend which was clearly evident twenty years ago continues and has become institutionalized. The original ideological commitment to equal participation in agricultural productive labor has given way to a clear-cut differentiation in work assignments. No women work in field crops, fisheries, fruit orchards, vegetable gardens, heavy machinery, and the garage; but they do work in vineyards, dairy, and poultry.

[5] "Sex-Role Differentiation in an Equalitarian Society," in T. E. Lasswell, J. H. Burma, and J. H. Aronson (eds.), *Life in Society* (Chicago: Scott, Foresman and Co., 1965), p. 145.

They do no maintenance work (carpentry, electricity, plumbing), but they do office work (accounting, book-keeping, secretarial), and they clearly predominate in the kitchen, clothing workshop, laundry, and education. There is overlap, of course, especially during a "draft," and there are the "symbolic" males-in-the-kitchen, but the institution-alization of sex-linked economic roles along the lines of traditional sexual differentiation is rather marked.

The same conclusion holds for kibbutz governance, as the following list of committee assignments (for 1969) reveals.

Secretariat:	4 women (incl. one of the sec-retaries), 9 men	*Culture*:	6 women (incl. head), 7 men
		High School:	4 women, 1 man
Education:	9 women, 2 men	*Maintenance*:	no women
Welfare:	6 women, 5 men	*Garage &*	no women
Politics:	1 woman, 5 men	*Eqpt.*:	
Finance:	1 woman, 8 men	*Basketball*:	no women
Work:	no women	*Assembly*	
Soldiers:	3 women, 2 men	*Hall*:	2 women, 3 men
Music:	1 woman, 3 men	*Health*:	3 women, 1 man
Library:	2 women, 1 man	*Clothing*:	6 women, 2 men
Security:	no women		

This growing differentiation of sex roles has to some extent generated much comment. There have been sym-posia and articles, discussions and meetings about the problem at every level of kibbutz organization. Mainly they have focused on the question of how the woman's life can be made easier and more satisfying. Feminine dissatis-faction has been the prime cause of a growing familial trend, and it remains (as it always was) a constant threat to kibbutz cohesion. ("Since I'm doing the same kind of

work I'd do in a private home—only now for 400 people—
I may as well have the benefits of my own home and
family.")

Since (unlike some of their mothers) there is no interest on the part of female sabras in moving into the male
occupational sphere (and since, moreover, such a move
would not be consistent with the kibbutz need for ration-
alized, progressive farming) the kibbutz has sought to satisfy feminine demands in other ways. For example,
whereas service occupations, it will be recalled, were always under-budgeted in the past, today new and more
efficient equipment is used to make this work easier and
(if not more interesting) more "modern." Improved efficiency makes it possible for more women to be rotated
into other (albeit similar) types of work. More important,
the kibbutz has afforded a kind of professionalized status
to many of the service branches, which has resulted in an
enhanced sense of pride and esteem in these "female" roles.
Women are sent for home-economics training, dietician
courses and, most especially, educational seminars, courses,
including university study. At the same time, with the new
rule of offering each post-army girl a year's training in
some field, there has been an expansion in the work possibilities open to female workers. Thus, some of the girls
(as has already been mentioned) have studied physiotherapy, some have studied arts and crafts, and one has become a trained beautician.

Still the "problem of the woman" remains. It is recognized by all that, for the most part, kibbutz life provides
much more satisfaction for men than for women; and the
"problem of the woman" is no longer a question of "equality," but of satisfaction in the roles allotted to women.

Given this problem, there is great pressure on the "unfulfilled" female to find fulfillment along the usual pathways of marriage, childbearing, and work. One bright, unmarried young woman, very much in search of some higher goal and adventure in life, commented, rather mordantly, "Sometimes I think that here in the kibbutz you should just get married, have children, and not bother with all those other things [art, politics, culture, etc.]." Perhaps we can say that, relative to its original formulation, the problem has been "solved," while another, more universal (as well as more specifically kibbutz) problem has arisen. And this, one might add, is normalization of a sort.

INTERGENERATIONAL CONFLICT AND THE PROBLEM OF THE AGED. Although there is certainly far more intergenerational *contact* in the kibbutz than is found in outside society, this is primarily formal and task-oriented. Otherwise there is little cross-generation interaction and there are few cross-generation friendships. In the first place, group socialization makes for a homogeneity of language and experience among the sabras, and a feeling of comfort in being among known individuals, so that there is little desire for relationships outside the peer group. In the second place, the changing realities of kibbutz and Israeli society militate against intergenerational relationships.

Beginning with the family group, it may be said that the relationship of adult sabras to their parents remains, for the most part, "friendly but not familiar." There is an abrupt transition, however, between the pre- and post-marital state. Prior to marriage there is very little visiting and very little closeness between adult sabras and their parents, so little indeed that even the researcher often has difficulty in identifying genealogical relationships. Still, regardless of whenever else they do or do not visit their parents, even the unmarried sabras have tea with them on Saturday afternoon. This has become an embedded institution, the one time when all families and all members of each family are together.

Marriage, however, and especially the advent of children, dramatically changes this desultory visiting pattern. Visits become frequent and regularized, the focus of the visit being very much on the children. Children also create occasional problems between mothers and grandmothers when (as often happens) the former are annoyed by the greater tension and drivenness of the grandmothers in their interaction with the children. The fact is that the older women—those who first gave their children over to the children's houses—are still not entirely sure about what to do with children; whatever they do tends to be done clumsily, embarrassedly, confusedly. They are, of course, generous to a fault with them, and they provide an important "baby-sitting" service for parents when the latter take their vacations or are gone from the kibbutz for other reasons.

Still, the generation gap between sabras and vattikim remains, a gap which is importantly fostered by the latter's "disappointment" with the former; a disappointment compounded of their own sense of personal decline, nostalgia for their youth and the golden age, an inability to adjust to and understand the changing needs of youth, and a realistic drop in the idealism of the type which sustained them in the past. This being so, it might be suggested that this gap is a transient one, and that as the sabras themselves age the gap between older and younger sabras will be

much smaller; first, because of the normalization alluded
to above, and second, because of a diminution in the neu-
rotic ambivalence found in the present generation of older
people. To be sure, with old age the sabras, too, will exhibit some of the "universals" of the aging process—pro-
jection, denial, withdrawal—and these will necessarily
interfere with their relatedness, but their aging will probably be less traumatic and discontinuous than their
parents'.

For the vattikim, the generation gap is only part of the
problem of the aged, a problem which, if anything, is
even more acute today than it was twenty years ago. Much
of the problem is related to the feeling of the older generation that somehow the dreams of their youth have not
been realized, and to doubts concerning whether it was
all worth it. But there are other elements as well. There
is—as might be expected from any group in the kibbutz—
the depressing feeling that they are "taking" from the kibbutz and not doing their share in return. There is also the
sense of weariness with it all, with the same faces and the
same places. There is, too, the classical problem of old age
—the problem (in Erikson's terms) of coming to terms
with the last crisis of the life cycle, the crisis of ego integrity versus despair; this was my one life to live and have I
really lived it well? Added to all this is the problem discussed above—the absence, for many of them, of a close
relationship with their children.

Finally, there is the problem of work which, for a generation for whom work was the paramount value, is acute;
and the factory (as we have already indicated) does not
represent a satisfactory solution to this problem. When it
comes to work assignments, the older people can become

highly wrought-up and irrational. Take, for example, the vattika—a warm and generous person—who had been assigned to the kitchen for a turn. She railed endlessly against this assignment, insisting on returning to the fields for olive picking. She finally prevailed and, of course, worked hard and well. But there was an air of such drivenness about her that all one could feel was a sense of despair about her future. Another vattika was permitted (because of her age) to work in her beloved garden only four hours a day. One day, a very hot one, all the other workers took a break for a drink and called to her to join them. She refused, saying: "All they let me work is four hours here, and I don't want to waste any of it sitting down."

But the problem of the aged is not only "psychological." Today more than 150 individuals are nearing sixty or older, and with this there has arisen a whole host of new problems of caring for them. The kibbutz has found no answer to these problems other than providing the aged with more comfortable accommodations and more amenities. (Short of religious solutions, are there any other answers?)

Despite these—and other—problems the kibbutz continues; indeed, it is flourishing. The perhaps necessary rigidities of the past have generally given way to a more flexible, pragmatic, "no nonsense" approach to problems. In response to these problems the kibbutz is changing, but it is changing within the framework of its original charter. That is, despite the changes, the kibbutz very much remains a kibbutz.

Having survived for this long the kibbutz may now be said to have taught us that a cooperative venture of unprecedented intensity can, despite enormous pressures from

within and without, flourish and succeed. If it continues
to flourish it may well prove to be the model for a society
which balances individual and group needs in a productive,
satisfying, and psychologically "healthy" way. If the children of the kibbutz continue to open themselves to the
world while maintaining the psychocultural filter through
which the various elements of the world are selectively
admitted, they will surely achieve something of great importance. Dangers, of course, are present, and they are
two-fold: centripetal pressures for action and freedom beyond the kibbutz (or beyond its normative structure) and
centrifugal pressures for maintaining an inbred, sectarian
enclave. This is, no doubt, a difficult balancing act, and
one that will continue to be fascinating to watch.

BIBLIOGRAPHY

BIBLIOGRAPHY

Becker, Howard. *German Youth: Bond or Free*. New York: Oxford University, 1946.

Dayan, Shmuel. *Moshav Ovdim*. Palestine Pioneer Library, n.d.

Dubnow, Simon. *The History of the Jews in Russia and Poland*. Philadelphia: Jewish Publication Society, 1920.

Gide, Charles. *Communist and Cooperative Colonies*. London: G. G. Harrap, 1930.

Holloway, Mark. *Heavens on Earth*. New York: Library Publishers, 1951.

Infield, Henrik F. *Cooperative Living in Palestine*. New York: Dryden, 1944.

Joffe, Natalie F. "The Dynamics of Benefice among East European Jews," *Social Forces*, 27:238–247 (1949).

Kaufman, Yehezkel. "Anti-Semitic Stereotypes in Zionism," *Commentary*, 7:239–245 (1949).

Kurland, Samuel. *Cooperative Palestine*. New York: Sharon Books, 1947.

Levensohn, Lotta. *Outline of Zionist History*. New York: Scopus, 1941.

Lovejoy, Arthur O. and Boas, George. *A Documentary History of Primitivism and Related Ideas*. Baltimore: Johns Hopkins, 1935.

Maletz, David. *Young Hearts*. New York: Schocken, 1950.

Mannheim, Karl. *Ideology and Utopia*. New York: Harcourt, Brace, 1936.

Mosensohn, Yigal. *Derech Gever*. Tel Aviv: N. Tversky, 1953.

Muenzner, Gerhard. *Labor Enterprise in Palestine*. New York: Sharon, 1947.

Murdock, George Peter. *Social Structure*. New York: Macmillan, 1949.

Nordhoff, Charles. *The Communistic Societies of the United States*. New York: Harpers, 1875; Schocken, 1965.

Nottingham, Elizabeth K. *Religion and Society*. Garden City: Doubleday, 1954.

Noyes, Pierepont. *My Father's House*. New York: Farrar and Rinehart, 1937.

Parker, Robert. *A Yankee Saint*. New York: G. P. Putnam, 1935.

Rosenfeld, Eva. "Social Stratification in a Classless Society," *American Sociological Review*, 16:766–774 (1951).

Schauss, Hayyim. *The Jewish Festivals*. Cincinnati: Union of American Hebrew Congregations, 1938.

Spiro, Melford E. "Is the Family Universal," *American Anthropologist*, 56:839–846 (1954).

——— "Education in a Collective Settlement in Israel," *American Journal of Orthopsychiatry*, 25:283–292, (1955).

Statistical Pamphlets. Tel Aviv: Brith Pikuach, 1951.

Troeltsch, Ernst. *The Social Teachings of the Christian Churches*. New York: Macmillan, 1931.

Weingarten, Murray. *Life in a Kibbutz*. New York: The Reconstructionist Press, 1955.

Wilson, Edmund. "The Scrolls from the Dead Sea," *The New Yorker* (May 14, 1955), pp. 45–121.

Zborowski, Mark and Herzog, Elizabeth. *Life is With People*. New York: International Universities Press, 1952; Schocken, 1962.

Note: since this book has gone to press, one of the founders of Degania, the first kibbutz, has written a most interesting personal account of its history. See Joseph Baratz, *A Village by the Jordan: the Story of Degania*. New York: Roy Publishers, 1955.

INDEX

INDEX

and women, 235. *See also* Ideology

Population, 60–63

Power: as function of ability, 218; possibilities for, 25–26, 94. *See also* Managerial positions

Prestige: avenues for attaining, 25, 26–27; as function of ability, 218; as a function of achieved status, 26–27; as a function of intellectualism, 156–158, 160–161; not a function of marriage, 116; as a function of physical labor, 16–17, 19, 76, 160–161, 218–219; as important motive for work, 76, 85

"Primitivism": as characteristic of The Movement, 44–46, 243

Privacy: and social control, 98–99; compared with *shtetl*, 31–32; desire for, 204, 209–210, 216, 221, 246, 247; desire for a function of age, 216; desired by women, 221; viewed as threat to existence of group, 31

Private property: attitude of *sabras* toward, 208n, 250; consequences of, 196; desired by women, 221; opposition to, 100, 168; presence of, 207–208. *See also* Collective ownership; Property

Proletariat, 192

Property: prestige not a function of, 87–88; collectively owned, 19–20, 195. *See also* Collective ownership; Private property

Prophets: comparison with, 172

Provincialism, 165–166

Psychiatric values: attitude toward, 31n

Psychoanalysis, 175, 185n

Psychological characteristics: candor, 99; conservatism, 165, 166–167; ethnocentrism, 34–35, 165–166; naïveté, 165, 167; of *sabras*, 250

Public opinion: as factor in work

motivation, 85; as form of social control, 100

Pueblo Indians, 241

Purim (Feast of Esther), 141, 144

Puritanism, 111, 114n

"Race" prejudice: aggression in, 107, 108–109

Regimentation, 204

Religion: contrasted with that of Utopians, 169–170; ideology as, 194–195; opposition to, 169–170; and other federations, 6; and problem of Jewish holidays, 140, 141, 142. *See also* Ideology

"Religious" community. *See* Sect

"Religious" faith: importance of, 197

Religious *kibbutzim*, 148, 148n, 196–197

Resignations: as cause of crisis, 206; incidence of, 177, 179, 196, 205–206, 252; as instigated by women, 221

Responsibility: compared with that of private farmer, 89–90; reluctance to accept, 96–97, 210–211; training of children for, 135

Rosenfeld, Eva, 24n

Rosh Hashana (New Year), 141, 142–143

Routine: boredom of daily, 151–152; of children, 132–133; work, 176

Russia. *See* Soviet Union

Russian Revolution, 151, 188

Sabbath: observance of, 140–141, 147–148

Sabras: attitudes of, 208n, 233n, 249–250; and collective education, 233n; definition of, 61, 61n; incidence of resignation, 252; and lure of "the world," 251–252; and private property, 208n; psychological characteristics of, 250

SUPPLEMENTARY INDEX

Aging: problem of, 289–291
Aronson, J. H. *See* Lasswell, T. E.
Asceticism: trend away from, 263

Burma, J. H. *See* Lasswell, T. E.

Children of the Kibbutz, 273
Collective education: changes in, 277–278

Equality, social, 269

Family as center of *kibbutz* life, 270; and conflict between generations, 288–289
Family structure: and aging, 288

Higher education, 279–281
Holidays: functions of, 256

Judaism: attitude toward, 256–257

Labor: and industry, 267; improvement in service occupations, 286–287. *See also* Work
Lasswell, T. E., Burma, J. H., and Aronson, J. H., 285n
Leadership: rising importance of secretariat, 268
Life in Society, 285n

Marriage: its role in *kibbutz* life, 269–270, public admission of relationship, 271; and relationship within the peer group, 273; and the role of The Federation, 274

Population: results of increase in, 268–269
Private property: increase of, 263

Sabras: and "lure of the world," 264; as parents, 275–276; dependence on peer group, 279; attitude toward collective education, 277; wish for "normalization," 278–279; desire for higher education, 279–281; and group orientation, 283
Sex: activity before marriage, 271–273
"Sex-Role Differentiation in an Equalitarian Society," 285n
Sexual morality, 271
Six Day War: influence of on *kibbutz* life, 253–256, 261, 264, 269–270
Socialism: and Soviet Communism, 259–260; and collective ownership, 260–263; as way of life, 262
Soviet Union: attitude toward, 258–259; in belief system, 259
Spiro, Melford E., 273

Talmon-Garber, Yonina, 285
Town meeting: decrease in importance of, 267

Voltaire, 254

Women: attitude toward clothing and the "world outside," 264; and differentiation of sex roles, 284–286; dissatisfaction of, 287
Work: changes in attitude toward, 265; outside the *kibbutz*, 265–267. *See also* Labor

Zionism: *sabras'* attitude toward, 257–258